BLITZKRIEG
AND JITTERBUGS

Footprints Series
Jane Errington, Editor

The life stories of individual women and men who were participants in interesting events help nuance larger historical narratives, at times reinforcing those narratives, at other times contradicting them. The Footprints series introduces extraordinary Canadians, past and present, who have led fascinating and important lives at home and throughout the world.

The series includes primarily original manuscripts but may consider the English- language translation of works that have already appeared in another language. The editor of the series welcomes inquiries from authors. If you are in the process of completing a manuscript that you think might fit into the series, please contact her, care of McGill-Queen's University Press, 1010 Sherbrooke Street West, Suite 1720, Montreal, QC H3A 2R7.

Very best wishes, Aida!
april 2012

BLITZKRIEG
AND JITTERBUGS

College Life in Wartime
1939–1942

Elizabeth Waterston

Elizabeth Hillman Waterston

Preface by Michael Bliss

McGill-Queen's University Press
Montreal & Kingston • London • Ithaca

ISBN 978-0-7735-3976-1

Legal deposit second quarter 2012
Bibliothèque nationale du Québec

Printed in Canada on acid-free paper.

McGill-Queen's University Press acknowledges the support of the Canada
Council for the Arts for our publishing program. We also acknowledge the
financial support of the Government of Canada through the Canada Book
Fund for our publishing activities.

Library and Archives Canada Cataloguing in Publication

Waterston, Elizabeth, 1922–
Blitzkrieg and jitterbugs : college life in wartime, 1939–1942 / Elizabeth
Hillman Waterston ; preface by Michael Bliss.

(Footprints series ; 16)
ISBN 978-0-7735-3976-1 (bound)

1. Waterston, Elizabeth, 1922–. 2. College students – Québec (Province)
– Montréal – History – 20th century. 3. McGill University – Students –
Biography. 4. Women college students – Québec (Province) – Montréal
–Biography. 5. World War, 1939–1945 – Canada. 6. Canada – History –
1939–1945. I. Title. II. Series: Footprints series ; 16

LE3.M219W38 2012   378.714'28   C2011-907834-1

Cover and book design by Pata Macedo
Set in Minion 10.25/14

CONTENTS

LIST OF ILLUSTRATIONS

PREFACE

Michael Bliss

Elizabeth Hillman Waterston entered McGill University as a freshman in September 1939, the same month that Canada went to war against Hitler's Germany. At first no one knew what to call the war. Between 1914 and 1918 Elizabeth's parents' generation had participated in what was known as "The Great War." As Elizabeth notes here, her generation came to know the conflicts as World War I and World War II. World War II finally ended in 1945 with the defeat of Germany and its principal ally, Imperial Japan.

Wars are strange, surreal times in the affairs of nations. For some, usually soldiers but often civilians, they are characterized by fighting, destruction, death, and misery, as well as service and heroism. Behind the lines, (everyone who resided in North America during the world wars was effectively shielded from fighting and bombing) life went on. Children laughed in their mothers' arms; boys and girls danced and dated; dads went off to work; weekends were spent at the cottage; and on campus, the literature students read their Shakespeare and Jane Austen and argued about Plato and Socrates. The fighting was a long way away, to be read about in the newspapers, heard about on the radio, viewed in gritty black and white newsreels at the cinema.

In the first eight months of World War II, Elizabeth's first year at McGill, there wasn't even all that much fighting, just the defeat of Poland, a nasty war in Finland, skirmishes on the sea and in the air. It all got serious in April 1940 when Hitler unleashed his *blitzkrieg* assault on Western Europe. The fall of France, Dunkirk, the Battle of Britain, the invasion of Russia, Pearl Harbour: by the time Elizabeth transferred from McGill to the University of Toronto in 1942, there was no doubt that Canada was involved in what came to be called "total" war. By the end of it more than one million Canadians had served in the Canadian army, navy, and air force. About half of the country's gross national product had been diverted to the war effort. Much had changed about life on the home front, including the awful knowledge that more than forty-five thousand young men would not come home at all. Another fifty-four thousand had been wounded, many maimed and crippled for life. People thought the country would never be the same again.

Blitzkrieg and Jitterbugs is a delightful, beautifully crafted portrait of the life of Montreal college students in the first half of the war. The disconnects between the war abroad and daily life at home are startling, beginning with the military tattoo Elizabeth writes about in September 1939. Torches and trumpets at Molson Stadium are to be followed by … a football rally! Then by "chatter and jitterbugs … music and moonlight," and as we see in later pages, debutante balls, Sadie Hawkins week, teas at the Ritz-Carlton, spring proms, and much more. Many of the young men, including the young professors, are thinking of enlisting, it's true, and their numbers on campus begin to thin out, but the *McGill Daily* pretty much carries on with its usual coverage of sports, parties, and potted war news. Elizabeth ponders the issue of the new problems posted by war. "Personally, I face none."

But she can't help but notice the reality of it, as news comes in of the first McGill men to fall in battle, as she and her classmates volunteer to greet and dance with recruits, as suddenly there is no shortage of summer work for women, and Canadians begin discussing the equity and desirability of requiring men to serve in the forces. The outside world seems increasingly stern, increasingly expectant that college students will button their lips when it comes to criticizing the war effort or carrying on with their frivolities. Soon there will be no Red and White Revue at McGill, no corsages at the junior prom. These are serious times – times of "fuzzy confusion" about how to live, and for women, how to live in a world where their men and their country are suddenly needing them in new ways. Is "knittin' for Britain" really enough, especially for McGill co-eds like Elizabeth, who are already proto-feminists, expecting to change the world for the better, and more than a little indignant that the province of Quebec, years behind the rest of Canada, still denies them the right to vote?

The women do get the right to vote in Quebec – in 1941 – and by 1945 they have advanced into area after area of Canadian life that had previously been a male preserve. Canada had changed in many other ways, not least in implementing a social welfare state (in part thanks to the work of McGill's dynamic principal,

Cyril James, whose absences from the campus at first upset his solipsistic students) designed to recognize the values of equality and service shown by the Canadian people during the war. When the soldiers come home in 1945, it is to a more equitable country, and to sweethearts and wives who never quite agreed that the old ways were the best ways.

Except that a lot of the idealism that caused so many Canadians to sacrifice in the service of their country during both wars had something to do with the homely virtues of the old ways. As the young men and women of Elizabeth's generation began to face up to the seriousness of the struggle, they knew that one of the causes they were fighting for was the right to be young and free and frivolous. They were fighting for the right to go to a Valentine's Day dance and hear Oscar Peterson playing eight to the bar. They were fighting so that young girls like Elizabeth Hillman Waterston could grow up and become a scholar and a university professor and spend her life telling us about the life and writings of Lucy Maud Montgomery, a woman from the earlier generation whose classic celebrations of the timelessness of a delicate social order were also disrupted by the chaos and agony of the earlier war.

In war you didn't exactly fight for king and country. You fought for the freedom to read and write good books and jive to "In the Mood" and dominate the men during Sadie Hawkins week and cheer for Old McGill. And it all began in a terrible September for the world, but a month when life in Montreal was mellow and the young folk were callow, but so full of the promise of life.

PART ONE

1939–1940

McGILL UNIVERSITY

September 13, 1939

TO THE STUDENTS OF McGILL UNIVERSITY.

During the war period the essential academic activities of the University will, in so far as possible, be fully maintained. Hence all students who, previous to the outbreak of war, were intending to return to the University are strongly advised to do so.

The University is establishing a War Service Advisory Board which will advise past and present students who are British subjects and who wish to offer their services to Canada's war effort how they may make their most effective contribution. A full explanation of the War Service Advisory Board is enclosed.

The tuition fees of students who leave the University on military service before the end of the session will be remitted for the period of such service.

All enquiries concerning war work or military service should be addressed to the Executive Secretary, McGill University War Service Advisory Board, Montreal.

Sincerely yours,

[signature]
Chancellor.

[signature]
Principal.

The Students' Executive Council has been in close consultation with the University authorities and gives its unqualified endorsement to the above letter.

President, Students' Society.

[signature]

PRELUDE

Of course there is a prelude. It is drawn from the diary I kept in the summer of 1939.

It begins on Labour Day. Thin edge of the wedge of winter; time to shut up the summer cottage. Lots of work for everyone: pulling up the boats, shutting off the water line, putting away the chintz curtains, wrestling the big shutters into place over the windows in the glassed-in part of the verandah, collecting brushwood for the final beach bonfire. All as it always has been.

But this year is different. Doubly different. First, high school is finally over, and I have been checking the college catalogue for regulations and courses, planning the best way to get from home in Montreal West to the McGill campus in downtown Montreal.

The other difference is not a happy one. All week the radios in the cottages have been buzzing with troubling news: Adolf Hitler threatening, claiming that Poles have fired on German government officials; Poland complaining that German soldiers have already begun shooting; France cutting pontoon bridges in the north; England calling up reserves. "And that is the news for today, August 29 … August 31 … September 1 …" A frightening end-of-summer, over there, in the world beyond the cottages.

On Sunday, September 3, we huddle beneath the radio on the mantelpiece. "London calling, in the overseas service of the British Broadcasting Corporation. Great Britain has today declared war on Germany."

"What will Canada do?" asks my young brother, Don.

Dad answers, quietly, "The cabinet's in special session now."

My mother snorts, "But of course we're at war if England is!"

Not necessarily "of course" any longer. High school lessons have taught about the British Empire devolving into a commonwealth of independent nations. Maybe

[left]

P.1 Chancellor's letter to students

Canadians won't rush to enlist the way they did when the Great War broke out twenty years ago. But maybe they will. Don won't be eighteen until 1943 so he is safe, but my summer cottage friends, Harold and Colin, and all the boys in my high school class are seventeen or eighteen. Colin's brother, Bob, and Arthur Piers in the cottage two doors down are already twenty. Will they want to enlist as my father and theirs did in 1914?

Dad predicts, "If we do declare war, young men won't be called up right away. They will be urged to stay in college and asked to join the Canadian Officers' Training Corps. That's what happened at the beginning of the Great War."

"At the beginning?"

"Don't worry about this one lasting like our war," he says.

Mother says, "The British navy is ready this time. Already they've captured the Bremen – you heard that on the news."

"No air force, though," Don says. His friends are all mad about aircraft, longing to fly; they have been boasting that they will get over to England and join the RAF if war comes. And now it has come. "Will they take girls into the forces this time, Dad?"

My mother snaps to her feet. "Regardless," she says, "we've got to close up the cottage. Breakfast is ready – has been ready for an hour now. Turn off the darn radio, Dan, and let's keep our sanity for the rest of today at least."

Later in the day, Colin and Harold come over for a last swim. They say their mothers are waging the same campaign, to keep things normal "for today at least." So we swim in the chilly Lake of Two Mountains, the wide water where the Ottawa River meets the St Lawrence. We sun ourselves and talk about getting ready for college, as if this were any other year, and not 1939.

CHAPTER 1
DAILY DEBUT

On September 13, each of us – girls as well as boys – receives an official letter from McGill University. Intended to reassure us, it announces, "Essential academic activities will, in so far as possible, be fully maintained." But, it adds, "A War Service Advisory Board will help students wishing to offer their services to Canada's war effort, and tuition fees will be remitted to anyone leaving the University on military service." The letter is signed by Sir William Beatty, chancellor; Lewis W. Douglas, principal; and also by Russell Merifield, president of the McGill Student Council.[1]

Medical students are already in their classes; students in engineering, the Library School, and the Conservatorium of Music are registered already. We students in the Faculty of Arts and Science must wait until Thursday, September 28 to begin our studies.

We are prepared. With my Montreal West friends, Gibson Beatty, Frances Tyrer, and Mary Scott, I have spent hours mulling over what the proper clothes are for university "freshettes." In high school we wore skimpy navy blue uniforms, lisle stockings, oxford shoes. Now we're out of uniform. Gibson's father teases us. He digs out his old McGill yearbook and shows us what young ladies wore in his day: long-sleeved, ruffly, high-necked blouses, full-length skirts.

1.1
McGill co-eds, 1914

1.2
Gibson, Elizabeth,
Frances, 1939

1.3
Roddick Gates

1.4
Arts Building

"Shoes barely visible. High style in 1914," he says.

"You were in college when the Great War was on?" we ask him.

"No. I graduated in May '14 and the war didn't start until the fall of that year." Like most of our fathers, Mr. Beatty doesn't like talking about the Great War. He swings away into nostalgia. "I was editor of the *McGill Daily* from 1913–1914. As soon as you're settled into your classes, you girls should join the *Daily* staff. You learn a lot, working on a college newspaper, and it's fun too."

We girls have other ideas of fun – dancing, sports, singing in the McGill choir, meeting new people in classes. (By "new people" we really mean "new boys.")

On September 28, Gibson, Mary, Frances, and I walk through the imposing Roddick Gates.[2] We are wearing new plaid skirts, white blouses, and V-necked dark sweaters. No stylish white-and-tan saddle shoes though, because all the mothers agree they are too hard to clean. In our despised old oxfords we tramp up through the campus, between arched elm trees to the grey-stone Arts Building.[3] To the left, at the doors of the registrar's office, a long line of students noisily waits. Inside, faculty advisors sit at rows of desks to check, advise, and adjust. Once safely registered, we flow with the mass of first-year students into the big assembly room, Moyse Hall, to hear greetings from the dean of Arts and Science, Dr Hendel.[4] Rumours fly about him: an American, he is planning to leave Montreal and go back to the United States. Because of the war? Maybe. The Americans are not prepared to join the Allies yet. Maybe this dean wants time to think about his obligations. His remarks are not memorable, but then, we are too excited to hear exactly what he has to say.

Released from the ceremony, we move on to the new Sir Arthur Currie Memorial Gymnasium, named for a soldier-hero of the last war. In spite of the gym not being quite complete (the official opening is still a month away) the main doors are open and tables have been set up inside for registration in exercise classes or sports. Badminton for me: we will play in the indoor courts at the Royal Victoria College, the women's college at McGill.[5] The girl ahead of me in the gymnasium lineup says, "I feel over-privileged here, considering."

Indeed. The *Montreal Gazette* this morning carried a story of British troops set to embark for France, and showed pictures of a first convoy of supplies setting off from Halifax for England, escorted by Canadian destroyers. Germany's blitzkrieg strategy, so dreadfully successful in middle Europe, is now being unleashed on London, Glasgow, Coventry – all the British places we have heard about all our lives. A long way from indoor badminton.

For the boys signing up for college, the war seems a little closer. Part of their compulsory registration procedure is an interview here in the big gym at the Canadian Officers' Training Corps (COTC) desk. Under the portrait of Sir Arthur Currie, a young officer assigns times for medical examination for all the young men, even the ones who are obviously not very fit (one fellow is on crutches). They aren't forcing anyone to join the COTC, we hear the officer explaining, over and over – just speeding up the process of the medicals that everyone has to take anyway, making registration a little more efficient. Classes will go on as usual, but all the men are urged to consider adding COTC drill to their schedules.

Now we are registered and can trail back down to Sherbrooke Street to board the number 73 bus and go home to Montreal West. Seven of us girls from our small high school class are now McGill freshettes. It seems that the academic world is open to young women now in a way unimaginable to our mothers.[6]

Over the weekend the radio pulls my family into a shocked circle: "Children are being evacuated from the big centres like London, sent to country places in northern England or Scotland, where they can escape the bombing." Maybe some of them should be sent to Canada? But then we remember the headlines about the torpedoing of the *Athenia* on the day the war began. The seaways are no longer safe, even for little children.

On Monday, October 2, the first real day of college, we girls have been invited to an afternoon freshette tea at Royal Victoria College, so we go to our first classes in new dresses and "Cuban" heels, and each of us has a pretty hat and a pair of gloves stashed in our bookbags. At 9 am, directed toward the French class, we climb the stairs at the far end of the Arts Building. In this French-speaking province, everyone has had French lessons since grade two, although there is rarely an occasion to speak the language in the west end, the anglophone end of the city. We hope that college courses will make us truly bilingual. We slide into the small classroom where the French lecture has already begun. A prim young student is reporting in careful, slow French that the textbooks for the course are not in at the bookstore yet.

"*Alors, on parle!*" cries the French professor, and she launches into a tirade on current events, the German threats to France, the news about action in Alsace-Lorraine. The prim student, obviously from outside the province, looks totally lost in this barrage of rapid comment. She breaks into the torrent: "*Parlez plus lentement, Madame, s'il vous plaît!*" But Madame Furness[7] continues in full spate, and the war-centred hour passes without any attempt to start the previously announced course of study.

After the class ends, we pause to pick up copies of the *McGill Daily*, worrying a bit about the war news on the front page.[8]

AROUND THE GLOBE | MONDAY, OCTOBER 2, 1939
Nazi-Soviet tie strengthened …

Puzzling news. We have been taught that Nazis and communists are polar opposites – how can Germany consider Russia an ally? This first issue of the *Daily* looks effective and serious. (Years later, Malcolm Davies, then editor-in-chief, remembered the challenge of bringing out that particular issue. "The October 2, 1939, edition was published only three weeks after Canada's war declaration and our 72-point headline ran: UNIVERSITY ASSISTS CANADIAN WAR EFFORT."[9])

But Latin class is next at 10 am, so I must dash to the other end of the Arts Building, all by myself this time. Gibson and Mary are taking history instead of Latin, and Frances, who is registered in science rather than arts, is facing her first physics class. I don't know a soul in this small Latin class, but it feels as though it will be relaxing. Soft-spoken Professor McCullagh[10] explains that the focus will be on the Latin love poets, Ovid and Catullus. It sounds very congenial.

And now, with growing excitement, I head back to the main floor and struggle through crowds of freshmen into Moyse Hall, the big auditorium that holds hundreds of students. Seats are assigned alphabetically – "H" for Hillman. I am in a row almost at the back of the right-hand section with a big young man – presumably another "H" – next to me. I smile at him, but he is busy trying to pull his textbook out of an overstuffed bag, while balancing a big notebook on his knees. I wave to Gibson, who,

1.5
Dr Cyrus Macmillan

being a "B" for Beatty, has a seat very close to the front. Mary Scott and Fran Tyrer are in the middle of the left-hand section partway up. Finding the proper places is a cumbersome business, but attendance is compulsory and graduate students will be cruising up and down the aisles noting absentees as the term wears on.

Everyone must take the freshman English class, English Literature I: The Great Tradition, from Chaucer to Hardy. The great *British* tradition, of course. Naturally, no American books are on the list, and certainly no Canadian ones either. All across the country, every freshman in every Canadian university is launching into a similar course. Here at McGill, the atmosphere in Moyse Hall is like the moment in His Majesty's Theatre just before the houselights go down and the curtain rises. Silence falls as a middle-aged man, wrapped in an academic gown, bursts through the curtains at the back of the stage and strides across to the lectern. He introduces himself as Dr Cyrus Macmillan, our English professor.[11]

This will not be a formal lecture, because none of us has brought textbooks to class, but since folklore is Professor Macmillan's specialty, he chooses to open the year's lectures by talking to us about ancient English and Scottish ballads. His voice lifts into a chant: "*Why does your sword sae drap wi' bluid, Edward – Edward?*"

The lecture is brief but powerful, but perhaps a little too poignant in this week of a new bloodletting. We have all heard stories of the trenches in the Great War twenty years ago. Now we think about British troops crossing the Channel again. The headline in a recent *Gazette* haunts us: BRITAIN CALLS 250,000 MORE TO THE COLOURS.

By the end of the hour, breathless with trying to take notes and think about the poetry at the same time, I struggle into my jacket. Here comes Gibson, shouldering her way through the crowd at the front of the hall. We slip through the wide hallway and out the big doors to the broad stone steps. We are free now until after lunch. Dozens of other students are gathered here. We sit down carefully because of the dresses we are wearing in preparation for the RVC freshette tea party later this afternoon.

"Should we go over and register at the library? Coming?" I ask.

But Gibby, basking in the October sunshine, laughs. "We'd better enjoy ourselves before we have to start serious work."

Someone has left a copy of the *McGill Daily* on the Arts Building steps. Scanning the paper, Gibson asks, "Should you and I go to the *Daily* office now? They are asking for reporters to register and I did promise my dad that I would sign up."

"Better wait till later in the afternoon. Maybe on the way to the freshette tea."

We have lunch on the steps, like dozens of other students, then go upstairs in the Arts Building to the first tutorial session for our second English course, English II: Composition. This double-barrelled emphasis on English language and literature is again standard in every anglophone Canadian university. A young graduate student tells us with enthusiasm that we will be using Professor Noad's composition text. "It's not only good on construction and clarity, it's also great on metaphors, tone – all that sort of thing."

The composition class ends and our first day of lectures is over.

Gibby says, "Time for the *Daily* now? My dad has been hounding me to check in there." She, in turn, hounds me to hurry down the campus to the Union Building. "Let's get this over with. I'm just going to the *Daily* office to keep my dad happy. But you're a good writer. You'll enjoy writing for them. Give it a try!"

So here we are now, Gibson and I, slipping down the campus under the elms, through Roddick Gates, and across to the Student Union.¹² Signs direct us down the narrow stairs to the basement office, and a smiling young man greets us. Not too many freshmen have been signing up to work for the *Daily* and there is a decided shortage of reporters. In fact, someone is needed to cover the freshette tea at Royal Victoria College this afternoon at four-thirty.

1.6
Student Union
Building

"Well, I had sort of planned to go to the tea anyway, so it would be no trouble." But I feel a little queasy at such a sudden plunge into journalism. How will I manage my metaphors and tone?

The young editor ignores my reluctance. "Perfect. We just need about two hundred words. And you," he says, turning to Gibby, "could you go up to the gym and cover the basketball practice? Get your notes back here by five-thirty. We'll show you how to set up the story."

A bit daunting, but we are both ready to give this journalism a try.

Then, as we start through the door, heeding his directions, he calls, "Hey, maybe one of you could do an 'Around the Campus' report after you get back with your stories? 'Around the Campus' is just a boxed summary of what's going on next week. Big week, the initiation week, trying to get all the freshmen out to as many events as possible. Could one of you do that?"

"Okay," I say, with a grin at Gibby. "Last one back gets to do the extra job."

I think I'll be the first one back. I assume that I can just drop in briefly at the tea party already in progress at Royal Victoria College. But the freshette tea is quite formal, and it doesn't prove possible to slip out as soon as I have gone through the reception line. All the girls wear pretty dresses (teal blue, mine). And hats. (Mine is maroon felt, a forward-tilted pillbox with a big flat felt bow at the back. Very fetching.) When we enter the RVC, heavy coats are laid in the cloakroom, but the hats stay in place for the tea.

The drawing room at RVC is dark and grand. So is the warden, Mrs Grant.[13] The students stand in groups, drinking tea, accepting sandwiches from the serving-maids. Phrases for my story begin to form: "*Voices rise so high that banging on the piano is necessary before the speeches of welcome can be heard.*"

Back at the *Daily* office, I find Gibby already smugly handing in her final copy. "He has blue-pencilled out half my material about the basketball team," she tells me.

"Yes, but it's still a good story, Gibby," says the editor. He turns to me and introduces himself. "Pete Wyman.[14] And what's your name?"

"Elizabeth. Elizabeth Hillman."

"Too long. If we ever give you a byline one of these days, it'll have to be shorter." I am not sure what a byline is. He goes on, "Don't worry, only really good stories get a byline. Take what you got about the tea, type it up fast, and I'll go over it. Be sure you get a good strong lead."

I wrestle impatiently with my notes. I want to get out of this stuffy basement office and back to the tea party. The lead comes to me, good and strong (I think): "*Where's my junior?" wailed the freshies, and "Where's my freshie?" asked the juniors. Bedlam for a while in the halls of RVC, then new girls and senior students found each other and milled into the common room for the first tea of the term.*

By the time I finish, it is obviously too late to go back to the tea. "Reporters don't worry about tea parties," the student editor laughs.

Meanwhile, Gibby reminds me of our earlier bargain: last one finished gets to do the "Around the Campus" résumé of events for the rest of the week. "That's you, old dear," Gibby says. "But I'll wait for you. I'll phone your family and mine, and tell them we'll be too late to get home for supper. We'll get something here. But hustle."

I hustle, skimming the notes on coming events, kindling to the fun of all the things planned to welcome freshmen to the campus. I begin pecking out my story for tomorrow's *McGill Daily* on the old Underwood.

> *Torches and trumpets – it's the military tattoo at Molson Stadium tonight. Bonfires, ballplayers, and burning effigies – it's the football rally that follows. Wieners and Wurlitzers – that's the roast afterwards. Chemical vats and cables – engineers' open house tomorrow. Chatter and jitterbugs – it's the SCM Conversat on Thursday. Sandwiches and spiders – the picnic on Friday; music and moonlight – the dance afterwards. Blood pressure and breathing tests – the medical examination whenever you can work it in. Don't forget any of 'em, girls and boys!*[15]

The night editor pulls the copy off the roller and scans it. "'Torches and trumpets.' Hey – that's good! Good enough for a byline." I still am not sure what the famous byline is but I suddenly want one. "This is good. 'Chatter and jitterbugs.' You've got it." (My hopes for a byline seem rosy.) Then he sighs (and my hopes sigh too). "But we NEVER give anyone a byline for the 'Around the Campus' box." Another sigh. "That's an unbreakable rule. I had forgotten. Well, now you can both scoot off; get yourselves a beer and something to eat."

No beer, since we have tried it at home and found the taste bitter and the smell unpleasant, but we are ready to wolf a sandwich at the cafeteria, since it is too late to go back to the freshette tea party.

Gibby says ruefully, "I'm going to bow out of the *Daily*. Can't manage my classes plus running around to things like that athletic event and then back to the *Daily* office and still have time for any fun. And I'd like to try out for the McGill Fencing Club." She smiles. "But I'll tell Dad I'm submitting a substitute, and you'll be editor-in-chief before you're done, just like him!"

"Not very likely," I laugh, wondering whether I too will find it hard to fit in the thrills of reporting with the requirements of all my courses. "I'll try for a while though," I promise. "If they'll let me."

CHAPTER 2
GOING WITH THE WIND

Tuesday morning opens with a disappointment. We've been looking forward to starting philosophy, a subject never touched in high school, but a note on the classroom door reads, "Professor Maclennan cannot meet his classes today. Please bring a copy of Plato's *Republic* to class on Thursday." So we waste an hour, and then face another first: our class in trigonometry, designated this year as the one course in science or math obligatory for first-year arts students. We rush over to the Macdonald Physics Building and take our places in the large lecture hall.[16]

The lecture turns out to be an exciting introduction to advanced math in general, presented by a senior professor, Professor Gillson,[17] who promises that we will enjoy our math class. "*This guy's world-famous*," comes a whisper from the student sitting next to me.

I have my own first dose of fame later that afternoon when I slip back into the *Daily* office. The night editor says he is putting me on his list of regular Monday

2.1
Macdonald Physics Building

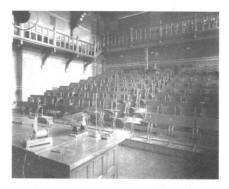

2.2
Lecture room, Physics Building

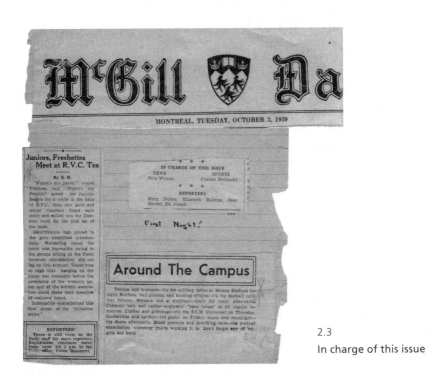

2.3
In charge of this issue

2.4
Military tattoo

reporters. I have already gloried in the masthead on this morning's *Daily*: "Editor-in-chief: M.N. Davies"; then managing editor, news editor, sports editor, women's editor – all the great names. Then, "In charge of this issue: night editor, Pete Wyman; reporters: Elizabeth Hillman – " There I am, along with Norma Neilson, Ed Joseph, Irene Polson, Syd Segal, Norm Taylor …

I look at the marked-up copies of the first issue on the bulletin board and see that someone has circled my "Around the Campus" piece in blue pencil down at the right-hand corner of the page and printed "GOOD" diagonally across it. Good indeed! It is WONDERFUL!

Not so wonderful, the appearance of my story about the freshette tea at Royal Victoria College. Blue pencil again, large and fierce: "florid," "cutesy," and of course, no byline, and not just because I am a freshman, obviously.

Then my glance slides to the left-hand corner of the student newspaper, where, opposite from "Around the Campus," news of the world appears, titled "Around the Globe"; news from another world.

AROUND THE GLOBE | TUESDAY, OCTOBER 3, 1939

Mutiny in Czech Army. Russo-Estonian defence pact revises previous treaties with Soviet Union due to altered status of Latvia.

Clearly life in Europe is not as simple as life around the campus.

On campus, though, tonight is the time for the first big freshman event – the military tattoo. Gibson, Frances, and I join a river of students moving up University Avenue to Molson Stadium. It's getting dark and already we can see the searchlights raking the sky over the stadium. Brassy music floats down to us.

By the time we reach the stadium, the boys who have joined the COTC have marched in and are parading around the track. They are not in uniform yet, but they look pretty military all the same. They march past a stand where older men in uniform take the salute. So this is the tattoo.

Now the football rally gets into full swing, with different kinds of uniforms on parade: cheerleaders and football players. The McGill band is playing; the cheerleaders are forming a human pyramid, giving us a rhythm: "What's the matter with old McGill? She's all right, oh yes, you bet!" The football team – the big Redmen – are running ceremoniously onto the field to cheers and drum rolls, glorious proof of how "all right" McGill is. Extra joy, because the powers-that-be had debated cancelling the football season this year, naturally, on account of the war. Decision put off for the moment at least, and here is the big red team, hugely ready for the first game next weekend against Toronto Varsity. "*We're out for gore!*" the cheerleaders intone. "*Keep it low!*" Then, "*Let 'er go!*" And we are yelling again, "*M-C-G-I-L-L! Rah, rah, rah! McGill!*"

All of us have sore throats by the time we start for home. Down University Avenue to Ste-Catherine Street, down again to Windsor Station, and we barely catch our commuter train for Montreal West.

AROUND THE GLOBE | WEDNESDAY, OCTOBER 4, 1939

Chamberlain spurns Hitler promises … would welcome any peace proposals, which would "achieve the aims of this country in entering the war."

The next morning in French class, Madame Furness, still in a trance of disbelief, tells us the latest news from France in her rapid, beautifully accented, idiomatic French. Still no textbooks for French, but who cares?

We calm down in Latin: olden days, olden loves, measured stanzas, serene and gentle. And then it's time for the tumult of the Moyse Hall English literature class. Before the lecture starts, the tall blonde girl sitting in the seat beyond mine introduces herself quietly: Ruth Hill, from St Lambert across the St Lawrence River, obviously a serious student who takes copious notes in a clear hand.[18] She is nice, but we hardly have time for more than a few words before the lecture on Chaucer's *Canterbury Tales* begins. Professor Cyrus Macmillan has chosen to plunge directly into the tales of Chaucer's Knight, the Squire, and the Man-at-Arms – military men of six hundred years ago, Professor Macmillan says, idealized by Chaucer as "parfit, gentil" men,

2.5
Tom Hardwick

warriors of the Hundred Years' War. (However apt Professor Macmillan might think it, being reminded of a war that lasted a century is not very palatable to us.)

Professor Macmillan describes sarcastically the fine array of the Squire: a young warrior and a dandy, with his long stylish sleeves and his careful coif. We girls respond a little self-consciously to the professor's mockery of this obsession with clothes. We are dressed more casually today, but on Monday we were very much dressed up, perhaps as ridiculous in our vanity as the young Squire of old.

Ruth Hill and I leave English class together. Gibson joins us and we move out to join the throng of students sitting on the steps of the Arts Building in the September sunshine. Tommy Hardwick, a friend from high school days, comes crosswise across the stairs to join us. "How did you like that lecture?" I ask him. Tommy is in first-year science, but every first-year student has to take English I. In Moyse Hall I had seen him sitting in the row in front of me among the "*H*'s."[19]

His answer is scornful: "That recruiting speech, you mean? Professor Macmillan did everything but insist we join the COTC right off the bat."

"I thought he was just trying to be topical," Gibby laughs, and Tommy smiles at her and shrugs. Then he stands up, stretches, and moves off. The sun shines; the tumultuous Arts Building steps become more and more crowded; minutes slip away.

The week hurtles by as we scuttle to classes, clutching books and notes. On Thursday morning we have our first real class in philosophy. It is hard to grasp

2.6
Professor
Maclennan

the flurry of concepts that Professor Maclennan promises to cover this term.[20] Of the philosophers he will introduce – Plato, Butler, Hobbes, Hegel, Kant, and Schopenhauer – I only recognize Plato.

"It's going to be an interesting class," says the young man sitting at the desk next to me. He introduces himself as Neil Compton.[21] I reciprocate, and Neil says that he has seen my name on the list of people hoping to go into honours English. "Me too," he says, then adds, "but I didn't know that philosophy would be another possibility."

Our next class, trigonometry, is cancelled. The famous senior professor has been called by the government to help organize navigation courses for the Royal Canadian Air Force and he is leaving his duties in the department immediately.

"A substitute lecturer will be found and there will be no further interruption of classes," the old professor who makes the announcement proclaims. "You are dismissed today, but the class will meet at the regular hour on Saturday."

Maybe I should go to the library and start on the Latin exercise. Or maybe I should read some Chaucer so I can understand what the English professor will be talking about in class tomorrow. Instead, I drift down the campus, back to Strathcona

Hall, the handsome building next to the Student Union, to visit the SCM Conversat[22] – another item mentioned in my "Around the Campus" list of freshman activities. The Conversat is hosted by the Student Christian Movement and the emphasis today is on funny skits to entertain the freshmen. The skits mostly poke fun at Hitler and patriotically suggest that the COTC is the answer to fascism. Later, there is an informal dance; lots of movement – nothing very Christian about it.

AROUND THE GLOBE | FRIDAY, OCTOBER 6, 1939

US warships race to protect the American steamship *Iroquois* laden with Americans coming home from Europe.

On Friday at four-thirty, a big bus picks up a large group of freshmen at the Roddick Gates and ferries us to the sports field at St Helen's Island, halfway across the St Lawrence. The baseball game lasts over an hour, so we are over-hungry for hot dogs and Coca-Cola; over-tired too, and glad to doze on the bus back to the campus.

I am still over-tired the next morning but I have to go back to college for my regular round of Saturday classes. Yes, it's a six-day week for us university students, as it is for most of the working world. In philosophy, Professor Maclennan announces that our first essay will be on Plato's "Allegory of the Cave": a meditation on the real and the ideal, the substance and the shadow. Plato, he tells us, describes dwellers in a firelit cave who watch shadows cast on the cave wall and assume what they are watching is reality. What if the dwellers turned round and realized that they had seen shadows only, and that those were cast not by real beings living out in the sunlight, but by mere puppets, manipulated by some unseeable entity? Professor Maclennan asks, "What assumptions do *we* make about reality?"

We strain our brains to follow his questions and come up with some sort of platonic answer. Neil Compton says, "I think I'll stick with going into honours English."

As I rush toward the Physics Building for trigonometry, I run into Colin Spencer,[23] a friend from summer days at the cottage, now in first-year engineering, rushing in the opposite direction. "Going home for lunch, Colin?"

"No. I've got COTC drill. It takes a lot of time and leaves me limp. And now, limp or not, I've got to go work on my lab report on 'stress and strain.' Lots to work at over the weekend. You're lucky you're not in engineering, Elizabeth."

"But I have a full-length essay coming up on 'the real and the ideal' for my philosophy course."

"Yeah." Colin sounds grumpy, as if already swamped by the laboratory report before having even begun to work on it. Or maybe he's brooding about other things – the war, the COTC, the not-so-ideal reality.

When I enter the trigonometry classroom, I find a reality very far from ideal. A very young lecturer has obviously been dragooned into meeting the freshman class without preparation or warning. He stammers his way through the hour, writing formulas on the blackboard and then immediately rubbing them off before the class can copy them into notebooks. The class grows restless and noisy but then someone calls, "Give him a chance," from the back, and fair play reigns, at least for the rest of that hour.

Anyway, that hour is the last class of the week.

A whole week gone. Gone with the wind, to quote the big American book that is still a best-seller this year. In our case, gone with a northern wind, stirring the McGill elms on a rainy Saturday. Who would have thought that our first week at college would end like this? Philosophy classes and freshman picnics in the foreground, blitzkrieg bombs in the background.

War moves into the foreground on Sunday. The Black Watch regiment appears in its first wartime church parade, filling the Westmount streets with the skirl of bagpipes and the sight of young men in swinging kilts – a sight that stirs sad memories for the older generation. My family goes downtown by streetcar to watch and to be jostled on the sidewalk by a big crowd.

The pipe band plays the old tunes that have spurred regiments into battle in the past:

> The Campbells are coming, ho-ro, ho-ro!
> Wi' a hundred pipers and a', and a'
> We'll up and gi' them a blaw, a blaw!
> Wi' a hundred pipers and a', and a.

Strong music. High hopes that the British (and especially the Scottish) "blaw" will bring a quick end to the new war. But back home, bad news blows from the radio: the battleship *Courageous* has been torpedoed; and the Soviets (still technically our allies, although everyone suspects they have signed a secret pact with Hitler) have moved into Poland. Warsaw has surrendered; Germany and Russia are dividing Poland between them.

The first week of college has led into the Thanksgiving holiday – Monday, October 9. Usually we go to the cottage on Thanksgiving but this year the weather and the war are both so discouraging that we stay home in Montreal West. At the end of the rainy day I get my dad to drive me downtown to the *Daily* office. I've been reminded that the *Daily* prides itself on coming out every class day of the first term and there must be a paper tomorrow morning, Thanksgiving holiday notwithstanding.

Pete, the news editor, is sitting at the typewriter desk waiting for someone to come in. I am that someone.

"There's a talk at the Maccabean Circle meeting this evening, upstairs in the meeting room. Up you go! We have a tip that the speaker is witty. Could make a lively story." The editor looks me over as he hands me the assignment slip. "By the way, what's your name?" Before I can answer he says, "Oh yes. The 'torches and trumpets' freshie," then returns to his work.

I take a minute to phone home. "I'll be late. I'll probably miss the train so I'll come by bus and streetcar. Okay? Don't worry about me."

Upstairs at the Maccabean Circle, a Jewish debating and discussion society, I recognize many of my new acquaintances from the *Daily*: Syd Segal, Judy Jaffe, Ed Joseph. Brilliant people. They have to be exceptional students because McGill exercises a quota system for admitting Jewish students.[24] Those who do successfully complete their undergraduate degrees will have to work extra hard, yet again, to be admitted to medicine or law.

Professor Reilley is a good speaker and the students flash questions and comments. The Jewish community in Montreal is desperately concerned about the need to help European Jews escape Nazi persecution, but the Maccabean students this night seem carefree, intent only on the bantering questions they put to Professor Reilley. It will be an easy story to write; I can fill two pages without any effort.

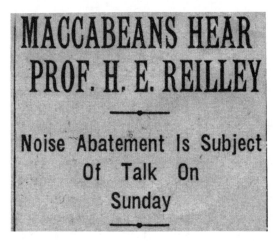

MACCABEANS HEAR PROF. H. E. REILLEY

Noise Abatement Is Subject Of Talk On Sunday

2.7
Maccabean
Circle

When I put my story on his desk quite late that evening, Pete piles on another assignment. "We have to put in something about the fall convocation last Friday. One of the university scholars took a bunch of notes. Can you boil it down to a short column?"

"I'll try." I explain about living in Montreal West; about there being no commuter trains at night; about how my parents don't want me travelling alone home late on the streetcar.

"Write up the convocation story fast and you can still catch your late train."

When I look at that front page the next day, I see that the editor has cut down my brilliant stories, each reduced to a short, dull paragraph.

At the bottom left-hand corner, another "Around the Globe" appears.

AROUND THE GLOBE | WEDNESDAY, OCTOBER 11, 1939

Finland empties cities as Soviets mass troops and heavy naval forces on frontiers.

CHAPTER 3
DANCE AND DEBATE

AROUND THE GLOBE | THURSDAY, OCTOBER 12, 1939
Great Britain has fulfilled her pledge to France by sending to the Western front 168,000 men and 25,000 tanks.

The second week ends with a dance. The *Daily* is holding a party on Friday, October 13, hoping to lure a few more students into volunteering one night a week as reporters. The *Daily* puts out thirty-two columns a day, five days a week, twenty weeks a year; it certainly needs lots of workers. Maybe Gibby should give it another try. She is at least willing to go to the party, and we talk Frances into joining us. Fran's father drives us downtown and drops us off in front of the Student Union. "Call me when you're ready to come home. Doesn't matter how late. I'll come and pick you up."

We make our way through the big doors, but this time, instead of turning down to the *Daily* office we ascend the broad stairs to the assembly room, already crowded with people. We move to the right where a cluster of girls is standing, trying not to look as though they are waiting to be asked to dance. Luckily, I am swept up before I can join the group. Pete, my night editor, moves in from the left, where upper-classmen cluster, looking over the new crop of students. Pete is long and lanky, not a good dancer, but a welcome start for the evening.

"Cutting in!" calls another of the *Daily* gang, a sports editor this time. "We have to encourage our new *Daily* reporter!"

And yet another, and the evening swings on. Soft drinks are being served at the bar at the far end of the assembly room. Fast music, good dancing. I spot Frances across the dance floor. Her ash-blond prettiness has caught the eye of Russ Merifield. Everyone knows Russ – hero of the football team and president of the Student Council. He had come into the *Daily* office when I first began working there

DAILY MAKES FIRST PARTY ASSIGNMENT

An assignment for all the Daily staff and editors will be given to-night in the form of an informal gathering in the Union Grill Room at 8 o'clock.

All new reporters will have the opportunity to meet the other members of the staff, and that they may understand the policy of the paper and the procedure following in its production, these intricacies will be explained.

The first meeting of the season will be followed by an informal dance and refreshments. All those who intend to work on the Daily, but who have not as yet signed up will be welcomed to this party.

Jacoby Photo.

Ruth L. Hill

3.1

Daily party

3.2

Ruth Hill

to hand in a terse little note that read, "In spite of the war, it will be business as usual at McGill. Contrary to what happened during the last war, there will be no recruiting on campus." And now, here is Fran twirling by, chattering to Russ Merifield, as if he were a mere mortal.

At the end of the evening, just before the last dance, the *Daily* sports editor turns up again. He doesn't ask me to dance this time but pulls me over to the side of the swirling room. "I liked your first 'Around the Campus' piece," he says. "I wonder if you'd like to go with me to the next home football game. It's not for two weeks, but I'll have the *Daily* tickets and I'd like to take you." He is bright-eyed, smiling.

I smile back. "I'd love to." And then, "But I don't know your name."

"Why, I'm Wallace Beaton," he laughs.[25] "Don't you remember me?"

"Of course. Sorry!" But in fact, I haven't recognized him. Wallace's mother and mine had been school friends in Toronto, and when we were little, Wallace and I had spent time playing together. That was years ago, though. Now he announces, "I'll leave you a note at the *Daily* before the game and we'll get organized." He disappears into the dispersing crowd.

AROUND THE GLOBE | FRIDAY, OCTOBER 13, 1939

Germany to fight to finish. Termination of peace efforts occasioned by Chamberlain's reply to Hitler.

Monday afternoon brings my third *Daily* assignment.

"There's a debate on upstairs in the reading room," says Pete. "Competition for the Bovey Shield. Important to cover it. If you nip up there right now you can still catch the end of the debate and the announcement of the winner."

I trudge up the stairs to where the debate has indeed begun. The topic is "Resolved that a state of war should involve the immediate nationalization of industry."

The speaker on the podium is Ruth Hill, her smooth blond head held high, prepared to be noticed, if not to win the shield. She is forcible and eloquent. When she finishes her effort there is a loud burst of applause from three serious-looking men at the back of the room. Friends of Ruth's who have come out to support her?

A good guess. Ruth, descending from the podium, sweeps me along with her to the back of the room and introduces me to the men. The three are med students dressed in white lab coats. They have to excuse themselves at once, however, "No time for these side trips; we are really supposed to be in a histology lab right now. Just slipped away to hear Ruth perform." And away they go, long-legged, thin, all three of them serious and unsmiling.

Now the judges are ready to announce results. It's not a win for Ruth Hill, but she finds a place as runner-up. I will have to put the male winner in the headline of my story, but I can add a proud sub-head: CO-ED COMES SECOND.

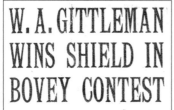

W. A. GITTLEMAN WINS SHIELD IN BOVEY CONTEST

Winner Opposes Nationalization of Industry in Wartime

COED COMES SECOND

Profiteering Denounced By Most of the Speakers

"The ability to make a good speech is a gift of the Gods", said Professor Humphreys, in opening the Bovey Shield Competion.

3.3

Co-ed comes second

Scots Shocked By Air Raid

But Rejoice in Fact Reich Was Unable To Reach Objective

Though shocked by news of the German air raid on the Firth of Forth, Scots wherever they may be can take pride in the fact that the German planes suffered four casualties and "got no change" out of the land they tried to raid, according to James B. Thomson, speaker at last night's meeting of the Scottish Schools Club in the Mount Royal Hotel.

Miss Hillman

Preceding Mr. Thomson's address certificates indicative of the fact that they had been awarded High School scholarships by the club were presented to Margaret Witts and Robert White. Presentation of a cheque to Elizabeth Hillman for her first year of study at McGill University under the Charles W. Powell Memorial Scholarship was

3.4

Scots shocked

For my lead, I will use the comments made by one of the judges, about the ability to make a good speech being a gift of the gods. "Speech" was in the news today as well.

AROUND THE GLOBE | MONDAY, OCTOBER 16, 1939

Lindbergh attacked by British press as "Hitler-minded" for speech criticizing Canada for entering the current war.

It's more than time to register at the library. I am a little shy about picking up a library card. My parents have told me (and told me again) that I must ask to speak to Miss Hibbard,[26] the assistant librarian, because Miss H. is an old friend from my Aunt Zoë's college days. Most students just register routinely by lining up at the front desk. It is embarrassing to be expected to march up to the information desk and ask specifically to speak to Miss Hibbard.

I walk through the heavy doors into the rich darkness of the Redpath Library. A little wait at the desk, and then the assistant librarian comes out from her office. Just as well I have obeyed my parents' instructions, because Miss Hibbard has expected me. "In fact, I was surprised that you did not come sooner, Elizabeth." Though her appearance is rather forbidding, her smile is friendly, and she speaks for a minute or two about her own days as a freshman "during the war. I suppose one must now say 'the last war.'" Then she tactfully leaves me to register in the regular way. The door to the librarians' office shuts behind the thin, upright figure.

I decide to sit for a little while in the library and plunk my books on one of the long, heavy wooden tables that stretch from end to end in the reading room. At intervals, green glass lampshades glow in the dark where students are concentrating on their books. I open my Chaucer and read. Lovely old stuff.

Not so lovely new stuff in the daily papers today. From the rack near the Redpath door I pick up a copy of the *Montreal Daily Star*. Very bad news. German planes are bombing Britain. Some have flown across Scotland to bomb the Glasgow shipyards. Glasgow bombed? We grew up in Montreal West singing Scottish songs, some of them romantic songs about Annie Laurie, but others more earthy: "*I belong to Glasgae – dear old Glasgae toon! But wha's the matter wi' Glasgae?*"

At home I read the story about the Glasgow bombing. Unlike the *Daily Star*, the *Gazette* headline reads: SCOTS SHOCKED. For me, the *Gazette* version of the story has a different – and embarrassing – interest. My picture appears right under the headline. At the meeting of the Scottish Schools Association last night, where the news of the Glasgow bombing was announced to a horrified audience, I appeared as recipient of a Scots-funded scholarship. The scholarship donors, in their fury and incomprehension of the bombing, paid little attention to a young girl gratefully receiving her award. And of course, the *Gazette* editors had no notion of mortifying me by printing, "Scots shocked" over my picture.

Maybe no one will notice. No such luck. Colin Spencer phones this evening to mock. I manage to laugh with him, but a sad song thuds in my head, drowning out my own discomfort: "*What's the matter wi' Glasgae ...?*"

Back in the *Daily* office, no one seems to have noticed my picture in the "real" paper. The editor hardly glances up as he hands me my next assignment. Then he stops abruptly. "You're the reporter we never see – the ghost writer!" He barks a laugh at his own joke. "Why haven't I seen you here in the evenings?"

I explain again about living out in Montreal West and having trouble catching a train for home if I stay too late on campus. "So I hope you'll let me write up my stories and just put them in the box after my Monday afternoon class."

"Okay. In the meantime do a good job on the Red Cross on campus." The Red Cross is organizing a contingent, open to female students, to prepare them for the war effort.

Today's "Around the Globe" has brought some encouraging news about the effort off campus.

AROUND THE GLOBE | MONDAY, OCTOBER 23, 1939

RAF frustrates Nazi raids. Four German machines disabled when a squadron attacked a ship convoy; a fifth brought down in a fight off the coast of Scotland.

The *Montreal Gazette*, however, serves up more shocking news on the weekend: U-boats threaten the convoys that ferry the first Canadian soldiers over to the English campgrounds. Yet more news: the ships the convoys have protected will return to Canada with boatloads of children. Thousands of London children have been evacuated from the dangerous bomb-threatened city to Scotland or to the north of England; now, many others are being sent to relatives in Canada or the States.

On Saturday my mother suggests that we write to our English cousins, asking if they will send their small sons to us "for the duration" – a World War I phrase, which sounds rather ominous. Of course my brother and I think it would be rather fun to have two little kids in the house, and my father is easily convinced, so the letter is sent off to London.

It no longer looks as if the war will be over soon. We learn now that in August, the Russians did indeed secretly sign a non-aggression pact with the Nazis. They have overrun Lithuania, Latvia, and Estonia, and that theatre of war is spreading. Reality darkens far away.

AROUND THE GLOBE | WEDNESDAY, OCTOBER 25, 1939

Five British merchantmen and a Greek vessel heavily laden with scrap iron sunk. Intense diplomatic exchanges over German seizure of the United States freighter, *City of Flint.*

Here at home, "The Nature of Reality" has been assigned as a topic for our first philosophy essay. Neil Compton and I meet in the library and compare notes. We spread our work out on one of the long tables in the Redpath Library, flip on the green-shaded light, open Plato's *Republic*, and begin. We argue (quietly as it seemed to us, until a library assistant asks us to move into the stacks to continue our discussion so as to not bother the other students with our talking). In the stacks, we return to the allegory of the cave. "Is everything that we see and believe to be real just a shadow on the back wall of a cave?"

"Hitler is real," I proffer, "and the bombing of Glasgow. And so are the things I write about – the Bovey Shield, the torches – and my stories are real because people read them." But Neil rejects my ideas as superficial and returns to the level of abstract and symbolic reasoning. We talk about shadows and caves and puppets until we are both dizzy.

After an hour-and-a-half we shut our notebooks, put Plato away, stretch, and glance upward to read the inscription scrolled in gold letters high up on the library walls, under the beamed ceiling: "*Of making many books there is no end, and much study is a weariness of the flesh.*"

I cannot agree! I'm not weary! I'm studying my head off, but I'm having a great time, war or no war!

Next day, the *Gazette* expands the story of Allied setbacks: GERMANS MASS 90 DIVISIONS OF 150,000 ALONG A 100-MILE FRONT.

At home in Montreal West, we count on the coming weekend being a happy one. We are going back to our old high school for October graduation exercises and the dance after the ceremonies. By nine o'clock the school band will be blasting it out: "*I'll be down to get you in a taxi, honey!*" But of course there will be no taxi, not in post-Depression Montreal West. And no thought of walking over across the tracks to the high school either; not while I am wearing my new long dress: candy-striped taffeta, with a ruffle at the neck and a wide swinging skirt, pink silk splendour, and me inside. My dad will drive me and my mother and Jack Liddy, my date for the dance. "*We wanna be there when the band starts playin'.*"

Before the dancing begins, we will endure the formality of the graduation ceremonies. I'm to read the class prophecy, though no one could have prophesied then what the future would hold for some of us. Robert Turner, already an accomplished pianist, will become an outstanding conductor and composer – a major figure in the development of the Canadian Broadcasting Corporation out west. Madeleine Thornton, now playing bit parts in the Montreal Repertory Theatre, will marry Robert Sherwood, the American playwright, and as "Madeleine Sherwood," will star on stage and on television, best to be remembered as Mother Superior in *The Flying Nun*. Tommy Hardwick will become a productive physicist at Chalk River, where secret experiments will soon work toward the application of nuclear energy.[27]

But there are other promising students who will join the armed forces very soon and many will be killed in action. Charles Crowdy, my "date" for last year's big dance will be shot down during the Battle of Britain; Wilf Bark will be torpedoed on a navy Corvette; and Jimmy Muir will be killed in Italy during the slow artillery slog toward Monte Cassino.

Even now, in the high school auditorium, there are three other boys already in uniform. They are the older brothers of kids in our class and they are stationed at the manning depot in Lachine, waiting to be sent west for basic training. One of them hopes to wangle a transfer to England to join the Royal Air Force rather than wait for the Royal Canadian Air Force to get itself organized. Meantime, all three of the "servicemen" are showing off a little, sitting stiffly in their new khaki uniforms.

City of Flint freed. Five German ships captured by Britain. Nazis await word to attack British forces in France.

After the ceremonies, the band strikes up. "*In the mood ...*" Time to dance.

Walking home, my friend Jack offers some news. He is going to stay at college this year, but next year right after his birthday, he will join the air force.

"But they tell us no one should leave college!" I say.

"That's what my family says too."

I can only say, not very hopefully, "Maybe the war will be over by then."

It turns out I am not very good at prophesying.

High school graduation festivities having concluded on Friday evening, we return to grown-up college life. The very next day brings the first big home game for the McGill football team.

"*Meet me at Molson Stadium, Gate B,*" Wallace Beaton's note has ordered. "*I can't pick you up ahead of time. Too busy. I hope you don't mind sitting in the engineers' section. It may be noisy.*"

3.5	3.6	3.7
Charles Crowdy	**Wilfred Bark**	**Jim Muir**

It is noisy. Twelve thousand sports fans are ready to let go with the cheers. At intervals the engineers bellow out, in full voice, their raucous song:

> We are, we are, we are, we are, we are the engineers.
> We can, we can, we can, we can, we can drink forty beers!
> So come, drink rum, drink rum and come with us –
> We don't give a damn for any old man who don't give a damn for us!

Several young fellows seem intent on drinking the forty beers before the game is over. Others seem ready to show they don't give a damn for any old man – or, more obviously – any young woman. But Wallace seems nice on the whole and I enjoy the game and the halftime show led by the cheerleaders and the marching band.

Here again are the trumpets I had reported in my first *Daily* piece. No torches, however, because the torch-light parade through town, traditionally part of the evening after the big game, win or lose, is cancelled "because of the war," the *Daily* had announced.

At game's end, Wallace puts me on the Montreal West bus to go home, pleading his need to go back to the *Daily* and write up his story rather than escort me all the way out to the west end of town.

On Monday morning I read his story. It's not very exciting. My own *Daily* stint on Monday evening produces an equally tame piece about the reorganization of the McGill Chorale Society. The bottom right-hand corner announces nastier news.

AROUND THE GLOBE | TUESDAY, OCTOBER 31, 1939
British reveal atrocities in Nazi concentration camps.

Along the block from the Student Union, Strathcona Hall offers the last social event in October: a Halloween tea dance hosted by the Student Christian Movement. The "tea" turns out to be Coca-Cola, and the dance does not begin until after a brief meeting in the second floor hall. There, student executive members explain what the Student Christian Movement stands for: "A sense of responsibility beyond the

ENLISTING IN R.A.F.

A. S. PIERS

3.8
Arthur Piers

ordinary concerns of student life; a moral awakening to the new problems posed by war, especially to those of us who have thought Christianity meant pacifism; a readiness to explore social problems; and a concern over the rights of union members and the position of women." It sounds very serious. I have heard that the Student Christian Movement has lately come under some surveillance by the university administration because of its support of several people suspected of socialist, or even communist, leanings. Among undergraduates involved in social justice activities – suspect activities – is Madeleine Parent, another SCM activist who speaks briefly at this "tea dance."[28]

But then a student jazz group strikes up "*Ain't She Sweet?*" and the dancing begins with a lightening of mood and a swelling of chatter.

Homeward-bound, I ponder the SCM's sense of "new problems posed by war." Personally, I face none. But over sixty thousand young Canadians, not much older than I am, have already enlisted and are in military training. Some of my acquaintances are indeed overseas already. Arthur Piers, one of the erstwhile "Young People's Club" at the cottage, has left Montreal to travel overseas with a friend to sign up with the Royal Air Force in England. The *Gazette* pays a little tribute to these young men and runs very flattering pictures of them, each looking thoughtful and smoking a pipe. Young people in Eastern Europe – Latvia, Lithuania, and Estonia–are resisting Soviet occupiers of their lands. English boys my age are beginning to fly against German bombers. The Scottish lads I danced with when we were in Glasgow a year ago, are moving *"wi' drums and pipers and a', and a'."*

CHAPTER 4
DAILY DISASTER

As November opens I have to acknowledge defeat by trigonometry. Our classes have become more and more chaotic, with the disastrous young substitute lecturer actually being pelted with paper balls by irate students. I get in touch with Tommy Hardwick, who was always a whiz at math in high school, and he helps me untangle the theory of sines and cosines that the inadequate young instructor is trying to convey. The lectures consequently become a little less frustrating for me, though the poor instructor is still rousing a lot of hostility in the classroom.

November actually begins with what seems to some a more important disaster. Big headlines about McGill University appear in the *Montreal Gazette*: F. CYRIL JAMES NAMED MCGILL PRINCIPAL.

"Goodness, he's young," my mother says. "Only thirty-six." That seems old to me, but looking at his picture I can see he is well preserved.

I smugly tell my mother that I knew about the new principal before the news appeared in the big city paper. Dr James has allowed the editor-in-chief of the *Daily* to interview him before the formal announcement. The *Daily's* account has reported the new head's honours and accomplishments, and his achievements on international boards. But the tone of the article is puzzling – it doesn't actually say that Dr James seems pompous and full of himself, but the implication is there.

When I run into Miss Hibbard, the librarian, at Poole's Book Store on McGill College Avenue, we discuss the *Daily* and she seems to have picked up the same implication. She lowers her voice and says, "I hear through the grapevine that the new principal is not pleased with that interview your editor did. Not pleased at all!"

PRICE TWO CENTS

-ELECT F. C. JAMES

4.1

Elect F.C. James

Censorship imposed by Finnish.

The *Daily* staff, however, are totally pleased. We have scooped the *Montreal Gazette*, beaten them to a first interview with the new principal.[29] We exult in our freedom to publish whatever we like about the principal or anyone else. Perhaps we sens a link with the "Around the Globe" at the foot of today's *Daily*:

On Sunday during tea time at Gibson's house, I find that her father has yet another angle on the new principal's appointment. As secretary of the Montreal chamber of commerce, Mr Beatty hears from insiders what is happening at McGill.

"The board of governors and the chancellor," he tells us, "had hoped that Principal Lewis Douglas would keep a throttle on student and faculty socialistic leanings. But Dr Douglas went back to the States when war was declared. I don't think the board of governors chose Dr James for the same reason, since there is less likelihood of socialist activism now that the war is on. Dr James will bring something new to the university. The students should make him welcome."

Then Mr Beatty changes the subject, perhaps thinking that mere girls are not up to understanding university politics and policies. "How about the *Daily*?" he asks me. "Still working there?"

I tell him my next assignment will be an easy one – covering a Gilbert and Sullivan show, *The Gondoliers*, being put on in Moyse Hall.

It turns out to be an excellent show, making for an easy story. The hyperbole in my coverage seems dubious, however, in the light of world dramas.

British and Polish warships rout Nazi planes in North Sea. Britain refuses Gandhi's demands, insists on participation in shaping of Indian Constitution. US communists again look forward to world revolution.

Off-campus, Montreal society is gearing up for another upcoming show. Mary Morris, one of my Montreal West friends, is going to dance rehearsal "for the St Andrew's Ball later this month, you know," she tells me.

"The debutante ball? But why?" The answer is that Mary's family has decided she should be presented with this year's group of debutantes. I worry. Mary didn't do well in grade eleven at Trafalgar, Montreal's best-respected private school for girls. In fact, she did not do well enough to meet McGill's entry requirements. "But her family had enough pull to get her in," the local gossip goes.

I sound a warning. "You won't have time for all that social stuff and keep up with college work too."

"It's my mother's idea, really," Mary says. "Two of my Lemesurier cousins are coming out this fall and Mum thinks I should too. We have to practice Scottish eightsome reels so as to perform well at the St Andrew's Ball. We'll be practising at the Windsor Hotel twice a week until the end of the month."

"Who are you going to go with?"

"Duncan Patterson. He's a medical student. His mother is a friend of Mum's. The good thing is that we will be presented to the governor general – I am a great fan of Lord Tweedsmuir."

I report this to Colin Spencer the next day when I meet him outside the Roddick Gates. "It seems funny to be doing all that stuff when there is a war on," I tell him.

Colin is too abstracted to pay much attention to the debutantes and their dance. He tells me about another "show" that is in the offing. The boys in the Canadian Officers' Training Corps have been marching and counter-marching in the central part of the track oval at Molson Stadium. They are getting pretty good at it. Now, at the official opening of the Sir Arthur Currie Memorial Gymnasium, COTC ranks will parade as part of the opening ceremonies. Colin shows me the publicity photo of the regiment. He finds it hard to maintain his cynical pose.

AROUND THE GLOBE | FRIDAY, NOVEMBER 10, 1939
Nazi troops move behind Netherlands frontier.

In early November, I have been working with Neil Compton, analyzing, discussing, arguing about the "Allegory of the Cave." Then, separately, we finish our essays.

Neil and I meet again later, with a little trepidation, at Professor Maclennan's office. It is his habit to interview students when he returns their essays. His opening comments to both of us are amiable. Then he says, "Interesting points of similarity between your essays, Miss Hillman, Mr. Compton."

Oh gosh! I think. Plagiarism? We have heard endlessly about this sin while we were in high school. Have Neil and I committed the unthinkable?

I can hardly hear Professor Maclennan as he continues, "You each took a different tack. You have very different opinions about Plato's intentions in presenting the allegory. Nevertheless, your papers seem to follow the same order and to cite the same examples. Did you work together?"

Together we say, glumly, "Yes, sir."

"Good!" is his response. "Always good to follow the Socratic method when you tackle any theory. I'm delighted that you could work together, and pleased that you agreed to disagree. Good work, both of you." He returns the essays.

I am a little chagrined when a peek at Neil's paper shows "A+" at the top of the first page, whereas mine says merely "A." Well, a mere "A" is not so mere, but I can't resist saying to the professor, "I guess Neil's argument was just a bit the stronger of the two?"

His answer is an evasion. Or a generalization, at least. "Logical thought comes more naturally to male students, Miss Hillman." And that is the end of the interview.

When Tom Hardwick drops in at our house that evening, I recount the story of the interview and ask, "Do you agree with Professor Maclennan, Tommy? About logical thought, I mean." Tom's answer is a little evasive, but it emerges that he does indeed agree.

"But how's the trig coming along now?" he asks, and we settle into a session of hard work, clearing up puzzles, and moving a little farther into the next part of the course. Soon I'll be able to follow the instructor's mumbled lectures. Even better, Tom, who is going into honours math and physics, promises to have a word with one of his own professors and tell him how much trouble even good freshman students are having with the young instructor. He appears quite pleased with himself as a logical solver of problems.

On Saturday, November 11, classes are cancelled for Armistice Day commemoration. At a ceremony at the cenotaph near the town hall in Montreal West, the three local ministers will take turns praying, reading scripture, and saying a few words. Then, at eleven o'clock, the bugler will put the shiny trumpet to his lips and play the *Last Post*. All is just as it has been every Armistice Day since I can remember, except that this year, I am a college student. I don't have to go to the cenotaph ceremony. Instead I am off to Toronto on the football train to cheer when McGill beats Varsity. There are rumours that football matches will be cancelled next year if the war continues, so I better enjoy life while I can!

The noisy weekend over, I traipse into the Union late on Monday afternoon. Pete has a challenging assignment for me: I am to go up University Avenue to the front lobby of the medical school where one of the third-year students will brief me.

It is a good story and easy to write up. "In spite of the war, the Meds are harbouring a German," I write. "This Fräulein has soft brown hair and limpid eyes. The third-year med students are taking turns cutting anatomy classes in order to keep her happy ..."

Pete, the night editor, chuckles and puts a headline on the typescript: "Fräulein in the Med School" and adds my name to the list of reporters "in charge of this issue."

"I like the way you keep the punchline for the end," he says. "A stray dachshund the meds are keeping as a mascot. Good." The story reads well. It appears on the front page, opposite the "Around the Globe" news.

AROUND THE GLOBE | TUESDAY, NOVEMBER 14, 1939
1,000 Canadians with RAF in France.

The aftermath of my dachshund story is not good. When I drop into the *Daily* office the next afternoon to see how it has been marked up, Mac Davies,[30] the editor-in-chief, is there ruffling papers at the rear desk. He turns and gestures to me. "I want to speak to you about your piece," he says. "I had a letter about it." He hands over a neat typescript on McGill letterhead.

Dear Editor:

As a survivor of the Royal Medical Corps from the Great War, I feel impelled to write to you about your amusing but worrisome "Fräulein" story. As was the case in the last war, medical students will be exempt from military call-up until they finish their internships. Even arts students will be advised to join the Officers' Training Corps and to stay on campus until they graduate. Accordingly, it is not appropriate for the McGill Daily *to run stories about cutting classes or other high jinks of the kind acceptable in peacetime. The general public will be watching university students very carefully in the next few months for assurance of campus support of the war effort. A word to the wise.*

Sincerely,

E.W. Archibald, Professor, Surgery.[31]

I read the letter with dismay, but Mac Davies says, "Don't worry, um – Betty, isn't it? I've been to see the dean of medicine already. He seemed amused, but he feels I should take some action about your story. I apologized and told him I would suspend the responsible night editor for a couple of weeks."

"Suspend Pete? But it was my fault. I wrote the story."

"Doesn't matter. It's the night editor's responsibility. Pete won't mind. Give him a chance to catch up on course assignments he's been missing. Don't worry. And we'll see you next Monday." He has returned to shuffling papers on his messy desk before I can answer.

I leave, humbled and disturbed. Maybe I'd better distance myself a bit from the *Daily* and catch up on my own course assignments.

It is something of a relief to turn to English and French and philosophy, Latin – even trigonometry. Then the first snow of 1939 falls. The campus turns grey and slushy underfoot. This is the nature of reality in Montreal: you have to get through November, somehow or other. Surely happier days are coming, even in the dead of winter. The lectures in English, in particular, are growing very interesting.

On the other hand, "Civil engineering is my cup of tea," Colin tells me. We are sitting in the Strathcona Hall cafeteria – the "caff" – in the free period after the big English lecture in Moyse Hall. "It feels right for me. I'm even coping with statistics. It was tough at first but seems to get easier as we go along. Well," he says, reaching for his jacket, "I'm off to my lab."

I check my watch. "Oh gosh, I've cut my French class! Now I'll never know all the 'ou' exceptions that take a funny plural, like *bijou, caillou, chou, genou, hibou …*"

French class has settled down to work through grammar and a book of short stories by de Maupassant. Madame Furness still interjects comments on the war, but in a less frenzied manner. She comments flatly that the war has moved into a new phase.

AROUND THE GLOBE | TUESDAY, NOVEMBER 21, 1939
Nazis place 1,200 Czech students in concentration camps.

AROUND THE GLOBE | WEDNESDAY, NOVEMBER 22, 1939
Nazis open reign of terror in Prague; kill 124 students before the eyes of 8,000 fellow students and professors …

Sitting on the Arts steps, Gibson and I giggle together over the day's lectures, the students' manners, the professors' mannerisms. Mary Morris joins us with her tale of practice sessions for the St. Andrew's Ball. The Scottish instructor, she reports, calls instructions for the eightsome reels in accents so thick that none of the debs or their escorts can understand a word. "Not a word!" Mary's escort-to-be is excused from practices (much too busy as a medical student to take time off), so the instructor usually dances as Mary's partner, "and scolds me horribly when I misstep – and all in that foreign language!"

Gibby and I are half-envious, though still worried that Mary will have a hard time catching up on her class work because of the steady round of debutante parties before and after the St Andrew's Ball. The whole idea of "coming out" in society seems like something out of Jane Austen. Madame Casgrain, the head of the Women's Rights Movement in Quebec, has been speaking and writing letters to the *Gazette* and *Star*, deriding this antiquated social practice as degrading to young women.

Twenty German planes downed at front since Monday … Britain loses 5 ships, France 2 by Hun magnetic mines …

Undeterred, on Saturday, November 25, I attend Mary Morris's "At Home," a tea dance for her fellow debutantes and their escorts, plus a few non-socialites like me and Jack Liddy, who has rather reluctantly agreed to be my date. The party is fun but I feel pretty tired next day, almost too tired to write an essay for my composition class on Monday.

Luckily, this week's assignment should be an easy topic for me. We are to write an essay titled, "Wild Animals I Have Known," based on a light-hearted essay by James Thurber included in our composition handbook. Here is a chance to have fun re-writing the Fräulein story, turning the little dachshund into a German shepherd, harder for the med students to hide in their labs.

When I phone Mary Morris to thank her for the party she moans, "I just can't get the darn English composition written. Too tired. Done yours yet, Elizabeth?"

I offer her the use of my composition. "You could read it and do something like it in your own words. You're in a different tutorial, so no one should notice if the two essays are similar." She sounds very relieved. Her debutante ball is coming up this weekend; we hardly see her all week.

Frivolity is part of journalism, whether at the professional or the undergraduate level. After the weekend the *Gazette* runs a three-page account of the St Andrew's Ball.

With a famous Scot like John Buchan (Lord Tweedsmuir, since his appointment

Debutantes Attending
St. Andrew's Ball

SEVENTY-TWO young Montrealers will make their debut to-morrow night at the St. Andrew's Ball being held in the Windsor Hotel under the distinguished patronage of Their Excellencies the Governor-General and the Lady Tweedsmuir. The list includes the Misses Clothilde Baudoin Jean land, Joy Ledeatt, Josette Lacaille, Diana Laing, Rosilla Foss Leavitt, Lucille Lynch, Carol Jean Macaulay, Elspeth MacLean, Peggy MacMillan, Andree Maillet, Raymonde Marchand, Barbara McCombe, Gwyneth McConkey, Elizabeth McConkey, Renee Moncel, Mary Morris, Mary Mather, Patricia O'Brien, Mary Porter

4.2 Debutante ball

as governor general of Canada) presiding, the ball gets full coverage. The *Gazette* dubs it "the Khaki Ball," since General McNaughton has attended it on the eve of his departure for England, along with many officers in uniform. But the *Gazette* goes on to fulsome descriptions of all the debutantes, their gowns, their escorts, the food and wines they consumed at midnight, the Scottish bands that played in the intervals of the dancing, and the pipers drawn in for the special reels and strathspeys for which there had been so many anxious practices. It is fun to spot the description of Miss Mary Morris, "in white *peau de soie*, with scalloped neckline and a full skirt set into a Mary Stuart bodice." No doubt she looked extraordinarily pretty, with her gold-flecked curls "bound in a silk bandeau with pearl *broderies*." There is also a description of "Miss Morris's kilted escort, Mr. Duncan Patterson, Meds '40."

Mind you, the *Gazette* has also run a few letters this past month protesting that this kind of nonsense should be shelved for the duration of the war. But the presence of Lord Tweedsmuir has seemed to justify the coverage. As "John Buchan," Tweedsmuir has had such a large following in the United States that he served very effectively in liaison with Washington in the years before the war, strengthening American-British ties. Now, there are rumours that his appointment as governor general in Ottawa signifies a hopeful effort to keep pressure on the States to back or join the British war against Hitler.

I notice that Principal James is not among the dignitaries noted by the *Gazette* as "in attendance at the ball."

On Monday morning, the *Daily* features events different from the St Andrew's Ball:

AROUND THE GLOBE | FRIDAY, DECEMBER 1, 1939

Russia invades Finland … Nazi air raiders repelled over Scotland …

CHAPTER 5

WINTER

This Monday afternoon at the English tutorial when the previous week's assignments are handed back, there is none for me. "Please stay after class," the tutorial leader says noncommittally. When the class ends, she says gravely, "Sorry, but I am not to comment on your essay. Professor Macmillan wants to see you in his office as soon as you leave this class. Sorry, I also cannot comment on why he wants to see you."

Outside the professor's office I find Mary Morris. "Maybe our essays are extra good and he wants to congratulate us." But I have an uneasy feeling that the summons might be an aftermath of my *Daily* dachshund story, and not a happy aftermath.

Professor Macmillan leaves Mary and me standing as he speaks to us. "There is an unacceptable closeness of these two essays." He picks up the offending efforts from his desk. "Not exact copies, but much too close in phrasing and organization to be accidental. Your tutorial assistants passed them on to me as possible examples of plagiarism."

Mary begins to explain, but he cuts in. "It does not matter to me who copied from whom. In any case, plagiarism is a very serious offence. I can guess that you, Miss Hillman, wrote the original of this pair of essays. Both are in part copied from the story that I read a few days ago in the *Daily*. That also seems to me to be a form of plagiarism in itself. Because you are both freshmen and perhaps unaware of the seriousness of your error, I am not considering suspending or expelling either of you, as would happen if you were in a senior class. Instead, I am going to ask your tutorial assistants to simply enter a zero, not an 'F,' for both of you on this particular assignment."

"Please, sir – " Mary attempts, but the interview is over. The professor waves both of us toward the door. There is a small smile as he dismisses us. "All right," he says. "There are more serious problems in the world right now. Go and sin no more."

Outside his door, when we have caught our dismayed breath, Mary whispers,

"If we get a zero on one essay, will that mean our final mark is less than an 'A' in the course?"

Even as I am trying to reassure my friend, and to accept blame for my own foolishness, I do a little mental arithmetic. Yes, one mark of zero will have a disastrous effect. Goodbye to my hopes of a steady march to an honours degree at the end of my college courses. The tutorial assistant will no doubt be scrutinizing everything I write from this point on, looking for shady practices, and when Professor Macmillan assigns the final mark on the course he will probably remember my name.

Well, I muse, brightening a little, he has remembered it already since he has alluded to my work on the *Daily*. He has read the dachshund story. "And it was good," I tell myself defiantly. I have heard that Cyrus Macmillan was editor of his own college paper when he was at Prince of Wales College in Charlottetown, so he knows a good story when he sees one. And the professor's final words sounded like an absolution, a little more benign than his tone early in the interview.

News of the world encourages a modicum of optimism.

AROUND THE GLOBE | TUESDAY, DECEMBER 5, 1939
US continues diplomatic relations with Soviet Union. President Roosevelt promises all possible aid to Finland.

AROUND THE GLOBE | FRIDAY, DECEMBER 8, 1939
Second Maginot Line, just constructed, completes the formidable defences of France.

Bright winter weather also helps me cheer up. There is already enough snow for skiing in the Laurentians. Last year, up north as high school skiers, we had watched members of the McGill Outing Club flash by on the cross-country trails, their red and white scarves flying behind them. Now, Gibby and I have joined the club together. As we sit in the meeting room at the Student Union, a tall young man strides meaningfully toward us. Tall, dark, and handsome? Yes. Very tall. Dark hair,

5.1 Outing Club skiing

grey eyes. And very handsome. It is Gibson he is aiming for. He met her at a freshman dance, he explains. And now he settles in beside her, as the club president explains their system. Club members go north by train and then ski down together to a rail station lower on the Laurentian line.

On Saturday we make our way very early to the Montreal West station. There we are joined by Gibby's new friend. Tall, athletic, friendly, and as it turns out, a good skier. The trip is as good as the club promised: lots of crisp snow; a wonderful run from Mont Saint-Sauveur down to Sainte-Marguerite, and then back home, so tired we all fall asleep on the train. So tired both Gibson and I fall asleep again in church the next day.

On Monday, Ruth Hill invites me to something different. "I'm trying out for the Debating Union. I don't expect to get in this year but it's a good warm-up for next year when I'll have a better chance." She laughs, "So they say, anyhow. Will you come to the Union later this afternoon and give me a little moral support, Elizabeth?"

Moral support consists of sitting through two hours of round-robin debates, senior members of the team standing against a succession of junior aspirants. Ruth lands the topic, "Resolved that education is wasted on the young." She speaks on the negative, flushed and eager, rattling off a string of pseudo-statistics about young scholars who have proved their worth; pronounces on the perils of putting off education until the brain has turned yellow with aging, and pleads for a reduction of the age of college entry "to eleven or twelve years old, perhaps, when the sap is rising."

The senior debater begins with a drawl, "Now that we have heard from the young – " then continues, " – the *sappy* young – " and the audience guffaws.

When the whole series of debates is concluded and the judges huddle to award points to each debater, I whisper consolation for the way the senior demolished Ruth's argument.

But Ruth is elated. "He listened to me! He picked up my ideas! What a compliment!"

Her elation is justified. Hers are the highest marks of the freshman debaters. There is still little chance that she will get a place on the university team or travel with them after Christmas on their trips to Yale and Princeton, but she is in a mood of triumph. She tells me that she hopes to get into law. "They aren't accepting many women into law though. It would be a great boost toward being admitted if I could get on the team." She adds, thoughtfully, "I will have to get good marks in everything this year, and next year I will have to take jurisprudence and a couple of other prerequisites."

AROUND THE GLOBE | MONDAY, DECEMBER 11, 1939

Finns stop three Russian brigades as violent fighting continues on eastern and southern fronts.

Sporadic snow makes it harder these days to move between the campus and the homebound train. We keep the Finnish ski-soldiers in mind. Less nobly, we hope the Montreal weather will be clear enough for the Santa Claus parade this weekend. Traditionally, the parade offers students a chance to make a little money before the term ends. Eaton's Santa Claus Parade needs elves, clowns, snowmen, et cetera. Gibby and I decide not to look for jobs in the parade, but we arrange to watch from the room of one of the girls in our French class. Her window is right above the main door of Royal Victoria College.

It is still snowing when we take our places at the window. Big soft flakes settle on the regal statue in front of the college. We look down at the top of the statue of Queen

5.2 Queen Victoria

Victoria.[32] Her crown is fluffed up into a white topping. Her knees and her little shoes are white-tipped; on her collar, *broderies* of snowflakes. There is no doubt about her status. Victoria still reigns in Montreal.

The parade sweeps toward us along Sherbrooke Street. It pauses by the RVC so that all the extras hired for the parade can raise a hearty yell. Santa Claus joins the elves and reindeers in hollering out, "*M-C-G-I-L-L! What's the matter with old McGill? She's all right, oh yes you bet!*" The cry trails away as the parade shakes itself and moves off toward the rest of the city and the beginning of the Christmas season.

AROUND THE GLOBE | THURSDAY, DECEMBER 14, 1939

Three British cruisers attack German pocket battleship *Admiral Scheer* off the coast of Uruguay. Aggressive attacks on Rhine-Moselle front.

On Monday I am ready for another *Daily* job: a story about the musical side of college life – the RVC Chorale is contributing Christmas music on the local radio station. I turn in the copy at five, planning to catch the early commuter train home.

"How about a cup of coffee before you go?" Pete, the night editor, asks. He has just typed up a little note for tomorrow's paper to the effect that our new principal, Dr James, is away for a week at an international meeting in Boston. Even though I wish I could stay and gossip a bit about Dr James, I have to run to catch the last train to Montreal West.

Windsor Station is full – overfull – of people anxiously criss-crossing, each aiming for his own gate. The big steamy concourse seems like a monster cave filled with animated puppets, as in Plato's allegory. But there is music to lighten the hectic rush in this cave: a piped-in version of a gentle carol, "*Il est né, le divin enfant!*"

AROUND THE GLOBE

MONDAY, DECEMBER 18, 1939

Graf Spee sunk.

Christmas comes and we welcome family guests: Granny, Granddad, and

Singers Carol Over Montreal's Airwaves

By E. H.

People who run radio broadcasts have to be optimists. Imagine any one telling forty women "You will please all keep perfectly quiet for the next minute"—and believing it could happen! The R.V.C. Glee Clubbers, waiting to broadcast last night, were so astonished at this amazing request that they actually made no noise—no, not so much as a single giggle—for one whole minute. Then a "little man with a ducky moustache", as one co-ed described the announcer, breathed into the microphone that "In connection with the Quebec Musical and Literary Festival the R.V.C. Glee Club will now give two see-lections." The see-lections were "Oh, the Summer" and "The Coventry Christmas Carol." Having described musically both seasons, the girls wriggled their way through crowds of people waiting to go on the Amateur Hour—Could the Glee Club have hit the wrong program?—What one of the R.V.C.-ites said seemed to sum up the whole broadcast. "The music was better than we expected; but the evening would have been worth while anyway, just to see those forty co-eds, all in one room, and not one saying a thing!"

5.3 Chorale

Aunt Zoë Smith from Toronto, and my cousin, Clyde Hillman, from faraway Kenora. He has joined the army and is stationed at the Lachine manning depot. On Christmas Day, happy to be away from the depot, glad to be back with non-soldiers, hungry as a healthy young person could be, he is not at all overwhelmed by meeting so many of his extended family for the first time. Clyde's excitement about being in the army and training to go overseas is infectious. "They've already sent one Canadian division over to England. We'll be following soon. And then – Hitler, look out!"

AROUND THE GLOBE | TUESDAY, DECEMBER 19, 1939

First Canadian troops land safely in Britain. Scots cheer Canucks as ship docks in port "somewhere in England." Two province of Quebec by-elections show landslide for King's participation government.

Our little English cousins have not joined us. Their mother has been frightened by tales of ships torpedoed en route to Canada and she has decided to send them north to a friend in Scotland instead.

Granny tells the old story about the miraculous Christmas Eve during the last war, when the guns fell silent and soldiers sang, "Silent Night, Holy Night" and "*Stille Nacht, Heilige Nacht*" to each other across the darkness of No Man's Land. My father, who was overseas for four-and-a-half years (1914–1919) but never talks about the war, makes no comment.[33]

CHAPTER 6
POETRY

January at college opens with mid-term examinations. They begin on January 4 for engineering students like Colin, whose second term of classes starts on Tuesday, January 9. For us in arts and sciences, there is a longer time off after Christmas: our mid-terms will start on the fifteenth and classes will resume on the nineteenth.

Although January is usually cold in Montreal, it is also usually bright and bracing. The snow falls in slow drifts, or in sudden blasts, or in single stars. At McGill, the double row of elms that lead from the Roddick Gates up through the main campus to the Arts Building forms a fine archway, architectural in its tracery, enhanced by the snow.[34]

Up where the Arts Building bulks grey and solid, hurrying students make a blur of bright colour. The statuary of the *Three Bares* is now encased, its marble eroticism sheltered against the white drifts.[35] The new year on campus begins with a lift of the heart, in spite of the little nips of worry about the world outside our world. The *Montreal Star* headline tells us: BRITISH CALL "PHONEY WAR" A "SITZKRIEG."

6.1
Arts Building
in winter

Pete greets me as I come toward his desk in the *Daily* office. "Off you go, Elizabeth. There's a talk in the RVC common room by a man from India. Quite hi-falutin; lots of important people coming to make a fuss about him. See what you can get."

A crowd clusters in the common room, including people from the city as well as students. The far door opens and Mrs Grant, the warden of RVC, enters, ushering in a dark-skinned dignitary, his wife in a splendid gold-crusted sari, and finally a small brown man in an ill-fitting dark suit. This is the famous speaker, Dr Balachandra Rao, famous politician in India, famous poet in the larger world, as the warden explains. She turns the meeting over to him.

He talks first in a very quiet voice about the India we all know from books – Kipling's mostly – and movies – *Gunga Din* and so on. Then he speaks of another India, a new India, seething with a sense of change, ready for a different place in the world. Ready for Mahatma Ghandi. (The Indian consul stirs a little, and his beautiful wife raises her elegant eyebrows.) But then Dr Rao goes on to discuss "a third India," the India of the poets. He names Rabindranath Tagore, and begins to read from Tagore's work.

Taking conscientious notes, I struggle to get the name spelled right and only half-hear the first part of the poem that the little man begins to recite. In a moment he swings into a high singsong, hypnotic, strange. Suddenly, I am caught. Then his voice sinks to a slow, sonorous tone, and the poetry seems to rise, beyond and through the single voice.

On either side of me, listeners are as spellbound as I am. "Marvellous, eh?" I whisper to a dark-haired girl on my left when the speaker pauses and sits down for a moment to catch his breath.

"I cannot understand it, but yes it is a marvel," the girl whispers back. Then the second set of readings begins and the spell is cast again. At the end, I smile again at my neighbour, who offers, "My name is Sari, like the dress that Indian ladies wear. But I am not Indian. Though I am not Canadian either. I am Czech. Sari is my nick-a-name. My real name is Luissa. And you are – ?"

"Elizabeth."

"Elissabett. An international name," Sari[36] says.

As we move together toward the door, pushing a little through the slow crowd,

I say, "You speak English very well. You must have come to Canada a while ago."

"No. I was sent last year to finish high school and matriculate in Montreal. My idioms are mixed when I speak. But I read perfect and," she laughs, "I write flawless."

"Well, I'm glad to meet you. But I must fly, got to write up this talk for the *Daily*. Maybe we'll see each other again."

"Yes."

I pause to say a polite thank you to the warden of RVC. Mrs Grant remembers me from the story I wrote about the freshette reception tea. She makes a point of introducing me to "a fellow writer," a girl who has just come to Canada from Europe.

The girl smiles. "We have met before this, Mrs Grant." It is Sari again.

"Sari," the warden announces, "has published a little book of verse in Czechoslovakia. Her family is very, very artistic." Then Mrs Grant moves away, saying, "I shall leave you two young writers together."

What does one young writer say to another, especially when one has only written newspaper stories and the other has published a book – and doesn't yet speak very fluent English? Not a problem. Sari and I giggle our way through Sari's troubles with idiom and share the feeling that the eloquent little man from India will stay in our memories a long time.

Then I dash out across Sherbrooke to the Union building. But when I get into the *Daily* office, I find myself not only out of breath but also out of ideas. "It's hard to write this story, Pete," I tell the night editor. "Too much to think about. India – and poetry – "

"Oh," says Pete, "not much copy in that, Liz. Just make it a brief news item: 'Famous poet speaks.' We've already got a pretty full page for tomorrow anyway."

I sit sideways at the news desk and peck out a quick minimal paragraph, hand it in and leave, still feeling strange, elated, unworldly. Then I catch the last commuter train home and amaze my parents, who expect my usual Monday evening bubble of *Daily* news, by going quietly upstairs to work on my English course notes. But first I pull down my old high school atlas and turn to the page where India appears. The deep triangle is coloured red on the map, like all the far-flung parts of the British Empire. Kipling's India, I say to myself. Maybe the map will change if the little man is right.

There are lots of maps in the Montreal papers these days – not of India but of

Europe. Dark arrows trace Hitler's new paths of attack: northward towards Norway – another blitzkrieg to keep his supplies of Swedish ore coming, for his dream of world conquest. Other maps show the possibility of movement into Europe by Hitler's ally, the Soviet Union. But the maps also show the Maginot Line – impenetrable, the line of defence that makes France safe. Nothing can happen to France, not like Poland. Troops are training in England to cross the Channel to back up the French forces, to buttress the Maginot Line. The newspaper articles are reassuring. It seems possible to concentrate on college affairs and assume that all will be well in Europe, that there will be no real change from the old certainties of England and France. Or could that certainty be as flimsy as the dream of Kipling's India?

AROUND THE GLOBE | TUESDAY, JANUARY 23, 1940

Twenty-five thousand Canadians volunteer for Empire Air Training Scheme.

Professor Macmillan is dealing with Milton in his English lectures these days, stirring the lecture hall with sonorous readings from *Areopagitica* – on the freedom of the press, and on freedom of thought.

"*I cannot praise a fugitive and cloistered virtue*," he quotes and thunders out his own response to Milton's vigorous pursuit of freedoms, his indomitable fight against tyranny.

"I suppose Tommy Hardwick would call this another recruiting speech," I mutter. My old friend Tommy is hard to find these days. He seems to slip away from sight, burrowing in his laboratories, never available for a little chat between classes.

I bump into Sari as we struggle up the aisle toward the door of Moyse Hall. I ask if she would like to go out for a cup of coffee together, but Sari answers regretfully that she has a German class in the next hour. "But we will assemble together for freedom of speech soon!"

The Red and White Revue is going to begin casting for its spring show. Pete wants me to write something up.

"It's always a great show," Pete says. "Of course if the war goes on it may be cancelled next year, but for now, give it your best."

I give it the best puff I can. "Calling all co-eds! Try out for a place on the Revue chorus line. Sign up now. Help make this year's spring show as good as its predecessors."

But next day when I look at the office bulletin board, I see my story has been fiercely marked up. Someone has scribbled a comment in the margin: "A girlie show!" I get a gentle scolding from Colin Spencer's brother, Bob,[37] who is one of the night editors, when he phones late next evening.

"I read your piece on the Revue," he says. Then without any small talk, "If you are going to be a journalist, Elizabeth, you really should work on serious stories. There are bigger things than the Red and White Revue tryouts to write about."

AROUND THE GLOBE | WEDNESDAY, JANUARY 24, 1940

Russian troops to the number of 1,000 killed in land engagements with Finns … Allied dispute with US over neutral zone continues; French doubt ability of American navy to enforce it.

Attention Fan-dancers, Engineers: Red, White Revue Can Use You

By E. H.

Is there a fan-dancer at McGill? Is there a pirate? If so, there are parts for you in the Red and White Revue this year. Other parts still empty are Crusaders and Engineers. Now we don't know just what would be the effect on a Crusader of the prospect of playing opposite a fan-dancer, but if we know Engineers, there ought to be a stampede to the casting office when this news becomes known.

Yesterday afternoon, in place of the regular sophisticated chorus routine, the Union Ballroom saw the Revue executive staging a little kindergarten work as would-be actors tried their voice on "Alice in Wonderland."

The results of the try-outs were quite satisfactory, but there is still lots of room for actors. Almost everyone who was in last year's Revue came back for more, but the doggone Freshmen, who don't seem to realize what they are missing, stayed home. Judging from some of the girls who tried out for the chorus, there's plenty of talent among the first year students, according to director Pat Little; why be discouraged because you didn't get a place in the mob, girls? Come on out and try for a star spot!

6.2

Red and White Revue

In philosophy we are now studying Bishop Berkeley and idealism. Professor Maclennan explains the difference between *eros* (ἔρως) and *agape* (αγάπη) – two kinds of love. I wish I had taken Greek instead of French this year. I wish the Americans felt a little more love for the Allied cause. I wish the war would be over.

AROUND THE GLOBE | FRIDAY, JANUARY 26, 1940

King government dissolves eighteenth session of Parliament. Soldiers will have right to vote under War Measures Act.

Though I hadn't felt able to write a news story about the poet from India, it seemed to come easily for the next essay due for the English composition course. "A small brown man from India sat cross-legged on the dais. He read poetry by Tagore. He spoke about peace." I try for "clarity, use of detail, rhythm" – all the rhetorical devices our composition text exhorts us to use. Professor Macmillan has mentioned some of the same rhetorical devices in his Milton lecture. The essay flows.

Yet it is a surprise when the tutorial assistant tells me at the end of class a week later, "Professor Macmillan wants to see you," and adds, "don't worry, it's not trouble this time. I liked your newest essay so much that I passed it on to him. He liked it too."

"Maybe he will write-off the zero for your first essay, Elizabeth," says Gibby. I am dubious, but pleased at least to be going for an interview. "I'll wait in the hallway to hear how it turns out," Gibby says.

Professor Macmillan is expansive. "I like your essay. Yes. I like it very much. You made me want to read Tagore, and I plan to do so. And that is rare for me. I don't read new books anymore."

My face probably reveals my horror at the thought that there might ever be a time when one would not want to read new books.

Professor Macmillan ignores my expression and continues, "I presume you are planning to go into honours English next year?"

"If my marks are good enough. But – "

"I remember. Your plagiarizing zero will not help, though it will not necessarily doom you. Keep up the good work as a writer." He pauses. "Frankly I have a pretty strong prejudice against young ladies who indulge in plagiarism, whatever the extenuating circumstances." He pushes his glasses down on his nose, peers over them at me. "But you have disturbed my prejudice, Miss Hillman," he concludes.

"Well, you have hurt my pride," I answer. Both of us laugh, me tentatively, him uproariously.

Then he says, "At any rate, we will admit you to the honours program, whatever your final mark in the first-year course may be, on the strength of your creative writing." He sweeps a hand toward the door; the interview is over.

Gibby is indeed hovering outside. "Well? Did he offer to wipe out that bad mark?"

"No," I say slowly. And then, in a glad rush, "But who cares?"

Our next English class is about Alexander Pope's *Essay on Man* and "The Rape of the Lock." Moyse Hall rings with laughter as Professor Macmillan mimics the silly voice of Arabella, ready for battle because some admirer had marred her beauty by snipping off one of her ringlets. It didn't seem quite as funny to me as it did to the boys sitting around me. I am becoming a bit bristly about the status of women, and I don't like this kind of mockery.

At the end of the lecture, Sari catches up with me. She has a request to pass on. The warden of rvc has asked her to entertain another poet, this time from Trinidad. His name is Anthony Douglas. Will I help? "Mrs Grant thought that because we liked Mr. Rao, the Tagore man, so much, we shall very much also enjoy taking the Trinidad poet around the campus."

"Fine by me. When?"

"Today, I am afraid. Could you telephone to your home and explain? We shall meet this Mr. Douglas at four. We shall take him to tea at the Ritz-Carlton Hotel and then come back to the campus and show to him the library. We are invited to dine with him at the Royal Victoria College at the warden's table. The warden," she adds, "will send us in a taxi each to home."

"Sounds all right," I reply.

At four, in the hall of the Arts Building, Sari and I are joined by a flamboyant young man. Very tall, very dark, with a flashing smile. "You are my guides, my hostesses?" he asks. "I'm afraid your dean has been misled about me. My old headmistress in

6.3
Ritz-Carlton

Trinidad was a friend of the dean, and I am afraid she has over-sold me. I am not a famous poet."

I laugh. "Never mind! We will all get a good tea out of this, and you can tell us what you really do and what you are in Montreal for." I add, "But Mrs Grant isn't called 'the dean' at McGill. She is the 'warden' of Royal Victoria College."

The young man from Trinidad finds that very funny.

The Ritz-Carlton is somewhat amazed when we turn up for tea – an unlikely trio. A large dark young man accompanied by two seventeen-year-olds clad in the campus uniform of the bulky red-and-white sweater and toque, are not its usual clientele. But laughter bubbles over the elegant *épergne*, the dainty teacakes, the fragile teacups, the white-gloved waiters.

"But why are you here, and under false poetic pretences?"

"I was destined for Cambridge. Most clever chaps in Trinidad go to Cambridge. But the war, the U-boats, the torpedoes are interfering now. By the time the Trinidadians realized that sea voyages were no longer possible we had lost a full college term. Not really lost, you know – we practiced our steel band and drank rum, you know! But our parents did not find it so amusing, so they decided that we should come to Canada instead of Cambridge. And here I am on a fact-finding mission, entertained by my fellow poets. Because I really do write poetry. I'm just not famous."

"The warden means to ask you to read some of your work at dinner," Sari tells him.

"I shall surprise her," he answers. "I shall make a dreadful rift between the dean – I mean the 'warden,' excuse me – and her friend, my old headmistress."

Surprise her he does. When the tea and the tour are over and the three of us have returned to Royal Victoria College and the dignity of the high table, Tony Douglas rises to the occasion with a double dose of his poetry. First he reads two little lyrics, very modern, hard to understand, wrought out of twisted West Indian metaphors. Then he announces, cheerily, "Now I will give you the real West Indian poetry – a calypso that I have just composed. I need everyone to clap in time, and perhaps to tinkle on their glasses with a teaspoon. Or a fork, if no teaspoon is present. It is called, 'A Song to Montreal.'" He throws back his head and swings into rhythm:

> O, Canada! I don't like you' wintah!
> O Trinidad, I miss you very bad!
> I land Montreal city
> McGill University.
> I thought I was robust
> Till I feel the wind on the campus
> As for the co-eds there are none bettah,
> Dressed up in they red-and-white sweatah
> But I've had enough of this weathah.
> O, Canada: I don like yo wintah!
> O Trinidad, I miss you VERY BAD!

The warden is still clapping and banging on her water glass when he stops. She is roaring with laughter when she thanks him. "I hope you learned enough about McGill to tell your friends in Trinidad that they should come to us now that the path to England is barred. And we hope you will come back yourself and sing your poems to us again."

"Good for her," Sari says, when the two of us are bundled into a taxi and sent off home. "I did not think the warden could relax this much. She always speaks to me so very seriously about my poetry. I tell her it is not my principal concern."

"What is your principal concern, Sari?"

"Like Tony from Trinidad, I mostly try to keep warm in this terrible winter!"

In our next English lecture, Professor Macmillan makes his usual grand entry, bursting through the velvet curtains at the back of the Moyse Hall stage, striding to the lectern and soaring into *Gulliver's Travels*. An old familiar book, as I thought. Not so – Professor Macmillan opens up strange levels of complexity in Swift's tale. We are on a trip not to India or Trinidad, but to Laputa, the land of foolish scholarship and automatic writing.

Winter has its compensations – sports, skiing, skating. On Saturday, January 27, Colin takes me to a hockey game: Princeton at McGill. We feel a little condescension toward these American boys. Their country is not at war. Lucky them. But it makes them seem younger than "our boys." And they don't skate as well as our team. We wish there was some way to have a chat with the boys on the American team. We are all hoping that the United States will see the light and join in the war, strengthening the Allies. We hear that President Roosevelt's wife supports the idea of American entry into the war.

I muse, "If women ran politics, maybe there wouldn't be so many wars."

The war doesn't seem to be going that badly right now though. We still call it the "Sitzkrieg." A new name begins to pop up optimistically in the news from England.

AROUND THE GLOBE | MONDAY, JANUARY 29, 1940

Winston Churchill, First Lord of the Admiralty, denounces Nazi treatment of Poles and Czechs; forecasts new offensive.

CHAPTER 7
POLITICS

Canadian political life has taken a surprising turn. To defend his stand on the war, Mackenzie King has called a sudden election, to the dismay of many.

AROUND THE GLOBE | FRIDAY, FEBRUARY 2, 1940
Less than 13 hours of campaign broadcasting allowed the four political groups over the CBC …

Among the irate is Madame Thérèse Casgrain,[38] who has been agitating for extending the vote in Quebec to women. (Everywhere else in Canada women have that right.) Obviously Madame Casgrain is too late to win this particular battle; getting the vote for Quebec women can't happen in this sudden election. She is also leading a general fight by the League for Rights of Women of Quebec, to give women the right to hold office and to make contracts without permission of a husband (or other controlling male) to buy and sell property.

The *Daily* assigns me the job of covering a talk, sponsored by the Canadian Student Assembly, to be given by Madame Casgrain: "Votes for women in the province of Quebec, and the status of women in the province." Serious stuff: Bob Spencer will be proud of me. He is on the executive of the local branch of the assembly – the body of which every Canadian university student is automatically a member. There have been some rumblings that the CSA has been making pronouncements about the war and other matters, but the *Daily* has been playing down any controversy. Anyway, the talk I am to cover is on a very serious and very controversial topic.

Alas, the talk itself, even though it is delivered by the famous Madame Casgrain, is rather dull. Anyway, I have only been allotted an inch-and-a-half of space to cover it. I don't think Bob will count my glum little story as making amends for my lighthearted pieces. I worry what he will say about my next assignment.

Sadie Hawkins Boldly Chases McGill Males

Finds Dates for Spree, Tea Dance

By BE. 0111

Sadie Hawkins, happy that her picture, clipped from yesterday's Daily, now reposes over many a fluttering male heart, is becoming bolder and bolder as her week of power progresses. Invitations for the Spinster Spree and the Junior Tea Dance are now flying thick and fast.

On Thursday, from four to six. Sadie and her sisters, on presentation of a nickel (5c) can dance with their Abners in the Union Grill to the music of a nickel-less nickelodeon. Or, if she can't get her own Abner to go, Sadie can attend the dance anyway, and on presentation of the same nickel (5c) can dance with other people's Abners. The Juniors are admitting outsiders to their Tea Dance—"For the '41 lady, and Freshette O'Grady are sister Sadie Hawkinses under the skin." By the way, if this dance is successful, a series of informal social functions like it will probably be held later, according to the Secretary of the class of '41. These will probably include skiing, skating and roller-skating parties.

As for Sadie's night of nights—the Spinster Spree on Friday, all the glamour girls on the campus

(Continued on Page Four)

(Continued from Page One)

say that that night they'll show men a thing or six about entering your light of love. Over hundred people are expected; dance will probably be as big a cess as it was last year. One last year's batch of eligible sp sters sent her date a large corsag of vegetables! What are you do about it this year, Sadies? Arc Etienne will play for the dance from 9 to 1 and at 11.30, the hung males and their escorts will served refreshments in the Co mons Room (which incidenta will also be the sitting-out plac As patrons, the Spinsters will ha Mrs. Grant and Dr. Ross, and De and Mrs. Hendel have also been vited.

Remember, girls, though there men who can boast that they ha had three or four invitations these events, there are still lots mals just **panting** to be taken. Yo, Sadie! Get going ol' girl!

7.1
Sadie
Hawkins

The first week on campus in February is Sadie Hawkins Week (an American import). The idea of a period when girls could take the initiative in inviting boys out – for coffee, or dinner, or to the big dance at the end of the week – began a couple of years ago in American colleges, then came to the University of Toronto in 1938, and has drifted to McGill this year. Something new. I have written a lead-up story in the *Daily*, although no one has taken much notice of it.

Bob Spencer joins me in the caff on Tuesday afternoon, where I am having a cup of coffee to warm up. It seems he still feels the need to lecture me about seriousness in journalism. I'm too in awe of Bob, who is after all a third-year student, to tell him (as I would like to do) to mind his own business.

"I read your piece on Sadie Hawkins," he says. Then adds, "I do feel that you should try writing more important stuff for the *Daily*. There are major problems everyday – the threat of censorship, for instance. Even the *Daily* may be subject to control if the war gets any worse. That's the kind of real topic you should be treating. Not girls chasing boys. And there is the CSA. I'm worried about some of the policies they are formulating."

"I thought they were just working to get increased numbers of scholarships, Bob?"

He shakes his head. "That's the story they have been giving the *Daily*. You should come to some of the assembly open meetings, Elizabeth. You could do a story about what is really happening. Give your readers a little dose of reality." Bob shakes his head again, picks up his books, and leaves.

But I am not so keen on reality these days. In fact, I have given up reading the *Daily* except on Tuesday mornings, when my own articles appear in it. I don't even read the *Montreal Gazette* anymore. The news is so pointless. Everyone going overseas and then just sitting in England waiting for things to start. And on the way over, the ships are helpless, sitting ducks for torpedoes from the U-boats, even with the navy convoys.

This all does seem to make Sadie Hawkins look silly. Yet after I finish my coffee, I find myself going back to the *Daily* office to invite sports editor, Wallace Beaton, to be my date at the Sadie Hawkins party. I danced with Wallace at the first *Daily* party, and enjoyed going with him to the first football game; since then I have seen him occasionally. Why not give him a tryout as "Li'l Abner"?

Well, at the first *Daily* party I must have been too excited to notice his lack of rhythm. Wallace turns out to be the worst dancer imaginable. His feet go every which way, regardless of the music, and apparently independent of his own direction. He seems surprised every time he missteps or bumps into other dancers, or treads on my toes. Not a matter for apology, just a surprise. At the end of the evening, I walk him home, as prescribed, and say a relieved good night.

"Lots of fun," he burbles. "We'll go out together again sometime, Elizabeth."

"Sure thing." But I am really sure it isn't a sure thing at all.

AROUND THE GLOBE | WEDNESDAY, FEBRUARY 7, 1940

New series of bombing struck England today, as the British Government prepared to hang two convicted members of the outlawed IRA. The blasts were blamed on the IRA.

When I go in to the *Daily* office next Monday, Wallace isn't around. Pete avoids comment on my Sadie Hawkins story. But Kitty Haverfield,[39] the women's editor, catches me by the arm and says, "I, for one, really liked what you did on Sadie Hawkins. And," she continues, "I liked your articles on the recruiting for the Red and White Revue. Well, Elizabeth, the Revue really needs publicity now. Maybe it should have been cancelled this year because of the war, but it wasn't. It'll lift spirits, a good funny show, satirical skits, a chorus line, solo singers. But it needs more publicity." Kitty makes her proposition. "I'm going to ask Pete if you can back me up for the next few weeks. We'll concentrate on the girls who are dancing and singing, and the chorus line – build up interest with a flurry of jazzy articles. Okay?"

I would have preferred to go on with the random assignments I had been doing, but Kitty is flattering, and I agree to help her. (But I wouldn't want to be women's editor, I decide in my own mind. Just like on the big papers, it would all be fashions and domestic stuff, silly tea parties.) Then I remember meeting Sari at a silly tea party and that softens my resistance a little.

Canadian Red Cross to aid the British branch in the event of emergency in France.

The national election is mostly about conscription. Should Canada draft young men for the army? The feeling in Quebec is strongly against it. Some of the election rallies are rather ugly, according to the anglo Montreal papers.

As we move further into February, we have other ugly feelings right here on campus. They concern the Canadian Student Assembly. The *Daily* reports that people at a CSA meeting on February 6 have been forcibly ejected from Strathcona Hall by "boisterous" students, calling for the dissolution of the McGill branch of the CSA. Those boisterous folk claim that CSA is trying to whip up student opposition to conscription.[40]

The disrupted CSA meeting will reconvene at a later date, the *Daily* says. The Montreal press gets involved in the uproar, reporting that many people suspect the CSA of serving as a front for communist interests. Another body claiming to represent all Canadian students, the NFCUS – the National Federation of Canadian University Students – promises to challenge the CSA at the reconvened meeting.

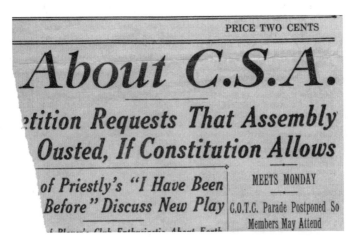

7.2
Canadian
Student
Assembly

The *Daily* professes to take no sides between the two contending organizations. A clear, forceful editorial pleads for calm and reasonableness. "The main purpose of the university is to teach those who are passing through to think. As long as we have campus controversies we know that the university process is succeeding and we have no cause for concern." I can hear Mac Davies's quiet, intelligent voice in the rhythms of that editorial.

But a questionnaire circulated on the issue shows that most students – eighty-five percent – have no opinion about the two organizations, and indeed pay no attention to campus controversies. I am part of that eighty-five percent. I have been busy catching up on my reading assignments, enjoying the lectures, adjusting to this complex undergraduate world.

Besides, I'm still less focused on serious student politics than on frivolous entertainment. To please Kitty, I write "something sprightly" to get more girls to turn out for a second tryout session for the Red and White Revue.

It is no particular surprise when Wednesday brings a phone call. "Saw your story yesterday." It is Bob Spencer. He plunges on: "You should be writing

CHORUS STILL CALLS CO-EDS

Blondes Flock to Register For Revue

Vacancies Open For Specialists, Musicians and Mask-Makers

E. H.

The assistant producer of the Red and White Revue who yesterday took the names and telephone numbers of hundreds of co-eds aspiring to a place in the chorus, was considerably surprised when one would-be chorine countered by asking him for his name and number. "Getting in practice for Sadie Hawkins week, no doubt," was the comment of producer Pat Little. The turnout at yesterday's registration meeting, Little stated, was extremely satisfactory, but it is hoped that the supply of beautiful women at McGill is still far from exhausted. Among those who came

7.3

Chorus calls co-eds

instead about the clash between the CSA and the NFCUS."

I tell him, "I don't know the differences between them – and I don't really care."

In mid-February there comes a sad break in the normal college routine. The governor general, Lord Tweedsmuir,[41] beloved John Buchan, producer of everyone's favourite thrillers, has died. The *Gazette* carries stories about his service to the British Empire, including his most recent work as information director in the United States, trying to encourage the Americans to join the Allies in the fight against Nazism. College activities are cancelled for a day of mourning.

Mary Morris, in her own extra burst of mourning, reminds me how much everyone admired Lord Tweedsmuir at the debutante ball. "He looked so frail! But he was so brave!" she says. "At least that's one good thing about having come out this year – I saw Lord Tweedsmuir up close. But – " her voice trails away, "the darn parties are still taking up so much time, I'm falling behind on all my courses. One day off isn't going to help. I might as well just go on mourning, and I think what I'll do today is just re-read *The Thirty-Nine Steps*."

7.4
Lord Tweedsmuir

The British Empire that John Buchan had believed in is still strong.

Thirty thousand Australian & New Zealand troops arrive at Suez.

February mornings grow colder and colder. Even if the window is only open a little crack at the bottom, snow drifts in onto the sill and the radiator under the window. Too cold to get up; and then too cold to enjoy going out, waiting for the commuter train, climbing from Windsor Station up McGill College Avenue to the Roddick Gates, through the deep snow on the campus road, up to the Arts Building. Hearing Dr Macmillan pontificate about eighteenth century fiction hardly compensates for this frigidity.

Finns repulse attacks as Reds intensify attacks on Mannerheim Line … British sink two more German subs … Three British freighters and Danish ship lost in sea war …

Lana Turner's hair auctioned for Finnish Relief Fund.

As February drags on I go to a meeting of the Student Christian Movement, concerned still with the question of votes for women in Quebec. Fiery Madeleine Parent, now in her graduating year, speaks with passion and then veers into the topic of other rights: the right to strike, the right to unionize, the right to oppose the war. Someone whispers, "That's the communist line. Since Russia joined Germany, all the lefties are turning against the war."

Sweden protests against the bombing of border towns by Russia … Yesterday's toll of shipping was three Dutch, two Norwegian … A new Dalai Lama is enthroned today at Lhasa, Tibet.

The new topic in our philosophy lectures is the idea of right and wrong: "Is justice the interest of the stronger?" Does the working of justice simply reflect the views of those in power? Is justice a compromise brought by the necessities of life? Plato had quoted wise Socrates as arguing that as an attribute of the state, justice could keep wisdom, courage, and temperance in balance, lessen suffering in society, and balance the needs of the different classes of people. But we are now asked to argue *against* Socrates. Using Hobbes as a springboard, we are to make the argument that justice in practice buttresses the status quo, keeps the poor in their place, and rewards those already in power. Maybe the current put-down of women like Madame Casgrain and Madeleine Parent is an illustration of the power of the establishment?

Forty Nazi planes fly over Paris.

More immediate problems are emerging. French classes in particular have become increasingly tense again. Madame Furness keeps drifting away from the curriculum into diatribes about the lack of French Canadian sympathy for the plight of France. She is "French from France," she tells the class, but everyone who shares the great French heritage should surely bleed for the Nazi threat to France. Several of the students are becoming restless as these personal commentaries continue.

"Could I ask the meaning of the phrase at the bottom of page seventy-two of the text, Madame?" one young woman interjects, just as Madame Furness is reaching a peroration. It is the same American student who has been trying since the outset of the class to keep Madame Furness "on track." Mary Margaret Miller has been sent to

McGill by her parents in Virginia in order to perfect her French. (If the war had not broken out, she would have been sent to the Sorbonne, she tells us.) Deviations from the promised course do not suit her priorities.

Madame is not so much angered as stunned. She rises and leaves the classroom without even gathering up her notes and textbooks. The abandoned class breaks into a verbal free-for-all (not in French) and by the time Gibby and I leave the room there is still a furious hubbub in progress. We pick up a copy of this morning's *Daily* and shake our heads over the stories.

AROUND THE GLOBE | THURSDAY, FEBRUARY 29, 1940

Heavy gunfire from the North Sea audible at Amsterdam and the Hague … Britain, fearing peace in the Holy Land might be endangered, announced new restrictions on the sale of lands to Jews.

February – a short month, even in leap year – has seemed to last forever. On the leap year special day, February 29, I am suddenly very busy. First I must go to the Royal Victoria College to hear the famous Madame Casgrain again. A very different affair from the insipid talk I heard her give earlier. Madame Casgrain now returns with high drama to her special plea for women's right to vote in the forthcoming provincial election. She reminds us of the famous "Persons Case," a judgment set down just ten years ago by the Privy Council of Britain, asserting that Canadian law had no basis for treating women as "non-persons" legally classed with children and mental incompetents. She calms down, ends with a quiet suggestion that it is now time we Quebec "persons" get the right to vote.

I catch sight of Kitty Haverfield as we move through the front hall of the college. "How could we possibly not have the right to vote?" I ask her. "Women have been voting everywhere else in Canada since the Great War. I didn't realize – "

"Didn't you see the Villeneuve story in the *Daily* last week? They quote Cardinal Villeneuve: women don't really want the vote; women can get what they want through their clubs; they will be exposed to evils if they get into politics; and finally, having the vote would undermine the hierarchy of families. The *Daily* didn't really comment, just presented the cardinal's arguments as if they assumed everyone would see the fallacies."

"Goodness, Kitty, I must have skipped that page. Can't we do something?"

"There's not much we can do about it, at least while we are at university," she answers. "Anyway, most of the girls in college are more interested in boys and dates than in whatever rights they are missing." She shrugs on her winter coat.

I ask her, "Then why should you and I go on filling the *Daily* with stuff about cute girls in the Red and White Revue chorus line?"

She echoes the words the older men, former editors of the *Daily*, have offered: "We mustn't rock the boat; we should feel lucky they are leaving our fellows in college rather than conscripting them." We both know there isn't an obvious answer to this kind of pressure from our seniors, despite what Milton might have written centuries ago about freedom of speech.

But this day is far from over. Our local unpleasant politics are coming to a head. There is a CSA meeting later today and I plan to attend it. This is the follow-up to the hectic meeting broken up a couple of weeks ago. It is bound to be exciting, and I expect Bob Spencer to play a part in the excitement. Sitting in the crowded Union meeting room, I follow the intricate arguments offered from the floor and from the executive with moderate interest. I perk up when Bob rises from the seat beside me and begins to talk, very seriously indeed. He speaks of the original values of the Canadian Student Assembly as a grassroots movement.

"I accepted a position on the executive of the assembly," he says, "because in past years this group stood for all that was best in Canadian student life."

"Still true!" someone shouts from the back of the room, but others boo. Bob drives on. "I suspected, as many did, that the headquarters staff were pro-communist, but that seemed unimportant to me, because the communists were clearly our strongest opposition to fascism. Now we hear rumours of a secret pact between Russia and the Nazis. And now the more I watch this assembly at work, the more I believe it is not just pro-communist, but also anti-British. Anti-Canadian. Against the war effort. Against what most students really believe."

The murmurs around Bob are rising into a shouting match. His voice outrides them all. "I am resigning my position on the executive of the Canadian Student Assembly." He begins moving toward the door. By the time I can get out of the turbulence in the room, he has disappeared. I rush down the Union stairs, grab my coat from the cloakroom, and exit into the cold night air. No sign of him.

I had better get to the *Daily* office. This is a big night for me. Tomorrow morning the masthead will carry magic words: "In charge of this issue: Elizabeth Hillman."

What kind of account of that tumultuous meeting should the *Daily* publish? Our student paper has become quite timid lately about tackling controversial topics.

When I get to the *Daily* office I find the account of the Canadian Student Assembly meeting is already in, written by Judy Jaffe. It is just a careful statement of facts. I set the careful headline: CSA TREASURER RESIGNS POST. No use stirring up feelings.

Anyway, this is my big day of glory. I am to "put the paper to bed." I organize the paste-up of stories on all four

PAGE TWO

McGill ✠ Daily

THE OLDEST COLLEGE DAILY IN CANADA

❖ ❖ ❖

Member, Canadian University Press

❖ ❖ ❖

Published every week-day
during the college year at
690 SHERBROOKE ST. W.
Telephone LAncaster 2244.

❖ ❖ ❖

Opinions expressed below are those of the
Managing Board of the McGill Daily
and not the official opinions of
the Students' Society,

❖ ❖ ❖

MALCOLM N. DAVIES...Editor-in-Chief
JACK L. GREENWOOD..Managing Editor
PETER H. WYMAN........News Editor
NORMAN CARDON........Sports Editor
G. H. FLETCHER..Advertising Manager

❖ ❖ ❖

ASSOCIATE EDITORS

Feature Editor.............Kitty Haverfield
C.U.P. Editor ....Sydney Segal
Exchanges.................Kalman Kunin
Sports Features ....William Cairns
Women's Editor..........Katherine Aikins
Women's Sports Editor.Winnifred Fairhead
Music.................Ralph D. Rabinovitch
Drama....................Maurice Hecht

❖ ❖ ❖

News	Sports
Harriet Bloomfield	Shan H. Dunn
Elie Abel	Charles Bishinsky
Edward D. Joseph	Doug. Armstrong
Robert A. Spencer	Sydney Wagner
Jean Worley	Andrew Gibb

M. M. Malen

❖ ❖ ❖

IN CHARGE OF THIS ISSUE:

NEWS	SPORTS
Elizabeth Hillman	S. C. Issenman

Montreal, Friday, March 1, 1940
Vol. XXIX—   —No. 86

7.5 My *Daily*

Feb. 29th, 1940.

Dr. Grant H. Lathe,
Natl. Secretary,
Canadian Student Assembly,
772 Sherbrooke St., West,
Montreal.

Dear Dr. Lathe:

This is to inform you that after due consideration I have decided to tender my resignation as National Treasurer of the Canadian Student Assembly.

You are no doubt aware of my enthusiasm for the C.S.A. program, especially those aspects dealing with National Scholarships and English-French relationships. These I hope will become two of the basic planks upon which a new national student organization will be set up.

However I have come to believe in the truth of the accusations that the C.S.A. is not in the control of truly representative Canadians.

Because of the fact that I am not in agreement with the National Executive and no longer care to be responsible for its actions, I am forced to tender my resignation.

Sincerely yours,
ROBERT A. SPENCER.

[top]
7.6a **Bob Spencer's letter**

[bottom]
7.6b **End of letter**

pages. On the front page I include the story about Bob Spencer and the CSA, and also my own story, again, typically, about the Red and White Revue skits. "Around the Campus" mentions the upcoming Meds Ball and Arts Banquet. "Around the Globe" on the first page recognizes famine in Poland, British restriction on sale of Palestinian land to Jews, and the failure of peace talks – lines of type less likely to stir exuberance.

Late in the evening I have to take the pasted-up pages through the dark streets of downtown Montreal to the *Gazette* building where it will be printed.[42] Harry Lash, one of the reporters on duty tonight, kindly accompanies me. A fabulous evening, all in all.

I do worry that Bob Spencer will be disappointed by the bland little *Daily* article reporting, simply and limply, that the Canadian Student Assembly has reviewed its bylaws in a meeting at the Union. And he will no doubt be annoyed that it is set side-by-side with yet another story about the inconsequential Revue.

The next issue of the *Daily* carries a long letter he has written, carefully setting out his point of view. It ends with a firm decision.

On the way to the library, I meet Colin. As Bob's younger brother he has his own comment to make: "Anyway, now that Bob is off the executive he'll have time to get back to work, catch up on his assignments. He wants to graduate with honours in history next year. Our dad expects it." He adds with a sudden smile, "If it were me, I'd stick to ancient history. Easier to take than modern developments."

My own favourite course is still philosophy. Professor Maclennan has moved a long way from Plato's idealism. He has been lecturing on Hobbes. We admit that the view of man's life as "nasty, brutish, and short" seems all too acceptable, given the current world news. Maybe both Plato and Hobbes were relatively right. Relativity seems tenable in the shifting sands of daily events.

CHAPTER 8
SILVER SWAN

At the English lecture on March 4, one of the younger English professors parts the curtain, steps to the lectern, and announces, "My name is Dando.[43] Dr Macmillan has been called to Ottawa for consultations with the government. In Dr Macmillan's absence, I have the privilege of talking to you today about John Keats."

The class sits up. We are caught out of our early March apathy. The young professor is dark-haired and very good-looking. He begins to speak about the rich, sensuous poem, "The Eve of St Agnes."

> Anon his heart revives: her vespers done,
> Of all its wreathed pearls her hair she frees;
> Unclasps her warmed jewels one by one
> Loosens her fragrant bodice ...

"You note the lush, voluptuous language," he says.

We do, indeed.

The rich voice goes on: "And now we turn to the 'Ode on Melancholy.'" His tone drops to a still lower register.

> Or if thy mistress some rich anger shows,
> Emprison her soft hand, and let her rave,
> And feed deep, deep upon her peerless eyes.

Sighs, ripples, flutters. And rustlings. And, from Tom Hardwick, sitting in the aisle seat right in front of me, a loud snort. At that moment comes the sound of the bell that marks the end of each classroom hour. The spell is broken. The poetry is over. We hunch into our winter coats and hump out of Moyse Hall.

The next morning, March 5, the *Gazette* carries a story about Dr Macmillan. He has been called to Ottawa to head a committee on methods of organizing classes in the army.[44] Important war work, the *Gazette* announces, and adds that Dr Macmillan's lecturing duties will be fulfilled by younger members of the faculty.

Younger and infinitely more gorgeous, I think, as I fold the morning *Gazette* and get ready to leave for school. Soon, I figure, all the younger professors will join up or be called up, clever fellows that they are – Dr Macmillan will conscript them into the teaching of army units – and we'll be left with a whole range of nitwits like our trig teacher.

AROUND THE GLOBE | TUESDAY, MARCH 5, 1940
RAF bomb sinks U-boat in Heligoland Bight.

Instead, on March 5, Dr Newton,[45] another fine-looking young man, steps through the velvet curtains and up to the lectern. He is more ethereal looking than the "lush, sensuous" lecturer last week. He offers a talk about Keats's contemporary, Percy Bysshe Shelley. "Such delicacy," he says, and he reads in a slow, quiet voice.

My soul is an enchanted boat
Which, like a sleeping swan, doth float
Upon the silver waves of thy sweet singing …

A kind of groan from Tommy Hardwick. Everyone nearby laughs and he slumps even lower than usual.

Dr Newton concludes his lecture. "When Professor Macmillan is unavailable, other members of the department will take his place. Meantime, I reassure you – Professor Macmillan will be returning at intervals from his war work."

His war work? The portly (euphemism for fat) professor? We know that he is also legendary as a scholar who collected folk and fairy tales while in the trenches of the Great War, but he certainly doesn't fit our idea of a warrior now. Not a Chaucerian man-at-arms.

8.1
Presenting
the colours

On campus, military training in the Canadian Officers' Training Corps has moved forward. The men are well organized, and our principal is ready to recognize them officially. Dr James hands over battalion colours.[46]

There is a lot of gossip around the *Daily* office these days about our principal: rumours of clashes between Dr James and some of the faculty, for instance. We know that when Professor Adair criticized Chamberlain's policy with regard to Russia, calling it "stupid" in a speech to the Montreal Rotary Club, Principal James let it be known that it was uncalled-for.

Dr James reads the *Daily* very carefully, again according to *Daily* gossip. Whenever there is some reference to him there, his secretary, Mrs MacMurray, calls the editor-in-chief to her office and explains Dr James's point of view. Amiable chats, but firm in tone. He would prefer that there be fewer references to his time away from Montreal. He is working on very important commissions and committees in connection with the imperial war effort.

College life always winds down in March. Though the February cold spell drags on, *Daily* assignments continue for a little while longer. I pick up my Monday assignment around four o'clock, scoot around the campus to collect material, and write it out in longhand while sitting in the caff eating a grilled cheese sandwich and drinking a glass of milk. Often Ray Rose and Bill Munroe, a couple of the other first-year *Daily* reporters, join me.[47] After the grilled cheese, we all scurry next door to the

Union to type up our stories on the old *Daily* Underwoods and hand them in to the night editor before seven o'clock. Then I catch a streetcar for home. Any later and my parents begin worrying about me.

I have one last duty for the Red and White Revue. Pete sends a photographer to go with me upstairs to the Union ballroom.

In the centre of the room a bunch of pretty girls stand, ready to go on stage in the chorus line. We interview and get some good shots – one of Student President Russ Merifield, surrounded by four of the long-legged girls who have already been chosen as dancers.

Now, like all the other students, I settle in to the final flurry of essays and begin preparing for early April exams. Faculty wind up the courses and brace themselves for the job of marking. Winding up, winding down.

8.2

Box office opens

[Quebec Premier] Godbout renews promise to give women vote.

But this year, in mid-March, the war is gearing up. There are frightening headlines in the *Montreal Star*: BRITISH TANKER TORPEDOED IN CHANNEL, and the *Gazette*: NAZI TROOPS MOVE TO SWISS BORDER.

In Finland, troops on skis are holding out against Russian invaders near Vilipuri. We think sadly of those snow-borne soldiers as we shoulder our own skis for a last trip to the Laurentians. Harold,[48] Colin, and I, with Gibby and her new friend, Vince, board the train for the north on this March weekend. Without regret, I have realized that if I go skiing I will miss the opening night of the Red and White Revue. Well, the chorus line will do just fine without me. The spring skiing is perfect. Sharp blue skies, soft powder snow. A successful day – a last carefree fling before the exams.

The more heroic skiers in northern Europe have had successful days too, according to the *Montreal Star*: FINNS HALT REDS ON THREE FRONTS.

So back to the final round of classes. It is soothing to turn from the barrage of war news to study Latin love poems with Professor McCullagh.[49] He is a wonderful teacher, warm and friendly, as well as learned; I hope to take another course with him next year. And the young trigonometry instructor who came in as a miserable substitute has at last found a way to clarify the conceptual structure of mathematics. He now sounds clear and reasonable. In philosophy, a different kind of concept: we have reached Emmanuel Kant, clearly Professor Maclennan's favourite. Our favourite too. Here at last are some clear "categorical imperatives." No relativity, but clear orders for life: "Act as if you lived in a kingdom of ends," and "Act as if your act were to be universalized." Technical language, but (in class at least) the concept is rational and acceptable.

We need clarity and rationality these days. We are still watching the news from Finland very earnestly. The thought that the ski patrols have given up the fight and signed an armistice with Russia is very sad; it seems that Europe is left with one less defence against enemy forces.

Stalin signs treaty with Finns.

The days fill up with end-of-term meetings, as clubs wind down their activities and elect new executives for next year. Some with clarity, some in fuzzy confusion – what will next year bring? Why bother electing a new executive when so many of this year's members may well be in the armed forces by fall?

Student politics rise into our consciousness for one last time this year. The Canadian Student Assembly is out of sight, the National Federation of Canadian University Students having taken its place. But there is a third national student organization with aspirations of influencing student lives – doomed aspiration, as it turns out. At the end-of-term Student Christian Movement meeting, there is a vote to break connections with the Canadian Youth Congress, now seen as communist. The meeting, however, votes to affirm the values that the Youth Congress stands for. Most students are obviously puzzled about the limits of left-wing sympathies in a time when attitudes toward Russia are so confused and complex.

On another note, Madeleine Parent again makes an impassioned plea for students to support factory workers in their demands that strikes not be outlawed for the duration of the war. For the majority at the meeting, this seems a less urgent matter than supporting the war effort – and finishing the final set of essays as the term end draws near.

Another notice in "Around the Globe" signals the swing of attention to a new front.

Turks fear Soviet-German attack.

With the Red and White Revue having concluded its performances, Moyse Hall is being readied for the springtime concert by the RVC Chorale. This I will happily attend, since both Gibson and Sari are prominent in the chorus. I choose a seat near the centre front, shuck off my coat and prepare to enjoy the concert. Young women's voices, sweet and true sopranos, strong, pure contraltos, blend into wonderful sound. Gibson, centre front in the chorus, her dark eyes shining, throws her heart into the music. Sari stands more shyly in the group. The whole chorale group seems lifted beyond their usual abilities by Dr Whitehead, who adds to his duties as organist at Christ Church Cathedral by conducting this choir. The songs swell, shift from a happy to melancholy mood, and conclude with a madrigal.

> The silver swan, who living had no note,
> When Death approach'd, unlock'd her silent, silent throat.
> Leaning her breast against the reedy shore,
> Thus sung her first and last, and sung no more.
> Farewell all joys; O Death, come close mine eyes;
> More geese than swans now live,
> More fools than wise.

I run through a spring snowstorm to the Union just in time to hand in my review of the concert. In the *Daily* office I find a bunch of geese at work. A group of noisy commerce students are putting together their annual special issue of the *Daily*. I recognize Wallace Beaton, now sitting at the night editor's desk. I tell him, "You'll be editor-in-chief soon," but he says, "Who wants it?" The atmosphere in the office is raucous, and as far as I am concerned, rude.

It is a *Daily* tradition that different faculties put out special editions at intervals all year. We have had an *Engineering Daily*, a *Theologs's Daily*, and now the *Commerce Daily*. The commerce one takes pride in being outrageous. We understand that the administration looks askance at these specials, which tend (except for the *Theologs's*) to be filled with dirty jokes. Principal James's secretary has called Mac Davies to his office after each one appeared and delivered critical admonitions.

At the end of the week, on March 15, a totally different group walks in procession from the *Daily* office to the upstairs ballroom, ready for the gala night of the awards banquet.

Mingling with us young reporters and editors are the people who had been reporters and editors in their time. These people, now in law or education, or working

8.3
Old *Daily*

as professional journalists, or businessmen, include Gladstone Murray, founder and editor-in-chief, 1911, and Senator A.K. Hugessen, associate editor, 1911. They have brought old copies of some of the original *Dailys* to show us.

Also present are Gerald Clark,[50] editor-in-chief from the previous year, 1938–1939, and Monty Berger, last year's prize reporter, now a graduate student at the Columbia School of Journalism. Gibby's father, Harry Beatty, is here too. He's very warm in greeting me, and full of hope for my great future career in the writing business.

Speeches and awards all round, and praise, even for lowly freshman reporters like me – I have won a *Daily* lapel pin, a first-year award. Special congratulations and honours go to Malcolm Davies, the editor-in-chief, who is planning to join the air force after his final examinations are over. When they rise to speak, however, several of the older guests launch hostile comments about the current *Daily*. The commerce students have produced that off-colour issue, and unfortunately that is the issue in everybody's hands tonight. The older men feel this is a bad climax to a rather inglorious year. We have not supported the war effort as we should, some say. Not enough stories about McGill graduates who are already overseas; too much "persiflage" about the Red and White Revue; not enough hard-hitting stories about issues like the status of women. I see-saw between defensiveness and pride.

In his banquet speech, Mac Davies does his best to spread a bit of oil on obviously troubled waters. Sitting quietly at a table near the back of the room, I opine that no one outside the *Daily* "retirees" cares that much about the *Daily*'s omissions.

AROUND THE GLOBE | FRIDAY, MARCH 15, 1940
Paris press demands abandonment of present siege warfare.

My year at the *Daily* is over. We are now in the final stages of lectures and assignments. Back in Moyse Hall for our English class, increasingly jittery with the approaching end of term, we find handsome young Professor Dando – "the Keats man, lush and sensuous" – in the spotlight again, talking about Dickens's *Hard Times*. He takes flight into an exposition of the connections between fiction and truth, and fact and truth. My galloping pen garners its crop of allusions, references to articles, witty turns of phrase. I can see Ruth Hill's pen in a blur of the same note-taking next to me. Turning from the seat ahead of me, Tom Hardwick scoffs in a heavy whisper. "Silly man. He wouldn't know truth if it cracked him on his handsome nose."

I lean forward and hiss, "I think he's both handsome – and right!"

The young professor shoots an irritated glance in our direction and resumes his lecture. Tom returns ostentatiously to his notes, then stumps away in a comic flurry when the class ends.

CHAPTER 9

FIRST FINALS

A good thing the Easter break is coming, with enough time off to lower tensions. Well – almost enough time. For college students, Easter brings only a very short holiday, stretching this year from Good Friday, March 22, to Easter Monday, March 24 – not like high school where the Easter break always lasted a week. We don't feel much Easter uplift, anyway. News from Europe is changing so rapidly, with all eyes on Scandinavia, while rumours circulate about plans by both Germany and the Allies to launch attacks in Norway or Denmark. A sombre time. The *Gazette* reminds us of the other world: 15,000 FINNS DIE IN WAR.

We go sleepily to our final classes. On Monday, April 1, Professor Macmillan is back on the podium, bringing the course toward a conclusion with a talk on Kipling and Hardy, representatives of "the modern world." There is another horrendous snort from Tommy, but he holds his fire till the lecture finishes. Then the snort becomes a ferocious tirade about the choice of "moderns." "Twenty years out of date! No idea what's been going on in the twenties and thirties! Poor old gink – left behind, and left on stage to fill us students with his out-of-date mush! And to think we have to hand all this stuff back to him in the final exam! At least this is my last course in English. Science all the way from now on!"

I laugh, but Ruth takes his comments more seriously. "Maybe Tom is right – Hardy can hardly be called modern, that's true. He died twenty years ago, and his books were published in the last century. It's hard to make a case for Kipling, too. All that Empire-building is surely out of date."

I nod, but with reservations. The Kipling story we have been assigned to read in this final week is "The Brushwood Boy." It might be mush to Tommy, and out-of-date to Ruth, but it seems very powerful to me. In fact, it's the most exciting thing I have read all year. Magic.

Mush or magic, the course is almost over. In the final English literature lecture, Dr Algy Noad[51] talks to us about early modern poetry. His gentle voice soars like the falcon described in Gerard Manley Hopkins's sonnet:

I saw, this morning, morning's minion, king-
dom of daylight's dauphin, dapple-dawn-drawn falcon, in his riding
Of the rolling level underneath him steady air, and striding
High there, how he rung on the rein of a wimpling wing
In his ecstacy!

We are breathless, lifted far above the crowded classroom. No one can fault this lecturer. This man, whose composition text has brought our own writing into new levels of metaphor and tone, speaks as well as he writes. This is "sweet singing" like the Silver Swan, or like the enchanted waves of Shelley's lyric.

We move inexorably toward the onset of exams. The *McGill Daily* no longer filters the world to us, but we snatch worried moments to peruse the Montreal dailies. Since the beginning of April there have been naval battles off the coast of Norway, and on April 9, the morning *Gazette* runs a troubling story about British ships withdrawing. News later in the evening *Star* headline is even more dramatic and depressing: GERMAN FORCES MOUNT SUDDEN ATTACK ON NORWAY.

When the adults hang over the radio it is difficult indeed to stay at the desk, reviewing Chaucer and Keats, Hobbes and Plato, sines and co-sines, irregular French verb forms.

Allied forces may try to make landings at Narvik and Trondheim, but the hard news is that Germany is beating down every effort at resistance in Denmark and pushing on to the western Norwegian coast, facing across to British shores. Northern armies and navies are locked in a terrible see-saw struggle.

In Britain itself times are very hard. We hear about the bombings from our cousins in England. Their children are back home again. They were so unhappy and homesick in Scotland that they were allowed to come home for the Christmas holidays, then remained in London. A little air raid shelter had been set up under the stairs, "with room for a card table where the children can play."

On April 18, I set aside my books. It's my birthday; and since Colin will turn eighteen at about the same time, our parents have tried to put together a little birthday celebration. Gibby and Fran plead that exams are too close – just ten days away. Bob Spencer, however, says he will join us. "My exam schedule is different.

I'm free for a couple of days now."

Except for a series of phone calls from all those who have not felt able to come, it is a quiet party. But it is a happy one – thirty-six candles on a fabulous cake to celebrate the double birthday. Then a shockingly serious moment: Colin says, "Well, now I'm the age for enlisting, I don't need to worry about exams next year."

Bob jumps in before their parents can react. "Don't be silly, Colin! If you keep on with your courses till you graduate, you'll be officer material when you join up and much more useful." It seems terrible to think Bob assumes the war may go on till we graduate. Colin subsides, a little resentful of Bob's air of seniority and superior wisdom.

My mother tries for a diversion. "I believe you've grown taller this winter, Colin."

Colin picks up her lighter tone. "Elizabeth too – she looks taller to me." I laugh, since I have no hope of growing beyond my present five-foot stature. Just the result of phys. ed., I explain, where the instructors always insist on standing up straight and lecture against carrying too many books, which make for round shoulders.

"Sounds like our COTC sergeants," Colin comments. "Only it wasn't just, 'Stand up straight,' it was 'Suck in yer gut! Pull in yer butt!' Your phys. ed. was badminton and track. Ours was drill, drill, drill. Not so bad in spring, when we were outdoors. But the winter in that stuffy gym, counter-marching – "

"Well, the final result is great!" his father says. But the laughter dims again when Colin announces proudly, "My last physical examination shows I'm in top form. 'Ready for active duty' is the way they put it."

Bob, tactful again, swings into a funny account of his own experiences with the COTC, marching from the campus to the barracks on Côte-des-Neiges, all led astray by a young officer who doesn't know Montreal well enough to know the difference between Côte-des-Neiges and Côte Saint-Luc. "We wound up asking directions at the Westmount town hall – very amusing for the old boys there who wanted to come over and tell us about their adventures in Flanders when all the road signs were turned around to fool the enemy."

"The kind of story we grew up hearing," Mrs Spencer laughs. "Same old army, same old muck-ups."

When the birthday party is over, I feel too tired to study.

Exams begin on Monday, April 29. The provisional time table has already been posted in the Arts Building. We will write most of our exams in the assembly hall in Royal Victoria College, cleared of its regular seating and filled with temporary writing desks.

So it's April 29 at last. My father treats Gibson and me to a lift downtown to the campus. Poor Frances has contracted a humiliating case of scarlet fever, a disease of childhood, and is in quarantine; she will have to write supplemental exams late in the summer to make up for the ones she is missing. Soon, tense and quiet, we crouch at those uncomfortable desks in RVC. Supervisors patrol, padding along the aisles between the desks. The odd sneezing fit breaks the tense silence, and at one point a student throws down his pen and storms out. But mostly it is endurance, furious speed, and solid, stolid perseverance as the examination hours slide by.

At the end of the English exam, Gibby waits for me. She is laughing but cries out, "That was tough!"

Tough, I agree. There was a really hard question comparing Chaucer and Dickens – totally unexpected.

"I don't think Dr Macmillan even made up the exam," Gibby complains. "It's hardly fair to ask things no one covered."

"And not to cover the things we did study!" There was nothing about Milton's defence of freedom of speech, which I spent hours dissecting. Nothing about Keats's lushness or Shelley's sensitivity, which overcame me again as I re-read my notes on the Dando and Newton lectures. But the exam is over, and though I don't let on to Gibby, I privately feel I have done well. "Next year we'll be back in stride," I offer.

Latin, philosophy, trigonometry, I tick each of them off and go on studying for the next ordeal. My last exam, French, will consist of sight-reading and explication – nothing one can really study for anyway. Better just go to sleep and study tomorrow.

The worst part comes after the exam time is over, when the horrible period of waiting for results begins. Everyone seems listless, disoriented. It is springtime; the crocuses and scillas are beading the gardens, but no one feels spring-like this year.

Gibson and I go downtown to see *Captain Fury* one day, and a few days later see a re-run of *The Lady Vanishes*. Gibby worries about Pete Williams, that boy she went around with in high school. He is in the process of deciding whether or not to chuck school next year and join the air force. His mother and his sister have both phoned Gibson, pleading that she should urge him not to enlist until he is older. But she feels she can't argue either for or against joining up. Even at the movies the feeling of heaviness and dislocation continues.

Then a great mood change comes with a *Gazette* headline: CHURCHILL REPLACES CHAMBERLAIN AS BRITISH PRIME MINISTER.

"The end of the phoney war," my mother says.

"Yes – now we can begin the real war." My grandmother, here in Montreal for a brief visit, sounds so ferocious that the others laugh ruefully, for all share the longing for a real war to start. We all still unconsciously assume that the British will of course win in a real war.

But a second bulletin comes in later that evening. The German Luftwaffe – air force – is suddenly pounding the Low Countries. The *Gazette* headline the next morning confirms the news: GERMANY INVADES HOLLAND, BELGIUM, AND LUXEMBURG.

No declaration of war, just sudden horror from the sky. The editorial speaks hopefully of Dutch resistance.

At breakfast I ask sombrely, "If only the Czechs had organized resistance two years ago, would the outcome have been different?" Then I pose a second question, "Will the French resist if the blitzkrieg turns on them?"

My father can only answer sadly that no one will ever know the answer to the first question, and that the hope for a positive answer to the second is slim.

"Madame Furness would say that the French will fight to the end."

But my father says, "Not if Paris were threatened. The French would do anything to save Paris from destruction."

The atmosphere at the breakfast table is so gloomy that I go back to my room to read *Pride and Prejudice*. By May 16 the newspaper headlines are worse: DUTCH LAY DOWN ARMS; INVASION OF FRANCE THREATENS.

Terrible to think that German tanks are driving our forces back from the Ardennes toward the English Channel. Even more incredible, on May 21 we hear that the Germans have succeeded in reaching the Channel coast. How can we celebrate Victoria Day this year? Well, May 24 is traditionally the holiday time for opening the cottages; we simply have no choice.

We drive out of the city, past Dorion, past Vaudreuil, turn off and drive through Belle Plage to Île Cadieux. All those French names drumming into us as we think about the French places far away where there is no holiday, no fireworks of the kind we will set off over our peaceful lake.

On Sunday, warm weather offers a preview of summer. At the tennis court, I stand holding a measuring stick up to the net while Colin and Harold tighten the ratchets at the side poles. The tapes are already laid, stapled in place by the boys earlier in the afternoon. Surely these preparations guarantee that summer will come for us. But in these last few days in May, we are marking time until we hear our first-year results.

Every spring, the downtown papers publish a full list of names of all McGill students who have passed their exams. The lists group students in each year by grades: I, II, and III. I grab and gobble today's paper. Here is my name, at the bottom of the I's. Good enough marks in every course, except English, to let me apply for a scholarship next year. Gibby has done better than she feared. Mary Morris has scored well too, in spite of the debutante dances, but Mary Scott, because of undiagnosed anaemia, has not done well and will have to take supplemental exams to get back into college next year. Fran's name does not appear because of that annoying case of scarlet fever. There are other names that interest us too – names of senior students we have come to know, graduating with all kinds of honours. Soon the *Gazette* and *Star* begin running pictures of many of them in a different news story, one about young scholars joining the armed forces as the summer begins.

In May, I attend the McGill spring convocation ceremonies, since so many of my *Daily* friends are graduating. The speaker is Dorothy Thompson.[52] She has attained an international reputation largely for her denunciation of Nazism in the years before the war. *Time* magazine featured her picture on the cover in 1939, with comments that she was the most important woman in America, next to Mrs Roosevelt. I stand in the May sunshine to hear her thunder.

But the war is pressing on us ever more forcefully. France is buckling under German pressure; the Germans are marching right now toward Paris, and the British expeditionary force has begun to withdraw from its northern position. Everyone believes – begrudgingly – that the French will sign an armistice with Germany rather than allow Paris to be bombed. Meantime, Italy has at last officially declared war against Britain and France, opening the way to another front of fighting: FRENCH AND BRITISH ARMIES WITHDRAWING TOWARD DUNKIRK.

PART TWO

1940–1941

INTERVAL

Summer of 1940: I settle into what my family considers "war work." In reality, it is babysitting. It seems that everywhere children are being shuffled around to "safer" locations. Our small Baldwin cousins were not among the 1,530 children sent to Canada under the British government's Children's Overseas Resettlement Scheme. On the other hand, two of our young Canadian cousins have been sent to stay with us for the summer. Their father has enlisted and gone overseas, and little Peggy and Shirley are coming to our cottage so that their mother can hold her job in Leamington. I am to watch them swim, take them for picnics, teach them the rudiments of tennis, read to them – anything to keep them busy and free from homesickness. (The first hope turns out to be possible, the second not so.) War work? Hearing about Dunkirk and swimming in the shiny lake do not seem to go together.

Meanwhile Colin, Harold, and Bob commute to real summer jobs in the city. On weekends we get together for tennis and for fierce arguments about politics. Nowadays, the United States is discussing a military "draft of all able-bodied men" even though their nation is still not at war, but Canada still hedges on the question of conscription. In June, the National Resources Mobilization Act allows the government to register men and women and move them into jobs considered necessary for wartime production, but does not allow them to be conscripted for overseas service.

I echo my father's view: "Since we are at war, Mackenzie King should bite the bullet and bring in Canadian conscription."

"Don't be ridiculous," Harold says. "There will always be enough volunteers. Girls just don't understand politics." To prove his point, he beats me at tennis and pushes me off the raft when we are swimming after the tennis game is over. A happy summer.

When Labour Day comes, Peggy and Shirley go back to their mother and get ready for the school year.

Our other small cousins in England have no such happy ending to their summer.

The day after Labour Day, Nazis launch new fierce raids across the British Channel. That night, three hundred Luftwaffe bombers, escorted by six hundred fighters, begin the long attack on London. Within the week we read of massive German air raids extending beyond London to Southampton, Bristol, Cardiff, Liverpool, and Manchester. Perth, the town in Scotland where the Baldwin children were sent as evacuees, is not spared. It was lucky that homesickness allowed them to return to their parents last winter. But in spite of them escaping the Perth bombings, they are still far from safe in London. News photos show children huddled together there in bomb shelters.

A terrible story in the *Montreal Gazette* marks the end of the idea of bringing English children to Canada for the duration of the war.

> On September 17, CITY OF BENARES, City Lines passenger liner of 11,000 tons (Captain Landles Nicoll) carrying some 400 passengers and ninety-nine evacuee children on their way to a new life in Canada, has been torpedoed by the U-48 (Captain Heinrich Bleichrodt) when 600 miles and five days out from Liverpool, its starting point. A total of 325 souls were drowned including seventy-seven of the children aboard.

That story scuttles our hope of ever having the little Baldwin children sent to us.

On September 16, as the summer of 1940 ends, another newspaper headline marks a worldwide tightening of tension: UNITED STATES PASSES MILITARY CONSCRIPTION BILL.

CHAPTER 10
KNITTIN' FOR BRITAIN

Our mood, returning to McGill on September 26, 1940, is mixed: saddened, and determined to help with the war effort if we can, but we can't help but feel delighted to be back into the energetic swing of life on campus. Befitting the second year of the war, no one wants to draw attention to the university by parades or torchlight processions. Instead, the Student Union is organizing an "aluminum drive" – a special day of collecting household materials that can be turned over to the government for use in munitions. I am on the sophomore committee organizing this, conscripted by Bill Munroe and Ray Rose, people who last year shared my experiences as cub reporters on the *Daily*.

We plan to send all the members of this year's freshman class out around the city, gathering old saucepans, metal railings – anything that can be turned to wartime use by the military. We will call for the city dwellers to donate these things when students come to their doors.

Preparing for this campaign in the days just before college opens, we have created distinguishing marks for the students. Bolts and bolts of bright green cloth have been torn into strips, tied in bows, and attached to loops of thin elastic, so that the freshmen can wear them around their necks as bowties and the freshettes can loop them through their hair as ribbons. First-year students will be expected to wear these badges at all times on the campus and also off-campus when they participate in "war drives."

Registration day goes easily. The welcoming address is given by the still-unfamiliar principal, F. Cyril James,[53] followed by Professor Macmillan, now dean of Arts and Science. We listen rather impatiently, anxious to get on to the registrar's office.

We are glad, though, to get a glimpse of our new principal. The city papers have written fulsomely about Dr Cyril James and his involvement in several important international committees, coordinating the economic measures that are being taken to add to the efficiency of the Allies's cooperative efforts. The principal's address in

10.1
Principal
F. Cyril James

Moyse Hall is brief. Someone whispers, "He looks as though his mama just shined him up and sent him to work." But Dr James speaks forcibly about the present parlous state of the war.

Now I must rush to the registrar's office to be advised on my choice of courses by one of the English professors. Dr Algy Noad, the scholar who read so movingly from Hopkins's poem last year, steers me to two courses compulsory for honours English students: Shakespeare with Dean Cyrus Macmillan, and History of the Novel with Professor Harold Files.[54]

After I register for French, Dr Noad advises that if I want to go to graduate school, I should take German, rather than Latin. ("German is still the language of scholarship," he says.) I tell him I would also like to try a new subject: sociology. I'm not sure what it involves, but other students say that Professor LaViolette is great. Dr Noad acquiesces, dubiously. Professor Noad himself is offering two half courses – one this term, the other after Christmas. Better sign up for them, I decide. Since he is adept in eleven languages, undergraduate gossip has it that this expertise may lead to his being requested to move to Ottawa soon to take part in military decoding. There is lots of action now around the multi-lingual Mediterranean.

British troops land at Malta without loss.
Italian fleet runs when sighted.
Spain to remain on sidelines; not to join fascist powers.

The uncertainty about what will happen in the English Department if faculty members continue to enlist or be called up is unsettling. With all the threats overseas, Canada will surely be drawn more deeply into the conflagration. Will the department close down with all these enlistments and secondings? Maybe I should consider changing from honours English.

How about math? It was my second best subject in high school, and I did pull off an "A" in trig, last year, in spite of the problematic young instructor. Taking the mathematical bull by its administrative horns, I go up to the second floor of the Arts Building, where the head of the Mathematics Department has his office. I introduce myself, and tell Professor Sullivan[55] that I hope he will accept me into the honours math program. I rattle off my qualifications.

Professor Sullivan looks me up and down (not far up, since I am only five feet tall), then he says firmly, "You couldn't handle it." He gets up from behind his desk and ushers me out of his office. I will learn later that there are no women in honours math and physics at McGill. The famous members of the department, like Professor Keys,[56] are working secretly on atomic theories that will ultimately change the way the war will end; they are much too busy to worry about whether there are any young females in their disciplines. Like Professor Sullivan they simply assume that women are not really interested in or competent at mathematics.

I decide I had better stick with honours English. That decision means I will see less of my high school friends. Gibson Beatty, always experimental, is taking modern history and political science – subjects untouched in high school days. Frances Tyrer is in science courses, undeterred by warnings (perhaps promises?) that she may be the only girl in some of her chemistry labs. Mary Scott has registered for all the courses that are prerequisites for getting into teachers' college after she finishes her BA. We worry a bit about whether gentle Mary will ever be able to handle classrooms of noisy kids. Ah well, we'll all be changed beings by the time we graduate; maybe Mary will emerge as a classroom tyrant like some of the teachers we remember. We picture it, laughing, as we walk through the Roddick Gates and hurry down to Ste-Catherine Street to take a streetcar home.

On the weekend before classes begin, our "aluminum drive" occurs. On Friday evening, over forty freshmen turn up to collect aluminum "for the war effort": pots and pans, boilers and cookie tins, all to be melted down for use in armaments. We travel in teams, two *Daily* reporters accompanied by four freshmen in each group. My partner is Ray Rose, my fellow freshman reporter last year, now one of the night editors. This year, no torches or trumpets, but gathering old metal objects for recycling makes a useful patriotic effort fun.

Our effort is publicized in the three Montreal English-language papers: the *Star,* the *Gazette,* and the *Herald.* The "real" papers want to help the university, glad to emphasize that McGill students appear to be contributing to the war effort. An alternative is clear: if Canada passes its conscription bill, all the male students will be at the manning depots, being enlisted.

On Monday, September 30, in his first class on Shakespeare, Dean Macmillan, back temporarily from Ottawa, makes a dramatic, rather military entry. He bursts

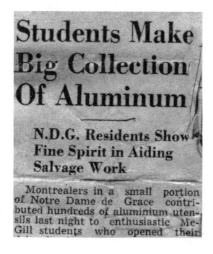

Students Make Big Collection Of Aluminum

N.D.G. Residents Show Fine Spirit in Aiding Salvage Work

Montrealers in a small portion of Notre Dame de Grace contributed hundreds of aluminium utensils last night to enthusiastic McGill students who opened their

10.2

Aluminum drive

through the Moyse Hall curtains, shouting the opening lines of *Hamlet*. "Who's there?" "Nay, answer me! Stand, and unfold yourself!"

Oh, yes! This theatrical course alone justifies staying in English.

Not so certain about Dr Files's course, History of the Novel. The senior professor walks quietly into the big second-floor classroom, sits at his desk, opens a bound notebook, and appears to be reading his lecture to us. But once we clue into what he is saying, there is drama of a different sort. He talks about the great fictions of the past as challenging puzzles, serious pleasures, constructs to be analyzed, experiences to be enjoyed. The lectures are the same ones he has delivered for years to similar classes, but the intensity of his interest rubs off on us very quickly. Flat delivery, yes, but far from flat in impact, these famous lectures on great novels.

This is a required course for honours students, so here I join the people who will be my classmates from here on: Neil Compton, Tom Mulligan, Honey Dickson, and others. Other than Neil, the only one I recognize is Mary Margaret Miller, the girl from Virginia who created so many scenes in freshman French. She seems happier now, glad to be back and on track for an honours degree in English. She and Neil have registered for Dr Macmillan's course on Old English in place of Dr Noad's courses. However, I still prefer the idea of Imaginary Voyages

AROUND THE GLOBE | TUESDAY, OCTOBER 1, 1940
Japan convicts 7 Britons as spies.

The first day of classes over, it is good to get back to the *Daily*. We fill the first issue of the year with exhortations to first-year students to wear their green cotton bowties and hair ribbons whenever they are on campus, and to plan to "get involved." The war effort is not about to diminish: the first *Daily* of the year notes the opening of another sphere of hostilities.

AROUND THE GLOBE | THURSDAY, OCTOBER 3, 1940
Messerschmitt not as maneuverable as the Spitfire or the Hurricane: carries heavier armament to cut down losses.

I go to my first German class with some misgivings. It makes sense to learn this "language of scholarship" but learning to say "*Ich liebe dich*" is not easy, given news of the day.

22,000 more men than was expected are enlisted in the NPAM ... First class of draftees to report to camps on Wednesday.

At our first *Daily* staff meeting, a discussion about the *Daily*'s role in wartime is led very firmly by two visitors, one from the morning *Gazette* and one from the afternoon *Montreal Star*. Many of the top journalists in Montreal are former *Daily* men. Many cut their teeth on the student paper and are glad to advise on tricky issues. "Just stay peaceful; don't give the people in the city, the war party, any excuse to criticize students for staying in college rather than joining up. You're doing a great job. Keep it up!" The two visiting professionals are cheerful but obviously anxious to keep the peace in the town-and-gown arena, even if the nation is fully at war now.

The college year has barely started before the Canadian Thanksgiving holiday comes along. Colin phones. "Going to the cottage for Thanksgiving, Elizabeth?"

The answer is a reluctant no. My grandmother is not well and my mum has to go to Toronto. So no Thanksgiving camp-out at the cottage for the Hillmans this year.

"So come and stay with us," says Colin.

"I've got to type up my first book review for Dr Files over the weekend."

"Yes, well – I've got to write up a lab report. Bob probably has work to do too. But there are two typewriters at the cottage. We can all work there. So we'll pick you up Saturday morning, not too early."

The lake looks perfect, sparkling with sunshine, and the Spencer family cottage is just like ours, same kind of cottage furniture, same air of ease and comfort. After lunch on Saturday, Colin and I bike up to the end of the island, climb the lighthouse stairs, walk the beach back toward the cottage. "You're in great shape, eh, Colin? All that COTC marching!"

"Bob too," he says. "He's ready – " and then he breaks off and talks about the theories he is studying in his third-year engineering courses.

Thanksgiving dinner is at noon on Monday so as to allow time to drive back to the city in daylight. Turkey, squash, mashed potatoes and gravy, pumpkin pie with whipped cream – a duplicate of all the Thanksgiving dinners I can remember. Colin and I can hardly find the strength to clear the table and do the dishes; then a last walk over to the clubhouse, shuttered for the winter, and a look at the tennis court, its net and tapes all stored away, and gold leaves beginning to drift down over the cedar hedge and onto the court. "A perfect weekend," I tell Mr and Mrs Spencer.

Our first lecture in sociology turns out to be concerned with matters close to home. Our term assignment, Professor LaViolette tells us, will be to produce a report on a single part of Montreal. Our city, the professor[57] explains to us, is a sociologist's dream.

This island metropolis rises in concentric circles, from the working class area at the waterfront – Pointe-Saint-Charles, Saint-Henri, and Verdun – through middle class and mercantile life in the island's mid-level, to elite upper-class homes and

10.3
Professor
LaViolette

temples on the two mountains: Protestant English Westmount and French Catholic Outremont. All like a sociological textbook on class and status, mores, folkways, ethos, institutions.[58] We students will research our home neighbourhoods this term, he says, using sociological methodology.

"What about students who are not from any Montreal neighbourhood, sir?"

Students from outside Montreal, Professor LaViolette says in reply, are encouraged to team up with Montrealers to collaborate in studying particular sectors: suburbs or city blocks. He asks, "Where do you Montreal people come from, specifically?"

The answers come from various points in the classroom: "Westmount" – "Notre Dame de Grace" – "Hampstead" – "Montreal West" – "Verdun" – "Lachine" – and then the suburbs at the outskirts, "St. Lambert" – "Chateauguay" – "Ville LaSalle."

Professor LaViolette seems delighted at the range of voices. "I am writing an article on Montreal," he tells us. "I hope to incorporate some of your findings in my work." He adds, "The connections between English- and French-speaking Montreal are of special interest to me. As an American, I feel there is almost as much separation here as there is between black and white citizens in the USA."

We bridle a bit at this. But I admit to myself that I really only know English-speaking Montreal; only once have I ever gone east beyond Saint Laurence Boulevard into the major francophone sectors. (That word, "sectors," will reappear soon in the *Daily* news.)

AROUND THE GLOBE | WEDNESDAY, OCTOBER 9, 1940

Thirty sectors of London bombed in one of the biggest raids of the war.

I have a chance to see our new principal up close at the fall convocation. In a grand display of academic ceremonials he is formally installed on Monday, October 7. Festivities begin with a procession up the campus to the newly renamed Sir Arthur Currie Memorial Gymnasium-Armoury. Preceded by members of the Red Wing Honour Society, and led by the freshman year in their green bow ties, the parade

GREEN-BOW AND GREEN-TIE FRESHIES GO TO CONVOCATION

McGill's freshmen formed up on the campus yesterday and paraded to the Sir Arthur Currie Memorial Gymnasium-Armory for the annual fall convocation ceremonies where 57 degrees and diplomas were awarded. In evidence were the green hair-ribbons of the girls and the green bow-ties of the boys, compulsory for freshmen.

10.4 Convocation parade

Elizabeth Hillman, Montreal, First Woman Winner in History of Gift

10.5
First woman winner

slowly moves through the campus. A sociologist would say this is a lovely example of the folkways of English Montreal.

The pomp and ceremony, the colorful medieval gowns and hats worn by the senior faculty, weave an unfamiliar spell.

Last year I wrote one of my first stories about this annual occasion; this year, as a recipient of a three-year scholarship offered by the Canadian Pacific Railway

Company, I have been cast for a tiny part in the ceremonies. I march with the university scholars into the new gym. The news item about my award took a gendered slant: the *Gazette* put the emphasis on "First Woman."

Something comparable has happened at the *Daily* over the summer. Replacing several of the men who have left to join up, a new managing editor has been chosen: Kitty Haverfield, first woman to hold this position in *Daily* history. We have a new sociological term for this also: "change of status."

In another bit of innovation in the status of women, we now have a new warden at Royal Victoria College. Mrs Grant has retired, and Dr Muriel V. Roscoe,[59] a distinguished botanist and member of the faculty, has been appointed to replace her. All previous wardens have merely been responsible for the moral and social life of the women at McGill, both the residents and non-residents. Dr Roscoe will change the idea of "wardenship" into something more like a "deanship." Though never called "dean," Dr Roscoe will become an academic model for McGill women, an intellectual, hard-working professional, a good researcher and administrator. We don't know – and she no doubt doesn't either – that she is also destined to become

10.6
Dr Muriel V. Roscoe

a close confidant of the new principal. Traditionally, no woman has much say in this very patriarchal university. By her example, Dr Roscoe will begin to reduce the chauvinism that has prevailed for so long. But for now, it is still a man's war on land and sea.

HMS *Ajax* sinks 3 Italian destroyers in fight with eight ships off Sicily … Nazi oil plant left in flames by RAF bombs; Berlin also bombed.

We girls are nevertheless encouraged to sign up with the Student Council to be assigned to appropriate "war work." Mine this term will be helping the Red Cross in its blood lab, just down Sherbrooke to the west of the Roddick Gates. Fran Tyrer

10.7
Knittin' for
Britain

and I have both been assigned to the lab: she, as a science major, will work in the testing section; I as a relatively useless arts student, will wash bottles, pack boxes, and prepare cartons for shipment overseas. Not heavy work, and emotionally rewarding to do late every Wednesday afternoon.

In all our classes, knitting needles flash. All co-eds have been encouraged to aid the war effort by knitting: sweaters and socks for the thousands of people in England and Scotland who have been bombed out of their homes in the terrible blitz that the Nazis have unleashed. "Knittin' for Britain" runs the headline in a *Gazette* story featuring a row of smiling co-eds wielding the needles. The story concludes with an estimate that two hundred and fifty thousand Londoners have been left homeless by the intensive German bombing. We take a grim satisfaction in news of bombs falling on Germany.

CHAPTER 11

AROUND THE WORLDS

Professor Noad explains his plans for our course on "The Imaginary Voyage." We will study writers who dreamed of other worlds, he tells us, from Thomas More and his *Utopia* to Aldous Huxley and his *Brave New World*. A welcome prospect, given the state of the real world we now live in.

AROUND THE GLOBE | MONDAY, OCTOBER 21, 1940
Blackout in Romania, followed closely by installation of anti-aircraft guns by the Germans.

AROUND THE GLOBE | WEDNESDAY, OCTOBER 23, 1940
Hitler and Ribbentrop confer with Laval. Vichy denies intention of joining Axis in war on Great Britain.

In the braver old world of books, we will begin by writing a short essay comparing two of the imaginary voyages on our list. Sounds good. Less good: half the marks for the course will be given for a library research paper due near the end of the term.

"When we have laid down a general theory of this genre, each of you will study one particular imaginary voyage. Maybe it will be the story of an ideal world, or a world of the future, or a nightmare – whatever the creative imagination of the artist fantasized. Some of you will write on a well-known work. *Gulliver's Travels*, maybe, or *Twenty Thousand Leagues under the Sea*. But," he continues, "some will study books that are unfamiliar – even to me!" He pauses, obviously expecting gasps of incredulity.

A murmur from the students. He hurries to reassure us, "The lucky students pulling those unfamiliar titles will be working in a new field. Virgin territory!" The term makes some of the students turn a little giggly. But the giggles and murmurs turn into growls as unheard-of imaginary voyages appear on individual assignment slips. I myself draw *Flatland: The Memoirs of a Dot*. What on earth? According to the notes on my assignment slip, *Flatland*, my book, is set not on earth, but in a universe totally different from ours: a geometric universe inhabited by dots and lines and cubes, where dots yearn to become lines, lines long for a third dimension, cubes and cylinders strive beyond their own three-dimensional limits.

Class dismissed. I put away my knitting and turn to the young man sitting on my left. "What book did you draw?" I ask him.

He fumbles his sheaf of notes together before answering, "My book is *We*, by Zamyatin."

Sari, seated on the other side of me, leans forward and interjects. "Zamyatin is Russian. I have read the book *We*. It shows the world of communism taken into the future." Her voice gathers momentum. "But nothing in the future can be more dreadful than what the Soviets are doing now in Finland. Or what they did in Poland last September. Or to Latvia last October – "

My neighbour breaks with surprising rudeness into Sari's tirade. "Latvia, Poland, Norway. That's all I hear in my boarding house everyday – war talk. I don't want to hear it in an English lecture." Then he adds, "I'm sorry," and asks Sari in a quieter voice, "What's your assignment?"

Sari, the wind out of her sails, answers flatly, "Aldous Huxley's *Brave New World*. Very interesting, very amusing, not difficult to read, since it tells the story of – "

Before she can continue, the young man repeats his question, this time addressing me. "And who is *your* author?"

How can I say, "A Dot"?

From the next seat over, another student gloats, "I've got *Gulliver's Travels*. At least that's one most people have heard of. I bet there's lots of stuff on Swift in the Redpath Library."

Maybe I had better start to work on the assignment right away. But it is Monday, and first comes an easier assignment: to write for the *McGill Daily* about the COTC parades around the campus. The boys look serious in these route marches. They shout in cadence: "LEFT, right, LEFT! ... I had a good job but I LEFT! ... I left my wife and twenty-eight children, an old grey horse and a peanut stand and I LEFT ... LEFT ..."

Not "Around the Globe," but here in the real world, I need to leave for a trip to an imaginary universe. I have written my first brief essay for Dr Noad on "The communities in *We* and *Brave New World* as logical extensions of modern Russia and England respectively." This was not easy to write. I have no difficulty believing that *We* accurately suggests the future of communist Russia; however, it is difficult to accept that Aldous Huxley's savage irony presents an acceptable view of Britain's future. In Canada, we are more and more sure as the war continues that England represents everything good, and Russia everything bad.

British bombers over Berlin early today pounding electric plants, railway yards and other targets.

Time to begin the longer assignment on *Flatland*. At the end of a busy week I make my way to the Redpath Library.[60] No one at the front desk can find any reference to the author of my assigned book. Finally I ask to see Miss Hibbard, the assistant librarian, and my Aunt Zoë's friend.

She offers a simple suggestion: "Maybe you'll find clues to the author's identity in the story itself. The book must be in the stacks." Then, in some puzzlement, as she checks the call number in the card catalogue, "It seems to be shelved in the mathematics section rather than in the literature section. Not sure why that should be the case, when an English professor told you to read it. Anyway, you'll find it in the stacks, Elizabeth. Fourth floor down, turn right, then look for the call number on the spine of the book."

My own spine tingling, I climb down to the lower reaches of the stacks. Iron grids serve as floors on each level of the stacks. You can look up five floors through the grids. All girls have been warned to be careful and wary where they stand, because

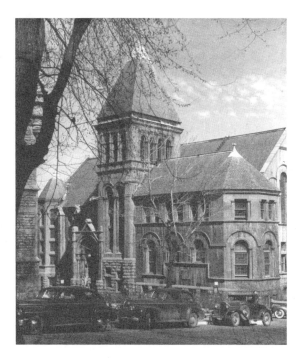

11.1
Redpath Library

there are oglers who try to slip inconspicuously into position beneath you, sometimes several floors down. It's very dark down here in the depths of the stacks.

Flatland: The Memoirs of a Dot. Here it is in the math section, and I begin reading. The dot makes friends with a line, and together they move into Flatland, a two-dimensional world. Okay. But beyond the opening, it becomes harder and harder to understand. The author was a mathematician, for goodness' sake. I'm good at math, but this –

Someone pauses; looks over my shoulder. "What's the diagram you're looking at?" I know the voice. I turn the page around to show the part that was most unclear. "I think it's something to do with going beyond the third dimension, but I'm not sure I know what that means."

A long finger reaches over my shoulder and begins riffling through the pages of *Flatland*.

"Hey, that's like Einstein, years before Einstein worked out his theory of relativity!"

I realize that this is Ray Ayoub,[61] another one of the *Daily* reporters. He is a friend of Ray Rose and Bill Munroe: they call themselves "the Gashouse Gang" and make a good deal out of the fact that they come from a less-than-savoury neighbourhood. But they went together to the old elite High School of Montreal,[62] which to my Montreal West eye gives them a brand of sophistication.

Ray Ayoub reads a bit to me, and expounds. "He's talking about parallel lines appearing to meet at the horizon, you know? You need to imagine – "

My new mentor is voluble, rapid, but clear. I feel like the poor Dot, slowly emerging into a new dimension, a field of energy.

"Would you like me to explain a bit more about Einstein for you? About relativity, and all that? And in return, you can pass this book on to me when you're finished. Bring it to the *Daily* office and leave it for me. My name's Ayoub."

"I know," I say. Before I can say thank you, he has slouched away.

AROUND THE GLOBE | FRIDAY, OCTOBER 25, 1940

Petain & Hitler hold secret conference.

Back upstairs in the main reading room, I lose myself in *Flatland*. Its hero, the Dot, like his friends the Line, the Cube, and the Cosmic Other, feels the urge to exceed his expected dimension, all with accompaniment of romances, feuds, escape plots, and inter-dimensional conspiracy.

The week goes by; the campus puts on its late October colours, and I have to leave *Flatland* and pick up on my sociology project. I must report on my own sector of this real city of Montreal. On late afternoons I walk the streets of Montreal West, drawing a map of the eleven blocks laid out as a town corporation, just beyond Montreal city limits.[63] I try to follow Professor LaViolette's instructions and remember Carl Dawson's textbook explanation about urban patterns.

Montreal West has its own peculiarities. Most of the streets are named for military heroes: Brock, Nelson, Curzon, Wolseley. Clearly the town fathers were in a warlike mood when they chose the names. Indeed, Montreal West developed at the end of the Great War. Most families moved out here around 1920, and almost all of the dads were veterans. Many are still called "Major Morris," "Captain Macrae," "Colonel Hillman," or "Colonel Holland," according to the rank each held in the Great War. In the early 1930s, however, the mood changed, and we were all pumped full of pacifist ideas, in school and at home. Our principal had a row with our eighth grade gym teacher when she wanted us to do a dance as toy soldiers in the school concert – no military displays in his school! Then in 1938, the pacifism began to dissolve. The parents who had forbidden toy guns began to mutter warlike threats against the Nazis and the fascists. All part of the local ethos, I decide, relishing the feel of professionalism in that specialist term. I can build this special quality of war-mindedness into my essay.

Another fact: ours is a railway town. The Canadian Pacific Railway cuts right through, bisecting the main street. Our public school is on the north side, the high school on the south. Shops are all on the north and so are the three churches: Pres-

11.2
War memorial,
Montreal West

byterian, Anglican, and United. There are only three Catholic families in Montreal West; their children go to Loyola school, so we seldom see them. South of the railway tracks stand the skating rink (the centre of social life), a garage, the town hall. Over half of the men in Montreal West and virtually all the college students commute by train from the suburb to the metropolis. This year, some of the regular trains have been cut and we are becoming used to being sidetracked when a troop train rattles through, hurrying to Bonaventure Station, en route for overseas.

The Montreal West War Memorial stands next to the town hall. As in most small Canadian towns, it is our only example of statuary. That statue of a young soldier from the Great War, looking upward, set on a grey granite slab, ringed by flowers, suggests the communal memory of earlier times. The old war, not the new war, which has no monuments yet, except the daily news stories.[64]

AROUND THE GLOBE | MONDAY, OCTOBER 28, 1940

German submarine U-32 torpedoes and sinks Canadian Pacific liner *Empress of Britain*, proud flagship of Canada's merchant marine in time of peace and sturdy transport in war.

Around the campus, in class and out, the war talk goes on, as we read news of disasters "Around the Globe" and closer to home. Early in November, we begin to focus on events in Greece. British troops have landed on the isles of Greece to help the Greeks ward off Italian threats. But how can that hold our attention? A week ago the Royal Canadian Navy auxiliary minesweeper *Bras d'Or* sank in the Gulf of St Lawrence with all forty of the crew. On its first convoy mission Royal Canadian Navy destroyer *Margaree* collided with freighter *Port Fairy*, four hundred miles west of Ireland, and 140 lives were lost. The Germans are threatening to bomb Iceland – much too close to home! The *Daily* continues to remind us everyday of other Canadians serving far from our province and our campus. The worst news is of convoys carrying soldiers overseas, attacked by the enemy before they could reach England. But the damage may be reversed.

Royal Canadian Navy destroyer *Ottawa* and Royal Navy destroyer *Harvester* sink Italian submarine *Faà di Bruno* off Ireland. Two U-boats, including the one that torpedoed the *Empress of Britain*, destroyed.

We are well into November already. Time to wrap up the sociological research. I take time off on Armistice Day, first to witness the town involved in the annual ritual of remembrance, and later to interview my parents and my high school English teacher.

A couple of young men at the cenotaph are in uniform this year. As always, the veterans of the Great War, middle-aged family men now, stand by, my father among them, wearing their medals. High school cadets parade in their new uniforms. We sing, fervently, "*O, hear us when we cry to thee / For those in peril on the sea!*" and think of the Canadian Naval Reserve people on board the little corvettes, guarding the convoys from the ubiquitous U-boats: "*From rock and torrent, fire and foe, / Protect them wheresoe'er they go!*"

The local bugler plays the *Last Post*. At eleven o'clock, the two minutes of silence. My father, like so many of the veterans, finds this a hard part of the ceremony. I can feel him shaking as I stand by his side. Then, as the minutes of silence seem to stretch unbearably on, the bugler breaks the spell by playing *Reveille*.

British strike Italian fleet, three Italian submarines sunk in the Strait of Gibraltar.

Home again, I sit down with my parents. They warn that neither of them ever studied sociology.

"No such subject when I went to college," my mother says. "Religious knowledge, now that was a compulsory subject."

I begin with a set of quick questions about the town's holiday rituals – Valentine's Day, Halloween, St Patrick's Day, May 24 – and then swing to their views on Montreal West schools: textbooks, discipline, games, boys' sports, girls' sports, tricks, jokes, taunts, school chants.

Under all my parents' comments runs a little melancholy refrain. My father says, "It is important to record all these things now, because if the war goes on, everything will change."

"Everything was changed by the end of the last war, you know," my mother adds. "Especially for women."

Later in the evening, I visit Miss Norris, the high school teacher who has kept an eye on my writing career. I hope she can freshen my sense of the folkways of our insular community.

"I certainly remember preadolescent courting rituals in your age group, Elizabeth," she says. "The boys walking the girls home from the skating rink, and in spring circling in front of their houses on bikes. Passing notes to each other in class, and pushing each other into snowbanks in winter. I sometimes wondered whether anyone ever paid attention to the books I was teaching you."

I admit I had felt the same wonder sometimes.

News from abroad reduces my focus on local mores to triviality.

AROUND THE GLOBE | WEDNESDAY, NOVEMBER 13, 1940

Nine missing from convoy Germans claim to have annihilated; merchant cruiser credited with saving most of convoy.

Two days later, we hear that Coventry has been bombed, blitzed, virtually obliterated. Another city, far from Montreal, but near our hearts through songs – "Coventry Carol" – and sayings – "sent to Coventry" – and on and on.

New friends at the SCM meetings also disturb my focus on Montreal West and its folkways. Cyril and Bill Powles were raised as sons of a missionary family in China and now treat Strathcona Hall as home. A very tall man from East Africa tells us he was a prince in Eritrea, his home country, before Italy invaded it, and will be a tribal chief if he can ever go home. Jimmy Panos is the son of the Greek consul; Charlotte Ferencz arrived recently with her family from Hungary. Tom Pavlasyk, like Sari, comes from Czechoslovakia. As the next week passes, the news intensifies the distress my European-based friends are feeling.

British pilots join Greeks for aid in air battle … Hungary is added to Rome-Berlin-Tokyo pact … RAF attacks Skoda works in Bucharest as a measure of protection … Cologne is again raided.

Sociology classes may create abstract understanding of terms like "ethos" and "mores," but I comprehend those concepts better when my African prince appears for an SCM party in his native robes, splendid in colour, flowing wonderfully around his tall figure as he drums for us, rolling his fingers, palms down, knuckles at incredible speed, his face grim and intent. On Sunday evening, all these SCM people collect in the chapel at Union College to sing in the choir.

I have also joined a fraternity this year. "Hellenic clubs" are known as "fraternities" at McGill, whether they enrol male or female members. In this pre-feminist time, we do not quibble with the fact that we belong to a "fraternity," not a "sorority." As with other terms, we accept the idea that the masculine-sounding word is assumed to cover the feminine component. College rules forbid freshmen from joining fraternities, but sophomore year brings the excitement of being "rushed." My friends on the *Daily* regard the fraternities pretty much as I regarded the debutante dances of last year. They feel that joining a fraternity is making a phony bid for social status.

But we Montreal Westerners rather enjoy being "rushed." Among senior students rushing us, Jean Douglas, my next door neighbour in Montreal West, is most insistent that we join her in Alpha Omicron Pi. Our parents, still scarred by the Great Depression, felt at first that joining a fraternity meant an unjustified expense. But Frances Tyrer's father and my dad (golfing partners in the summer, bridge partners in winter) have talked it over and then convinced the other parents that Gibson, Fran, Mary Scott, and I do need a safe and private place near the campus where we can have lunch and find a sofa to nap on if we stay late for extracurricular activities, or to study in the library. At the fraternity house we will make friends with other nice girls our own age. In fact, Ruth Hill and Sari decide to join the same fraternity, so it's old friends as well as new ones in this circle of girls who will become close in the next few years. We have to learn the Greek alphabet and master a few phrases in Greek: *Agape ou perpetuitai* – "Love – brotherly love (which we assume includes sisterly love) – lives forever." A good Greek motto, but ironic today, considering the new situation in modern Greece.

AROUND THE GLOBE | MONDAY, NOVEMBER 25, 1940
Athens announces that British troops are aiding the Greek advance into Albania.

Another irony, given the reports of the real combat, is the current excitement about the Fencing Club – Gibson has entered this field of combat. The *Daily* features a picture of her as an outstandingly beautiful member of the club, dressed in a stiff white jacket with a high collar, with her duelling foil in the *salut* position. We turn out as a solid group of fraternity sisters to support her when she competes.

A different kind of fighting engages Ruth Hill. She asks the Alpha Omicron Pi sisters to come up to the Union ballroom and support her. "I'm on the substitute list today at the McGill Debating Union[65] for the intercollegiate debate against Toronto Varsity. So pray that all the regular debaters get sick!"

Maybe prayers are answered. Ruth is called up to substitute for a senior McGill debater who is "unfortunately ill today." The topic is, "Resolved that the government should own and control all essential war industries for the duration of the war." Ruth's

> Turning to the novice tournaments; McGill should have several entries in the men's and has one definite entry in the ladies'—the highly touted Gibson Beatty.

11.3
Gibson as fencer

argument is clear, simple, and to the point. McGill wins by a narrow margin. We feel that Ruth has saved the day for McGill. The president of the Debating Union is less effusive. He thanks Ruth, but then he makes it quite clear that her inclusion today has been a fluke, not likely to be repeated until she is in third year. "But we appreciate your loyalty," he says. "And your persistence!"

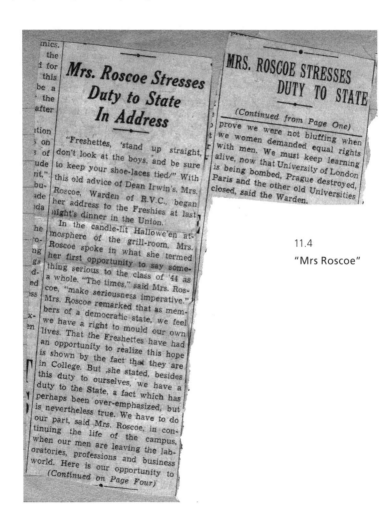

Mrs. Roscoe Stresses Duty to State In Address

"Freshettes, 'stand up straight, don't look at the boys, and be sure to keep your shoe-laces tied'." With this old advice of Dean Irwin's, Mrs. Roscoe, Warden of R.V.C., began her address to the Freshies at last night's dinner in the Union.

In the candle-lit Hallowe'en atmosphere of the grill-room, Mrs. Roscoe spoke in what she termed her first opportunity to say something serious to the class of '44 as a whole. "The times," said Mrs. Roscoe, "make seriousness imperative." Mrs. Roscoe remarked that as members of a democratic state, we feel we have a right to mould our own lives. That the Freshettes have had an opportunity to realize this hope is shown by the fact that they are in College. But ,she stated, besides this duty to ourselves, we have a duty to the State, a fact which has perhaps been over-emphasized, but is nevertheless true. We have to do our part, said Mrs. Roscoe, in continuing the life of the campus, when our men are leaving the laboratories, professions and business world. Here is our opportunity to

(Continued on Page Four)

MRS. ROSCOE STRESSES DUTY TO STATE

(Continued from Page One)

prove we were not bluffing when we women demanded equal rights with men. We must keep learning alive, now that University of London is being bombed, Prague destroyed, Paris and the other old Universities closed, said the Warden.

11.4

"Mrs Roscoe"

"Not my favourite qualities," Ruth mutters to us. "Clarity, yes. And logic. And brilliance, maybe?" We all know that there is a sure bet that they will put someone else – male (and not necessarily more brilliant) – on the team if there is another emergency. As Ruth's fraternity sisters, we are miffed, but not necessarily furious. This is the way of our world.

Female status is the topic of a story this week in the *Daily*. Dr Muriel Roscoe spoke at the freshman banquet in RVC. In her speech she did not emphasize the role of women in wartime, but instead offered a new model for women in academic life. Unfortunately, the *Daily* headline referred to her as "Mrs Roscoe."

Syd Segal, the editor for Mondays, is a bit upset. He says we must be careful in stories about those in the seats of the mighty.

CHAPTER 12

AUTHORITY

We are considering the traditional male role as warrior-king in Professor's Macmillan's Shakespeare course. We're working on *Henry V* (which we call "Hank the Cinq"). Professor Macmillan makes us very conscious that he too is playing a part in history. He has been elected federal MP for Queen's County in Prince Edward Island. Rumour has it that the government engineered his election – he got in unopposed on the understanding that he had a role to play in the national War Cabinet. The *Daily* congratulates him but doesn't mention the rumours.

AROUND THE GLOBE | MONDAY, DECEMBER 2, 1940

Italian submarine *Argo* torpedoes Royal Canadian Navy destroyer *Saguenay*, killing 21, but not sinking the ship. *Saguenay* was escorting an eastbound convoy 300 miles west of Ireland.

Dropping in to the *Daily* office next Monday, I am given a related, touchy assignment. Ray, as my night editor, says, "Someone has to take a story about Principal James from today's *Gazette* and rewrite it from the college angle."

The Montreal papers continue to write praiseful stories about Dr Cyril James and his work on national and international committees. At the *Daily*, however, the feeling is that it is wrong that Principal James is more concerned about his work on various committees than about our life on campus.

Ray amplifies his directions regarding my assignment. "Just cut the *Gazette* story to its bare bones. We don't want to overdo the homage to Dr James."

The story is interesting in itself. McGill's principal has been named chair of the National Conference of Canadian Universities. That body has been considering the use of Canadian personnel in the new war, relative to British authority. Twenty-five years ago during the Great War, the question of the authority of British officers over all "colonial" troops had been a dreadfully sore topic. If Dr James's conference can change the ground rules, that will be a major achievement. The *Gazette* story, in reporting the deliberations of the conference, has stressed our principal's background as an Englishman of high repute in Great Britain. That will not go over very well with any of the *Daily*'s touchy young Canadian nationalistic readers, whatever the *Gazette*'s older pro-British audience may think of it. Well, I figure I can do what Ray wants by cutting out the last few sentences and stripping out the Britishness of the principal's credentials.

The *Daily* in this fall season of 1940 is being careful not to offend the authorities. Some of the reporters, however, take private umbrage at some of the changes that the new principal is instigating at McGill. There are rumours that he is edging out long-established faculty members who don't measure up to his own standards of achievement. We hear that he is pressuring those who do not have a doctorate to either finish their graduate work or resign. My gentle first-year Latin teacher, Professor McCullagh, is among those threatened,[66] and so is Eugene Forsey, a more prominent (and controversial) faculty member. Some junior *Daily* staff members take a dim view of these machinations and urge the paper to run editorials about the situation. The seniors' decision is not to stir up trouble "in wartime." So the paper leaves this explosive story in the "rumours box."

AROUND THE GLOBE | TUESDAY, DECEMBER 3, 1940

Mass surrender of 5,000 Italians ... and the destruction of the fascist line which they had helped to hold were reported last night by the Greeks ... Marshal Petain announced that the French cabinet would move to Versailles.

In spite of such internal disagreements, everyone on the *Daily* continues to regard the paper as "the best god-damn fraternity on the campus."

I hand in my truncated version of the Conference of Canadian Universities story and turn to my next assignment: to report on the first speaker in the scm winter series of talks.

The SCM series begins with a much-publicized speech by Madeleine Parent in Strathcona Hall. She now has a new cause: the rights of the labouring class in wartime. Exploited always, she says, but now doubly so. Management can keep wages low and conditions poor by appealing to patriotism. Because of the war, textile workers are denied the right to unionize, while other unions – the Canadian Seamen's Union, for instance (in our own harbour) – are kept from asking for proper wages. Madeleine Parent reminds us that Pat Sullivan, president of the Canadian Seamen's Union, was interred for communist leanings last June. "Unfairly, against the right to free speech," Miss Parent says. "Meanwhile, others are capitalizing on the war to amass wealth. We students should join the labour unions' protests. They are our brothers!" She is in effect raising the old cries: "Liberty! Equality! Fraternity!"

Madeleine Parent is frightening in her intensity. Not an easy speech to report, given the *Daily*'s policy about playing down controversy. Labour unions and free speech are becoming controversial. But the Canadian Seaman's Union seems to do such essential war work right now.

AROUND THE GLOBE | WEDNESDAY, DECEMBER 4, 1940

British government turns to United States shipyards for 60 new freighters to meet immediate menace: Nazi raids on shipping …

When I take my story into the *Daily* office, I find Ray Ayoub at the night editor's desk. Luckily, I have brought the copy of *Flatland* with me and I hand it over to him with a repeat of thanks for his help. He chucks the book onto the desk behind him and puts my story into the "IN" box.

Next day, when I drop into the *Daily* office again to check comments on my Madeleine Parent story, I find the reporters here are concerned with something other than labour strikes.

"Dr James is off to England again today," Judy Jaffe tells Jack Greenwood, this year's editor-in-chief. "Shouldn't we take a stand? He's definitely becoming an absentee principal, always off to some conference or other."

Jack Greenwood is silent. Sydney Segal[67], the news editor, urges patience. "He's still new here. Give him a chance."

Another reporter pushes in, "New or not new, he's neglecting his job here. How can he run the university if he's off in Edinburgh or New Haven all the time?"

"Not all the time – "

Syd's voice is drowned out. "Most of the time! He's building his reputation, not working for McGill!"

And then, "Come on, Jack, are you going to take a shot at our absentee? In the past the *Daily* has attacked individual professors for less!"

"You owe it to the students, Jack."

The editor finally speaks, so softly that I can hardly hear him. "Most of the students don't know or care what the principal does. This is a student paper, and we should stick to what interests the students."

There is a chorus of "*but*'s" – Judy Jaffe dominating with a solo, "But we should *make* them care, shouldn't we?"

Jack's voice is still slower. "This year, the way the war is going, we'll have to be more careful and not draw attention to ourselves."

Syd Segal mutters, "You're probably right, Jack. There are plenty of people in the city ready to criticize. If we don't conform, they'll shut us down."

"Who is 'they'?"

Syd's answer is glum. "The board of governors. We'd better not start our own little war. We wouldn't win against the board of governors."

Jack moves further back in the room and stands looking out the dirty window. "I'll think about it."

The group of reporters straggles out. No one has said anything about my brief report on Madeleine Parent and the Seamen's Union.

More and more, I find that being interested in the Student Christian Movement presents awkward moments. People at their meetings argue fiercely about the assumption of loyalty to Britain and the Commonwealth. Among the questioners is an older member, King Gordon, brother of Ralph Connor, still one of my favourite authors. A calmer voice comes from a faculty patron, Frank Scott, a much respected campus professor and poet. He too, however, is a questioner of some other orthodoxies.

From the SCM meetings I take home controversial political ideas. My father has always been a Conservative, though he and my mother agree that Mackenzie King is doing a good job as prime minister, even if he is a Liberal. Now I bring home ideas endorsing the politics of the socialist party, the CCF. On Sunday at the breakfast table before we go to church our political conversation becomes heated. I cite some CCF ideas from a recent *Daily* report: "CCF calls for the end of profits, and nationalization of industry, and financial bodies." My father explains why he thinks they are wrong. My mother tries to spread oil on the troubled waters.

The trouble is that I have been invited to become a member of the SCM cabinet – the executive committee. How can I manage that? Outside of worries about stirring up more family controversy, I realize that I am already stumbling in my college course work.

As an SCM cabinet member I will be embroiled in urgent issues. Nevertheless, I accept the invitation to join the executive committee. At once I face internal wars in the cabinet about conscription – an increasingly bitter point of disagreement in every organization right now. The dominant members of the executive want the SCM to take a strong stand against conscription. I am not convinced. My father feels that the question should be debated at greater length in the Canadian parliament. Generally, however, he is in favour of conscription, and I tend to follow him in this. Indeed, in general I tend to follow the *Daily*'s policy: "Don't rock the boat." If the country votes for conscription, so be it.

Actually, at the rate our school friends are joining, it doesn't seem as though anyone needs to worry about conscription. On a date with my own high school friend, Jack Liddy, I find out he is definitely thinking about enlisting. Gibson tells me that Pete Williams, the boy she went around with in high school, is determined to join the Royal Canadian Air Force and to receive his commission by the end of this year. Tommy Hardwick is not talking enlistment, but he has joined the COTC.

AROUND THE GLOBE | WEDNESDAY, DECEMBER 11, 1940
Second contingent of Canadians trained in British Commonwealth Air Training Plan arrived in London last night.

It becomes increasingly hard to calm the waters in the SCM. The anti-conscription people become more and more ferocious. Maybe I should resign from the cabinet position I so recently accepted.

After one stormy meeting I emerge into the season's first snowstorm and push up University Avenue to our fraternity house. I have to calm down. Today, we are acting as hostesses at a professor's tea. Once a month we invite a professor for tea – and they always seem to enjoy talking informally to a group of eager (and pretty) co-eds. Our guest today is my dear classics teacher, Professor McCullagh. We ask him to explain the Greek motto passed along to us by the central office of our fraternity.

"*Agape*," he muses. "Well, it means love. Not romantic love – *eros* – but the kind of brotherly love – or sisterly love in your cases, I suppose – love that encompasses all humankind."

After he leaves, Ruth Hill, who has been preparing for a debate on the topic of conscription, counsels me to stay in the SCM cabinet, maybe try to calm things down there. Spread a little *agape*, she says.

AROUND THE GLOBE | MONDAY, DECEMBER 16, 1940
Italian communiqué admits war has shifted to Libyan frontier.

Somehow, before the first term ends, my sociology report on Montreal West is completed and handed in on time. I go for an interview with Professor LaViolette.

"A good sense of community patterns and values," he says. "I hope to use some of your material when I come to write my article on Montreal."

That sounds a bit like plagiarism to me. But of course when it is a professor, it seems to be another case of relativity.

Professor LaViolette doesn't ask me whether I plan to become a sociologist.

The *Flatland* essay is finished, too, and handed in to Professor Noad. He says, apologetically, that he may not have time to mark this set of papers before Christmas. He is being called several times a month to Ottawa, to consult on something to do with war secrets. What if he is snatched away from us like the famous trigonometry professor last year?

AROUND THE GLOBE | WEDNESDAY, DECEMBER 18, 1940

German troops are in Italy, concentrated at Naples and Bari, the troop embarkation point for Albania. Despite fine weather, Nazi bombers failed to make their customary night raids; not a single bomb fell anywhere in Britain.

AROUND THE GLOBE | THURSDAY, DECEMBER 19, 1940

Fascists retreat deep into Libya … Germans reported pouring into Italy … British forces effect raid from Kenya into Italian East Africa.

Classes end for the Christmas holidays on December 20.

Our family Christmas will be very different this year. We are not expecting cheerful cousin Clyde to join us – he is in England now, waiting for a spring offensive. Not much merriment there: the bombing continues as if the Battle of Britain will never end. Anyway, we will not be at home in Montreal West this Christmas. Granny Smith is ill and we must go to Toronto to celebrate Christmas there.

I spend time sitting by Granny's bed, reading P.G. Wodehouse to her.[68] I try out some of my political ideas on her and hint at our family controversies over the CCF and socialism.

She laughs. "You'll never get over political arguments in this family, Elizabeth! *My* father used to say that politics 'runs in the family – like a wooden leg.' So tell me some more about the CCF."

Granny and Granddad give me a fur coat for Christmas. Sheared mouton, soft brown, very light, wonderfully warm; it will be perfect for the daily walks from

Windsor Station to the McGill campus all through the wicked winter weather that is just beginning to settle in.

We return to Montreal to read frightening headlines in the evening *Star*: LONDON IN FLAMES AS LUFTWAFFE BEGINS FIRE-BOMBING.

Sari phones the day after we get back from Toronto. "My family has asked me to invite a friend to spend New Year's Eve with us. Perhaps you already have a party to go to on New Year's Eve?"

I cannot very well say that I am still hoping that one of the boys will ask me to go dancing that night – Harold, maybe, or Colin, or Jack Liddy. But how interesting to spend the evening with strangers! If my parents agree, that is.

Sari senses the hesitation. "If you prefer, I shall ask my uncle to telephone to your mother to make it the formal invitation."

My mother thinks this is a fine idea. The uncle phones. "I shall call for Elizabeth and return her to your home also." Sari lives with her family at the Gleneagles apartment, high up on Westmount Mountain. The uncle turns the phone over to Sari who adds, "We will not begin our celebration until eleven o'clock, and we will return you by one o'clock. It will not be very formal, although my grandmother likes us to dress."

I figure this means I should wear my pink taffeta evening dress, but my mother disagrees. "You can borrow my long black skirt, love, and wear the velvet bolero over your best blouse. I think that would look more appropriate."

Mother is right, as usual. When the door opens to Sari's apartment, a small group stands ready to greet me, rather sombre in dress. Sombre in mood too, although Sari's family puts on a brave show of making Sari's friend welcome. Over Sari's shoulder I see a strange scene. It is like a small stage set surrounded by a vast empty expanse. In the middle of the long room, a rich dark oriental rug, a set of carved chairs, and an elaborate table set with crystal, plates edged in gold, and heavy silver. Above the table, an enormous crystal chandelier, twisting and shimmering. But beyond the pool of light cast by the chandelier, there is nothing – no little chairs, sofas, side tables. No scatter rugs. No bookcases. A fantastic, theatrical setting. As her mother welcomes me with a smile, Sari explains, "We had a chance, two years ago, to send a trunk to my aunt here in Montreal. We chose to send the chandelier. So we packed it up, filled up the trunk with ends and odds. When we arrived, everything was in readiness."

If the goblets and silverware are the "odds and ends," I say to myself, how hard it must have been to pack! And imagine getting that incredible chandelier across international borders between Czechoslovakia and Canada. Sari continues, "We made the right choice, yes?"

Caught in the glamour of the chandelier's flickering light, I, of course say, "Yes!"

"And now," Sari's English-speaking uncle explains, "we must open all the windows to let the old year out." I gasp. All the windows? The weather outside is about three degrees below zero! Weather or not, the windows are ceremonially flung wide. Silence; sadness is palpable in the room, until way down, far below the Gleneagles eyrie, the bells of the city churches begin to ring out. Everyone shakes hands quietly, and then the grandmother claps her hand and says, very formally, as if she has practiced the phrase in English, "Now to the table!"

A babble of talk breaks out, Sari translating for me. Music, art, books – nothing at all about politics, the war, or their own adventures escaping from Europe just before their country was invaded. When the feast is over, Sari and I slip quietly out of the warm room into the cold starry air of the balcony. I ask, "Does your family never talk about the war? Or is it just when I am here?"

"We do not speak ever of our past. We are living now." Then, after a little pause, "It is indeed cold. Let us go back into the inner rooms."

Sari's uncle practices his formal English: "We drink to 1941!" But the grandmother abruptly rises and leaves the room. I know I should ask to be taken home now.

CHAPTER 13

EROS

The winter term at college begins – at least in Professor Noad's class – with a dose of romance. His second-term course is called English Lyric Poetry. Largely, he says, this means studying love songs, beginning with the poems of early Tudor poets; moving on to Donne, and finishing with some early Romantic poets. He begins however with Sidney's Elizabethan love song to Stella: "Loving in truth, and fain in verse my love to show …" Dr Noad's intense response to poetry is infectious.

In the bigger English class in Moyse Hall, Dean Macmillan has moved from Shakespeare's history plays to his romances, beginning with *Romeo and Juliet*. He takes us through the play, emphasizing not only how it works on stage, but also the poetic qualities, the imagery, the singing rhythms – and the powerful vision of youthful passion. Lovely to revel in this, in light of real news as the weeks go by: there is no love lost on either side.

AROUND THE GLOBE | FRIDAY, JANUARY 10, 1941

German dive-bombers attack British convoys to Malta; sink *Southampton* and cripple *Illustrious*.

AROUND THE GLOBE | FRIDAY, JANUARY 17, 1941

RAF makes heavy attack on Wilhelmshaven. Admiralty announces loss of 9,000-ton cruiser *Southampton*.

Few of the novels on Professor Files's first-term list were love stories: his choices consisted of virile picaresques, like *Don Quixote* and *Tom Jones*. In this winter term, though, he is talking about passionate books, books I almost know by heart: *Wuthering Heights* and *Jane Eyre*. Professor Files's lectures at first seem a bit disappointing. He focuses on the powerful, unconventional portrait of Mr Rochester rather than on

Jane. In *Wuthering Heights*, again, the emphasis is on Heathcliff as a vivid creation. Otherwise, both books seem to him overwrought and awkward in construction. Professor Files, however, promises we will find more meat, more to think about, in our next text, *Madame Bovary*. I take a peek. Doesn't look like a love story to me.

AROUND THE GLOBE | MONDAY, JANUARY 20, 1941

Personal message sent to Churchill from Roosevelt: Wendell Willkie favours Lend-Lease Bill "with serious modifications."

Romance is rearing its interesting head in our own lives. Gibson is becoming more and more involved with her engineering friend, Vince Griffin. Mary Morris is dating a young man who has decided to quit college and enlist in the RCOC, the Royal Canadian Ordnance Corps. As for me, Ray, my aluminum drive partner, has joined the steady (but less than ardent) circle of people who invite me out on dates.

Sari is threatened by *eros*, too. She waits for me at the end of the Lyric Poetry class to tell me that she has been invited to hear the Montreal Symphony by the rather rude young man from last term's Imaginary Voyages class. He has admonished her, "But no war talk!" I tell her I want to hear an exact report on what happens on this unexpected date.

She reports by phone. "Rubenstein was wonderful – he played three encores, two pieces by Chopin and Stravinsky's *Petrouchka*."

"But how about conversation? What did you talk about before the concert began?"

"Well, he said again that he did not want talk about the war. But then almost at once he asked me about our coming here, our escape, really. We never talk about those things at my home."

"What did you do?"

"I pretended I could not understand his English. And then I began to talk about music, about Gulliver, Huxley. I talked until my throat was hurting, and my head ached, trying to find the words. You know – "

"Your famous difficulty with idioms that you told me about when we first met."

We both dissolve in giggles.

In spite of giggles, and in spite of various kinds of romance, January has been a sombre month so far.

Hitler and Mussolini confer in secret at undisclosed spot … Bombing raids on London, Norfolk, Kent and Scotland.

On January 24 I go with Harold, my summer cottage friend, to a hockey carnival. I have other dancing dates, too, with new friends from the SCM, like Stu Polson and Homer Brady (the best jitterbug dancer on the campus), and with colleagues from the *Daily*, like Ray and Bill Munroe. Energetic dates rather than romantic ones, all very nice, all helpful in pushing away thoughts of war.

Are we all feeling a thin thrill of sexuality? I don't think so. Our approach to love, romance, and passion is cerebral still. We are still inhibited at the age of eighteen by the proprieties of our parents. This is a time when popular books and movies still cast a veil of glamour and reticence over any suggestion of physical lovemaking. But we are beginning to read more suggestive novels in our rare spare time: *Anthony Adverse*, *Kitty Foyle* – books which imply that physical passion can be overwhelming. We hope not to be overwhelmed too soon. Not before we finish all the overdue essays that are piling up, at least.

I have definitely slipped dangerously in the German class too. There is an odd atmosphere in that class, anyway. There are twenty-one of us, all aiming at graduate studies, but all slightly apologetic about studying German at this hostile point in time.

In British push near Derna, RCAF retains Canadian identity.

The British "theatre of war" has expanded into Africa – Ethiopia, Somaliland: these are the new names that catch at us. Professor Macmillan, lecturing now on *Othello*, raises the question of what Shakespeare meant by choosing an African – a

"Moor" – as a heroic figure. He sends us to our atlases to see the relative positions of Venice, Morocco, Somaliland, and Eritrea, as he dramatizes the too-passionate love between a Venetian woman and an African man.

AROUND THE GLOBE | WEDNESDAY, JANUARY 29, 1941
Free French Camel Corps captures Italians at the oasis of Fezzan.

Fezzan? Back to the atlases; and then back to *Othello*. Soon we read in the *Gazette* late news about Haile Selassie, Lion of Judah, returning to Ethiopia. An Othello figure, surely.

Less dramatically, Professor Files takes us to *Middlemarch*. Poor Dorothea – like Othello's Desdemona she is married to the wrong man. (This is not Professor Files's position: he focuses on the way the author interweaves several plots and a variety of Victorian themes.) But I identify fiercely with Dorothea, so assured of her status as an heiress when the novel opens, but suffering total loss of power once she marries the dreadful professorish scholar, Dr Casaubon. Dr Files does not discuss this topic.

In all our English courses, great works of art are presented to us by wonderful professors. All of them, as it happens, are male. Maybe women professors might deal a little more sympathetically with romance?

But there are no women in the Faculty of English at McGill. As a student who has been encouraged to plan to do graduate work and to hope for an academic career, I am beginning to notice this rather chilling fact. It seems to connect with what Madame Casgrain has been saying in her speeches about the status of women. It connects also with the themes emphasized in our second term of sociology: the function of role, status, and stereotype in modern society. Maybe literature and sociology can be mutually enlightening on the topic of status of women?

AROUND THE GLOBE | MONDAY, FEBRUARY 3, 1941
British women to be conscripted for war work.

Needing to choose a subject for a second-term sociology essay, I ask Dr LaViolette if I may write about the status of women in the province of Quebec. Professor LaViolette seems dubious. "Status is certainly a sociological term," he muses, "but this subject is emotionally charged. Hard to be objective, as a social scientist must be. Maybe you could limit the topic. Just do a little research on the laws governing the position of women in the province. Do you know a lawyer you could interview about property rights, for instance?"

Yes, I decide as I walk away from the Sociology Department offices, I can talk to Palmer Savage,[69] a distinguished lawyer who has always been very kind to me and who lives across the road from our house. This evening I phone to ask whether he is willing to help me. The answer is yes, and I can interview him next weekend.

Professor Macmillan has reached the end of *Othello*, and Desdemona has met her fate. A noble woman, trapped in what turned out to be a terrible marriage. That is not the way Dr Macmillan presents the story, but that is the way it strikes his listeners. A terrible ending for a love story.

AROUND THE GLOBE | MONDAY, FEBRUARY 10, 1941
British armada pounds Genoa.

A happy development in politics is that the "United States congress has now passed the Lend-Lease bill, rejecting all the cautious amendments of the isolationists. The new entente between Britain and the States has taken a turn we see as hopeful."

In a mood less than loving, the *Daily* has run some hostile letters about the frequent absences of Principal James. Moving in a well-established tradition, the principal's secretary, Mrs MacMurray, has called our editor-in-chief to ask, "Do you have a free period today? The principal would like to see you."[70] Rather starchily, the principal has reminded Jack Greenwood of his leadership in providing guarantees that college men who enlist will get privileged treatment when the war is over.

"So now," Jack says, "hostile letters will no longer appear on page 2." Instead, we will soon report that our principal has been appointed to chair a committee on reconstruction, concerned with demobilization and post-war admissions. But we groan in private about the notion of a post-war period. This war will never end.

Hostilities have spread in the larger world now as troops moving from Australia and New Zealand and India are coming under attack by the fascist forces, and German troops bolster their Italian allies in the Dark Continent.

But courtship takes precedence over world news when Sadie Hawkins returns for her annual visit to campus. Once again I have to write a story about it. The news editor asks me to take a sort of Gallup poll around campus on attitudes to this turnabout week. He gives me the questions: *"Do you take advantage of the week? Do you feel embarrassed when paying checks? Do you make new friendships, or take out people you already know?"* And the headline: A GALLOPING POLE.

Even before I do the interviews, I have worked out a lead: *"Although I'm not a Pole, I went galloping around as the editor told me, finding out what the girls think about Sadie Hawkins Week, and tabulating their answers."*

I corner everyone I know and ask the questions. Answers range from "A silly idea!" to "Never heard of it!" and "Sadie Hawkins Week is an American idea, wouldn't you know?" And yet I know that almost all the tickets for Friday's Sadie dance are already sold.

Finally I find four students in the caff willing to admit an interest in the "girls' take-over" week. Three of the four plan to take advantage, so there is one statistic: seventy-five percent for, twenty-five percent against. And one hundred percent say they find nothing embarrassing about being in charge, paying for the date, opening doors for the boys to walk through ahead of them – the whole works. Story in the bag and a small bright spot of fun in this dark month.

I am a little miffed when I go in to the *Daily* office on Monday. Ray Rose avoids comment on my Sadie Hawkins Galloping poll story. Ray Ayoub, lurking at another desk, sniffs. Girl stuff is not his line of interest. Well anyway, I think, Sadie Hawkins

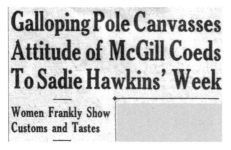

Galloping Pole Canvasses Attitude of McGill Coeds To Sadie Hawkins' Week

Women Frankly Show Customs and Tastes

13.1

"Galloping Pole"

Week maybe constitutes a tiny, mocking change in the status of women. For one week we've taken the lead. Maybe it's prophetic. But I doubt it.

Professor Noad has reached Shakespeare's lyrics. "O mistress mine," he intones.

> O mistress mine, where are you roaming?
> Oh, stay and hear, your true love's coming …

The news features a rendezvous, but not a romantic one.

Franco confers with Mussolini in the Italian Riviera.

Now Valentine's Day has come at last, the culmination of this love-fraught month. Ever since grade five we have worried, "Will there be enough Valentines in the classroom box? And from the right people?" At college, we should surely attain to sang-froid. I write a laughing *Daily* column about Valentine's Day.

Two unsigned cards arrive. I suspect Ray Rose, my friend on the Monday night roster of the *Daily*, may have sent the first. The second, with Harold's writing on the envelope, is no mystery but welcome. Would either have appeared without my *Daily* nudging?

On the evening of Friday, February 14, our fraternity holds its formal dance at the Ritz-Carlton. Nice to remember my earlier foray here, with Tony, the West Indian poet (we have never heard from him since). Now it is un-poetic Harold who walks with me through the elegant foyer and into the ballroom. My mother has concocted a new evening dress for me of rose moiré. I consider it extremely glamorous.

But Harold is obsessed with the naval news of the day. Indeed, he is talking about quitting his engineering course and enlisting in the RCNVR. Not the ballroom topic one could have expected, surely.

The idea of being at sea in this second year of the war is very disturbing. Why should Harold even consider joining the navy now before finishing his courses as all the students have been advised to do? The Germans are dominating the war at sea, as the radio news tells us. And the war at sea seems perilously close to our shores. The German battle cruiser *Gneisenau* has sunk Canadian merchant ship *A.D. Huff* east of Cape Race, Newfoundland. Two merchant seamen are dead, thirty-seven taken prisoner.

Even distant seas on the other side of the globe are fraught with unexpected danger.

Valentine's Day Finds Co-eds Most Anxious To Be Remembered

By E. H.

A while ago, the men of McGill had a chance to see how their line "went over" with the co-eds when Sadie Hawkins week rolled around. Now Sadie's turn to gauge her social success has come. If Abner **really** had as good a time that week as she hoped he had, says Sadie, he'll show it by sending her a Valentine tomorrow. "Gee! will I be scared to look in the mail-box," gulped one girl—"just think of the shame of it if I didn't get a Valentine! I'd have to go buy myself one!"

Students of McGill! Are you going to let an awful thing like that happen? Are you going to break a poor girl's heart just for want of a little kindness?

A thousand times no! Not when there are so many splendiferous Valentines in the five and ten cent stores. There's a very wide choice—something to suit the personality of any girl on the campus. The cards range from fluffy, lacy things, decorated with blue-birds and rose-buds, and bearing sweet sentiments like "For thee I pine, my Valentine!"—to cardboard squares, showing fat women, thin women, fluttering women, committee-sitting women, and so on. You know, even the most comical of all will at least give a girl the right to say "Yes" when the other gals ask, "Did he send you a Valentine?"

So come on, fella, have a heart! Send her **a Valentine on** Valentine's Day!

13.2 Valentine's Day

Britain announces that minefields have been laid around the port of Singapore to protect it against the suspicious movements of Japanese troops southward.

Japanese troops? Another field of aggression? Another area to start worrying about this week?

Tokyo's envoy tells US that Japan will expand to south, says force will be used if necessary.

We swing back soon to focus on the nearer east: Egypt. Cairo is cited as the base from which news of the desert war emanates.

Cairo: British command announces capture of Mogadiscio, capital of Italian Somaliland.

As if on cue, Professor Macmillan takes us to Egypt too. He opens the last of Shakespeare's romance plays, *Anthony and Cleopatra*, which he says is less about romance and more about passion. And, he adds, *Anthony and Cleopatra* is more relevant today than plays like *Romeo and Juliet,* since it is a play about war, as well as about love.

Love and war, war and love – not (as in the books and films we devour in our rare spare time) romance and marriage. Yet new roles, neither in love nor in war, are also opening for women. As an honours English student, I am especially interested in McGill's literary magazine, *The Forge*. I notice that Kitty Haverfield is its associate editor. How can she conceivably fill that role at *The Forge* and also be managing editor of the *Daily*? It is obviously possible to become over-involved in this bustling campus, war or no war. Yet it is hard for women to back away from jobs that would never have been offered to them before the war.

The status of women in the province of Quebec seems ever more important and controversial to me. I raise the topic at home, but my mother is too busy organizing the annual church bazaar at St Philip's to pay much attention. In the church, she says, the women do most of the work. They don't mind if the men are the ministers.

"It isn't worth wondering whether women should be ordained. Why bother? No one listens to the sermons anyway."

CHAPTER 14
STATUS OF WOMEN

When I cross the road to visit Palmer Savage, he pays me the compliment of answering my questions clearly and firmly.

"In Quebec, questions of civil law are governed by the old Napoleonic Code rather than by British precedents. The Napoleonic Code gives women many rights, if they sign a marriage contract before marrying. The contract makes her 'separate as to property,' giving her absolute control over any money she brings into the marriage. But if a couple were married elsewhere before coming to this province, the woman has very limited rights."

I say thoughtfully, "I suppose that would apply to my mother. She and my dad were married in Toronto."

"Your mother would not have much claim to control over her own property now that she is in Quebec," says Mr Savage. "If your father was away sometime and an emergency arose, your mother would be in a difficult position. She would not be able, for example, to sign you children into a hospital, nor to draw money from her bank without his signature, nor to own property in her own name." Seeing my look of alarm he smiles. "I'm sure they have some contingency plan worked out to cover such a situation. But the answer to your general question, Elizabeth, is that women have an ambiguous status under Quebec law: very good in some respects, but very limited under certain circumstances. I can get you copies of the relevant statutes so that you can use the details in your essay. An interesting topic, although I would not have expected it to be assigned as a project in sociology."

"It wasn't really assigned. I asked the professor if I could work on this. I have been hearing on the radio about Madame Casgrain – "

Mr Savage laughs. "The respected and redoubtable Madame Casgrain. She is regarded as a troublemaker by many people."

"Would it make much trouble to give all married women the same rights, whether or not they had a Quebec marriage contract?"

"I think it might cause quite an upheaval. I am not sure how I myself would plead in a court of law if some unusual hardship were argued. Yes, an interesting subject," he muses, and he promises to lend me materials on it.

I go back to *Middlemarch*. The troubles of Victorian Dorothea are not so very remote.

AROUND THE GLOBE | FRIDAY, FEBRUARY 28, 1941

French refuse Japan's terms for Indochina; Vichy balks at yielding territory to Thailand; ultimatum is reported; Tokyo is said to be demanding action from participants …

The university declares a "brief recess" in classes from March 1 to March 4. "No lectures will be offered except in medicine, dentistry, and music." Harold and I, with Colin and Mary Scott, go skiing. But while we are up north, the war abroad changes significantly. Bulgaria joins the Axis, so that the border between Axis troops and Russia now stretches from the Baltic to the Black Sea. British forces, already thinly strung out, hive off troops to support Greek resistance. Another Nazi offensive begins, with Rommel's "Desert War" in North Africa.

A lot to absorb when we open the *Daily* on the first days after our brief recess.

AROUND THE GLOBE | THURSDAY, MARCH 6, 1941

Greece defiant as Nazi troops mass on Bulgarian-Greek border … Ethiopian revolt routs 20,000 Italians near Addis Ababa. General Weygand at Vichy to confer with Petain.

Meanwhile, a *Daily* assignment waits. Not on the Red and White Revue – it has been cancelled for this year, so that is one less controversial job to be involved in. No, I am to do a piece on this year's plans for the McGill Players' Club. I go back to Moyse Hall, where the drama society members are trying out for roles in this year's play, *A Kiss for Cinderella*.

RED AND WHITE REVUE THIS YEAR CANCELLED

14.1
Revue cancelled

McGILL PLAYERS MEET TOMORROW

SEEK NEW TALENT

14.2
Players' Club

Almost without meaning to, I join the aspirants. I know, I know – I'm overloaded already. But this is such a relevant play! The characters in it are caught up in the confusion of the last war, the Great War, the "War to End all Wars." The director explains that it is about a young woman, a lower-class girl, who tries to set herself against the wartime regulations: the blackout, the limitation of aliens' rights. This Cinderella is a lovable little rebel, he says.

I go onto the Moyse Hall stage and read for a part. I'd love to be Cinderella, but instead I land a minor part as one of the children in the play. Like Peter Pan looking after the Lost Boys in Barrie's more familiar play, Cinderella cares for little waifs left alone because of the war. She hides them in crates in her dressmaking workshop. So my stage debut will take place inside a box. Rehearsals will start soon.

Theatre-going has always been a delight to me. I love the very air in His Majesty's Theatre on Guy Street. For the last year, my schoolmate, Madeleine Thornton,[71] has enlisted me as an usher for the Montreal Repertory Theatre. Madeleine herself is playing bit parts there, ingénue parts. Surely she can coach me in the McGill Players' Club drama – if I even need coaching, that is – for now that I read the play I learn that the children in it do little else than jump up and down and scream. Not a major role.

"Role" is a term that Dr LaViolette is exploring in the sociology class, along with "stereotype" and "status." I feel encouraged to raise a question about the role of women, but he is intent on following his own train of thought like most professors, no matter how much they claim they want us to question.

Soon, in intense rehearsals for *A Kiss for Cinderella*, I try to fit into the part of one of a group of children abandoned in London during Great War bombing raids. Charles Rittenhouse, a distinguished Montreal director, comes in to give our leader a bit of help. "All right, children, jump up and down," he calls. "Higher! More childishly please. Squeal more loudly please!" I enjoy trying to sound like a Cockney child.

That First World War London story becomes sharper when on Saturday, March 8, the morning radio brings news that Buckingham Palace has been bombed. We feel deep sympathy for the Royal family, the young princesses in particular, always held up as ideal young girls, now quietly accepting their public duty. The Queen is quoted as saying that the bombing of her home makes her feel more than ever a sympathy with other London citizens.

Well, we must carry on with an effort to maintain normalcy too.

AROUND THE GLOBE | TUESDAY, MARCH 11, 1941

Italian cruiser, sister ship of the *Bartolomeo Colleoni*, torpedoed in Mediterranean by British sub … RAF carries out three sweeps of English Channel, and heavy attack on Boulogne.

Normalcy means essays. *Cinderella* rehearsals have set me back on the sociology report on the status of women.

A date with Bob Spencer might be a good time to discuss the topic of women's rights. We are going to a party at the scm. Dates with Bob, however, are not really dates but information sessions. I mention the news items I have been reading and then he places them in a larger context. He is an honours history student and his classes are providing deeper insights into the global picture. Bob is also head of the Arts Undergraduate Society this year, so he knows about campus politics. After we finish discussing the war, he carefully explains the logic of strengthening the national federation of students.

I don't see any way of returning to the questions that are bothering me about the status of women. No use. So I just say, "Tell me more about your opinion on conscription, Bob."

He does.

The tone of news coverage changes briefly now. The American government halts its apparently endless discussion and actually implements the The Lend-Lease Act that promises invaluable help to the British.

AROUND THE GLOBE | THURSDAY, MARCH 13, 1941

Roosevelt asks congress for 7 billion dollars to protect against aggression and to aid Britain. More than 2 billion to go to aircraft.

Yet the war grinds on. In Africa, Rommel's Afrika Korps harasses Commonwealth troops. Photos in the *Montreal Star* show Scottish soldiers in kilts, suffering in the African heat. Back in Scotland, the Luftwaffe strikes the shipping industry along the River Clyde and at Glasgow itself.

Here in Montreal, cold weather continues.

"I find the dark so very depressing," Sari confesses. "I can hardly get up in the morning. Depression. When will it ever be sunny sunshine again?" Sari has phoned to invite me to her home again, this time for afternoon tea on Sunday. "Afternoon tea seems to us very British, and we wish to adopt British ways now that we are in a British colony."

I gasp, and then laugh. "We don't think of Canada as a colony anymore, Sari! But I would love to come to tea on the weekend." I sound a lot like my mother. Arranging a tea party: the role of women.

In my next class with Professor Noad I bring up the question of Donne's attitude to the role of women. It's not the kind of question that this teacher considers very important. He swings back to the technical intricacies of Donne's imagery and the shock value of the way his poems open. Revelations of what poetry can be.

Lately, the English Literature Society has become aflame with excitement about the relative values of traditional poetry and modern experiments. Two of my classmates in the honours group, Tom Mulligan and Mary Margaret Miller, debate fiercely about contemporary poetry at the Society. The topic seems a little less than world-shaking, but I write it up for the *Daily*.

Fortuitously, three days later I am assigned an interview with the celebrated British poet, Alfred Noyes, author of "The Highwayman." Mr Noyes is a "modern" rather than a "contemporary" poet, in Dr Noad's terms. But his poems are certainly very widely known, and "The Highwayman" is a standard for elocutionists. To me, the young colonial interviewer as he seems to see me, he explains the basics of poetic appeal, especially poetry in the great English tradition. He seems to have a particular grudge against Louis MacNeice (I've never heard of him, but I will read him now).

On the train homeward at the end of this day of my Noyes interview, I continue to fume a bit over the famous poet's patronizing attitudes to some one who is a) young, b) colonial, and c) female. I am also annoyed at his (as I see it) old-fashioned sense of what poetry is.

I have written an overlong story about the interview, but for once the *Daily* editor doesn't cut it. Arthur Noyes is a "name" in the modern world. I guess the *Daily* editors are glad to have

MODERN TREND OF POETRY NOT PUBLIC DESIRE

Noyes States People's Opinion Not Represented by Critics

JOURNALISM DIVERGENT

Believes Canada Can Help Restore Faith Lost in Europe

"Canada can set her face against the perversions which have attacked the poetry of the old world." This is the interpretation by Dr. Alfred Noyes

14.3
Modern poetry

something other than the war effort to present to our readers.

UK throws reserve bombers into attack on promise of more planes on the way from America. Early aid from US likely to include 30 torpedo boats. British warn Berlin the worst is still coming.

On Monday, Harry Lash,[72] my night editor this week, gives me an innocuous assignment. "No hurry on this one, Elizabeth. It's an okay story, but we have a pretty full paper. You have an appointment to interview a first-year med student. This will be your last story for the year. Make it a good one." Harry smiles ruefully. "We need to run more stories about students that do good work and fewer about rebels." He elaborates. "This fellow Ashdown chose summer work on a hospital boat patrolling the coast of Labrador. Good publicity for the serious things students are doing, just in case people worry about us having too much fun, now that the war is dragging on."

David Ashdown is waiting for me in the reception area of Douglas Hall. He takes me into the little sitting room for our interview and begins.

"I don't like talking about myself, but it's important for people to know about the Grenfell mission," he begins. "Dr Grenfell died last year, but every port in Labrador still shows his influence." He goes on eagerly with tales of the isolated ports, swarming with excitement when the Grenfell schooner pulled in. He describes roughly built chapels with taut fish-skins in place of stained glass, where the villagers roar out lustily the old Baptist hymns like, "Throw Out the Lifeline."

"And the Grenfell mission is the focus of trade. Ivory carvings and hand-woven tweeds and embroidery are exchanged on the boat for old clothing sent by charitable societies in Canada and the States."

David Ashdown's blue eyes seem to me to reflect memories of ice-blue caverns, blue skies over Labrador. "Are you going back sometime?" I ask.

The answer is a surprised, "Of course!"

It is a good story. It has repercussions. Harold comes calling, holding a copy of the *Daily*. "I gather you liked this ice-king, Ashford," he says. "But what do the natives

Rude Life on Rocks of Labrador Described By Grenfell Assistant

By E. H.

"This is the place where they give you new eyes."

That was what the Sir Wilfred Grenfell Mission meant to an old Labradorean, according to David Ashdown, first year medical student, who worked on the hospital schooner the summer before last. But the mission is far more than a hospital, says Ashdown. It is the centre and fountain of all community life. Through its influence the villages of Labrador and Newfoundland have changed from isolated stations in which people lived like animals on the proceeds of old-fashioned net-fishing, ill-fed, ill-clothed, uncultured, w i t h o u t churches, schools, or doctors. They are now centres, still without strong connections with the outside world, but with well-developed community life, flourishing crafts, and roughly-built chapels with taut fish-skins in place of stained glass.

When the mission boat puts into one of these little ports, everyone boards the fishing dories, and soon the ship swarms with everyone suffering from any ailment, as well **as those who** come aboard merely to visit and perhaps to join in the sing-song. The villagers are all very musical. They love to dance to accordion music, to sing the old Scottish and Irish airs, and especially to roar out lustily old Baptist hymns, like "Throw out the Lifeline." As well as fostering the religious and recreational life of these settlements, the mission is the focus-point of trade. Here ivory carvings, and hand-woven tweeds may be exchanged for old clothes sent by charitable societies in Canada and the United States.

The mission boats travel from half-way down Newfoundland as far as the North-West River, where there are a few scattered Hudson Bay Posts and little else entering every inlet on the way. Sir Wilfred Grenfell travelled as far as Cartwright, the most northerly of his hospitals, in what was to be his last visit to Labrador and Newfoundland before his death, during the same summer that David Ashdown was working at the mission.

He had a rugged, kindly appearance" the med. student stated. "with a deeply tanned skin, white hair and a square jaw." When the

(Continued on Page Four)

14.4 Life in Labrador

think of exchanging their crafts for old clothes?"

I sidestep. "David Ashdown says they don't like to be called 'natives.'"

"I gather that whatever David Ashdown says is bound to be true."

But I have had enough teasing. "Don't you have a lab report to write up this evening, Harold? Something about stress and strain?"

Next morning, I meet Miss Hibbard, the librarian, as I hurry up the avenue of elms. She smiles at me and stops.

"I liked your story about Dr Grenfell," she says. "Better than most of your recent efforts." She moves on toward the Redpath.

Dr Grenfell? But the story was about David Ashdown!

Maybe I won't be a journalist. Maybe I'll be a lady missionary. Spread a little *agape*, Ashdown style.

Now the *Daily* is folding for the year. March 17 brings the annual banquet. As last year, this is a rollicking meeting attended again by a cadre of "real" newspaper men, all regarding themselves as alumni of the *Daily*, as well as of McGill. No special award for me this time: I have been spreading myself too thin.

The banquet is a gala, applauding the announcement that Harry Lash will be editor-in-chief next year. The chairman proposes a special vote of thanks to "our managing editress," and Kitty Haverfield does not take offence at the term.

There is other news on the feminist front during this March of 1941. Dr Muriel Roscoe is agitating to replace two "residential advisers" – the official term for the youngish women who live in RVC and help organize residents' life there – with "academic dons," graduate students who will put more emphasis on intellectual and cultural concerns than social and moral ones.[73] Many on the campus are opposed to the change, including many of the men on the *Daily*. I am not sure why. They encourage women students to circulate a letter of protest. Dr Roscoe comes in for some ridicule. The men like their co-eds girlish.

The roles assigned to women look more and more unfair to me. In consequence, my sociology paper increasingly lacks the objectivity Dr LaViolette emphasized. I have done extensive library research on the status of women in Quebec and Palmer Savage has helped me with professional insights. We have had some good discussions about the basis of Quebec law.

presents

SIR JAMES M. BARRIE'S FANTASTIC COMEDY

"*A KISS FOR CINDERELLA*"

14.5 *A Kiss for Cinderella*

Indeed, Mr Savage suggests that I should try to get into law myself, after I finish my BA. He warns me, however, that so far although women may graduate in law, the Montreal Bar has never admitted women to its ranks, so there will be no chance of pleading in court, even with a law degree from McGill. Nevertheless, I think I might try for admission to law next year.

I consult Ruth Hill, who says, "Why not?" Then I mention the idea to Judy Jaffe when we are next in the *Daily* office at the same time. I have heard she has set her sights on being a lawyer. "Yes, well, maybe you could get into law. At least you're not Jewish," she concludes. I realize that as an applicant Judy will face a double discrimination as a woman and as a Jewish person. But Judy advises me to take the course in jurisprudence next year, just in case. It is an undergraduate prerequisite for law. "And you will enjoy it, given the amount of interest you have taken in the peculiarity of Quebec's Napoleonic Code." I gather I have been boring the whole *Daily* staff with my ideas about women's rights.

Never mind – the essay is finished at last and handed in.

Now, if I don't get down to more reading for the fiction course my marks won't let me stay even in honours English. I settle down to a sandwich of Meredith's *The Egoist* and Hardy's *Tess of the D'Urbervilles,* two late-Victorian views of the lives on women and men.

Neither are fairytales; no Cinderella endings.

It is hard to concentrate though, because now *A Kiss for Cinderella* is at last "on the boards" with performances from March 22 to 31.

At that final performance, the playbill announces, "The Royal Canadian Air Force is providing the guest audience for the evening." Seeing Moyse Hall filled with men in air force blue uniforms adds a fillip to our work on stage.

And that is the end of a potential dramatic career. I revel in the tiniest of mentions when the *Montreal Gazette* reviews our performance. We refugees, the review states, are "appealing"; "their squeals at the mention of treats … being completely disarming."

"Disarming" is a wonderful word these days.

During the run of our play, I take time for a different performance. In line with my current stance as a proto-feminist, on Monday afternoon, March 23, I have the honour of introducing Madame Casgrain at an SCM meeting in Strathcona Hall. Our speaker was to have been Madeleine Parent, but she has had to renege, and the redoubtable Madame Casgrain has graciously filled in for her. I, too, am a substitute as chairman – the senior student who was to have chaired the meeting has the flu. I am too much in awe of Madame Casgrain to exploit the chance to get inside information on the battle over the status of women. Anyway, my essay is out of my hands.

CHAPTER 15

AGAPE

Getting close to final classes, Dr Files winds up History of the Novel with Tolstoy's *War and Peace*. It is an appropriate way to end this academic year. Again, as last year, tensions about the coming exams mix with exploding news from the spring offensives outside the campus. We turn nervously to the paper for morning news in the early April days.

Germany has invaded Yugoslavia and Greece. Germans enter Zagreb on April 10 and push into Belgrade on April 12. Sari calls to discuss these events. They are almost meaningless to me, but to her a frightening set of developments in Eastern Europe, affecting some of her relatives. I go back to my atlas and trace the connections between Czechoslovakia, Hungary, and Yugoslavia. These were never part of our mental geography in the way that France and the Low Countries were, because of our parents' memories of the first war. (Nowadays, we are learning to call it "World War One" instead of using the old term, "The Great War.")

On Easter Day comes other news whose significance we don't quite understand. The USSR and Japan have signed a neutrality pact. What is going on? The great communist USSR and the ultra-imperialist Japan? Too much to absorb at a time when we should be cramming for exams.

Over the Easter holidays, Aunt Zoë visits from Toronto, and as always her Montreal friends have come to our house for tea. College classmates, McGill '15. They are an impressive group of women – three doctors: Dr Mary Child and Dr Eleanor Percival, obstetricians, and Dr Jessie Boyd Scriver, pediatrician; two teachers, Miss Dora Braidwood and Miss Win Hibbard; and her twin, "my" Miss Margaret Hibbard, the librarian. Aunt Zoë herself was formerly secretary to the Ontario minister of labour in Toronto. Only one of this group, Jessie Boyd Scriver the baby doctor, ever married. No lawyers are among them. Dr Percival explains that it was easier to get into medicine, since at the end of the first war there was a shortage of doctors and a tremendous need to look after the returning veterans. Another one of their classmates, Glad Cunningham, took her medical degree and then married a medical missionary and spent the rest of her life in China. "Lots of good work women can do, Elizabeth, married or single, at home or abroad."

I am tempted to say, "*Agape* – the good of humankind," but am afraid these snappy ladies would laugh at my pomposity.

They talk a bit, of course, about the last war, and the incredible number of young men who never returned. "The reason most of us are old maids," they laugh, shifting from the melancholy mood for a minute. "This time it's different, though," they console me. "No trench warfare. No bayonet charges. That was where the terrible loss of life came. Your young men will be back in ordinary life in no time, Elizabeth!"

Some of our "young men" – the boys who were in our high school class – are now engaged in the Battle of Britain as fighter pilots and bombers. We dread hearing news of them. England is being pounded; London, Plymouth, and Liverpool are hammered mercilessly night after night. The air force is countering by throwing everything they have into the air – semi-trained boys, over-tired men. The same Nazi battering hits Scotland, Northern Ireland, Wales, and we know that Charlie Crowdy and Jimmy Muir are being chucked up into the air in the defence (the seemingly pitiful defence) of all those places.

Gibson, Tommy Hardwick, and I are still singing in the St Philip's Church choir, as we have done since high school. The services are gloomy on the Sunday after Easter. Canon Ireland always prays for "our boys in the services" by name. The list has grown longer every week, and the canon manages to make his prayers sound even more doleful than they need to. Today, after the service, Gibson tells us that her high school boyfriend, Pete Williams, has indeed joined the Royal Canadian Air Force. He hopes to get to England in time to take part in the Battle of Britain. Canon Ireland will add his name to the prayed-for list next week, she says. In the end, it turns out the prayers are pretty useless.

The war continues badly, in spite of the insistent news of American willingness to help the Allied cause. The papers are full of hopeful prophesies about Lend-Lease. They say that the British have hustled lots of their reserve planes into use, in the hope that American aircraft are already on their way to English air fields, thanks to President Roosevelt's support.

PRESUMED DEAD

FO. PETER YEATES WILLIAMS, 23, who was previously listed as missing in action, has been reported officially presumed dead according to word received by his parents, Mr. and Mrs. Steuart B. Williams, 149 Westminster avenue north, Montreal West. Born in Ed-

15.1

Peter Williams

Canadians are inclined to idolize Roosevelt for his pro-British attitude and his success in procuring Lend-Lease aid "on an unprecedented scale."

Jokes go about that FDR gets his marching orders from his wife, a woman considered homely "on an unprecedented scale."

Eleanor Roosevelt, clearly, is a great source of strength and inspiration for the president, but never, ever likely to become president herself. Seen by many men as bossy, opinionated, a wrong-headed socialist, she appears to many women in America and many more in Canada as a model of the new independent woman, noted for her brain if not for her beauty, and dauntless in defending the underprivileged. Another example of *agape*. I have referred to her in a footnote to my essay on the status of women. But the jokes about her don't disappear.

Professor LaViolette hands back all the essays during his last class on April 23. My mark is an "A," but there is virtually no comment at the end of the paper. In the pause before the final exams, I call in at his office hoping for a little post-mortem discussion.

He tells me it was all right, but that he much preferred my first-term essay

on Montreal West. He reiterates that he wants to use it as part of a paper he's giving in Chicago in July.

"You are really going to use bits of it?" I ask with pleasure.

His answer is off-hand. Not bits – all the data on Montreal West. And of course he will mention my name.

I feel more than a little miffed. I feel – abused, maybe? Should I report this to my mentor, the anti-plagiarist Dean Macmillan?

But it is nearly exam time, and I can't let myself worry about anything else. Time to go back to *Tess of the D'Urbervilles*, a tale of real abuse.

The exams do indeed come. We have to withdraw attention from the real world, where the news is so very awful: Germany has broken the Greek defences; the British have retreated from Mt. Olympus and have begun evacuating troops to Egypt and Crete.

At least now we know the ropes so exams are less frightening this year. Even when writing them I feel a tendency to drift off into the charms of the lyric poems Professor Noad read to us, or into the intricacies of plot and character and setting, noted in Professor Files's lectures on that huge range of long, long novels. For Dean Macmillan, I quote extensively from *Othello* and from *Anthony and Cleopatra*. "My salad days!" Cleopatra cries, celebrating her lost youth. My own salad days seem to be wilting away.

On the very day of our German exam, we hear that Germany has captured Athens, in spite of fierce Greek resistance. I recite from memory, with genuine astonishment, "*Ich weiss nicht was soll es bedeuten …*" and translate it: "I don't know what is going to happen …"

The *Gazette* says that Rommel's desert march foreshadows a major Axis victory. But when the examination is over, we learn that things have changed: Rommel's drive through the North African desert has stalled.

The war news of late spring 1941 has meant more hunger for manpower in the armed forces, more urge to hasten the enlistment of young men, especially bright young men who can master the complexities of navigation for the air force or navy. Now, of our high school class of twenty-seven students, most of the boys have enlisted. Seven will be killed before the war ends. That ending seems far away right now.

On May 11, the day after our final exam, the city papers carry news of what sounds like the climax of the war. German bombers have turned their full strength against London. More than five hundred aircraft have dropped high explosive and incendiary bombs; there are many fires and many, many casualties. On the other hand, some twenty-seven German aircraft are lost – but how can this seem like "good news"?

An end-of-year meeting of the SCM cabinet stirs up a new controversy. Madeleine Parent appears to lay before us the plight of the trade unions. The Canadian Seaman's Union in particular needs student support. They are on strike at the docks. Will we go down and march with placards to show our support? Will we strike a blow for social justice?

I tell my parents about this request. I present it as an example of missionary work. *Agape,* in fact – love of humankind. They are alarmed. That would be a real blow against the war effort, they say. The Montreal docks must be kept working, making transport of troops and goods possible in this bad time.

"It sounds suspiciously like sabotage," my father says. "Madeleine Parent and her friends may not realize that they are perhaps being used by communists to hamper the war effort. The communist party is still anti-war, since Russia and Germany signed a non-aggression pact. Watch out, Elizabeth. Don't get involved."

Madeleine Parent has not mentioned any of this stuff in her rousing speech. She concentrated on the terrible conditions faced by the dock workers. Way out in Montreal West, my parents just don't understand the real situation. So indeed a small group of us do go down to the docks to support the Canadian Seaman's Union. All just part of a flurry of year-end activity in this busy time. We wear our McGill blazers to make a point about student support of the union. My blazer is a new acquisition; well worth the ten dollars it costs at Eaton's, but the colour and the insignia make me feel extraordinarily conspicuous.

Luckily, the Montreal reporters do not pick up on the story. In their low-keyed references to the seamen's strike, the papers make no mention of the little McGill presence on the strike-bound docks. Maybe they don't know about Miss Parent?

Soon our final marks are published in the city papers again. My only poor mark is in German.

Plans for summer settle into place. My hopes of a job seem reasonable. My father

McGILL BLAZERS

Expertly tailored, with McGill crest embroidered on pocket.

Red, for the undergraduate - - - 10.00
Blue, for the graduate - - - - 13.50

N.B.—Blazers sold only to persons bearing official order.

THE OFFICIAL McGILL BLAZER

FOR MEN AND WOMEN

Sold Exclusively by

T. EATON Cº

15.2
McGill blazers

has arranged an interview for me with a section manager at the Canadian Pacific Railway. My father's friendship with the manager in question ensures me a clerical job starting in June.

"Junior clerk," the man that hires me says. "In fact, it's the work that male college students usually do in our busy season. Three of the boys we promised jobs to have taken it into their heads to go down to the manning depot and join the army. So we're prepared to hire girls as summer replacements."

Ruth Hill phones with a similar story. She has got a summer job as a filing clerk in a law office – Gibb and Gibb, a famous old firm. They tell her what the CPR told me, that the young men are all leaving and they might as well hire young women "for the duration."

The duration looks increasingly likely to be long. But at least the heavy bombing of London halts in mid-May, and the British air force steps up its own bombing of places like Hamburg. On the Mediterranean, though, a see-saw of new developments. First, the papers feature pictures of German paratroopers invading Crete. Then distressing news ensues: the British evacuate that important isle.

On Friday, May 24, my family drives to the Île Cadieux cottage to do the spring cleanup. Everything is as it has always been on Victoria Day weekend. When we were young, my brother and I used to react to our parents' calls for help with the old chant:

The twenty-fourth of May
Is the Queen's birthday.
If you don't give us a holiday
We'll all run away!

Of course it's never a real holiday. This is the day every cottage has to be opened up and readied for the summer. The black flies are bad, and the mosquitoes just starting, so once the heavy shutters are off the porch windows, most of the weekend has to be spent indoors, straightening up, taking the dust covers off the furniture, putting the ornaments back on the mantelpiece and the china back on the shelves. Everything as it has always been.

The lake is so beautiful in the early morning, with the gold-sided birches standing still as sentinels against the darkness of the pine woods. How can we believe in a world at war? But the *Montreal Star* is reporting the onset of a battle at sea involving the dreaded German battleship *Bismarck*.

Just before noon on Saturday, Colin bicycles up the path to invite the whole Hillman family up to his place for tea. "Mum says she especially wants to talk to you, Elizabeth. But she says no favouritism, she'll be glad to see the whole kit and caboodle of you."

My parents have not seen the Spencer boys to congratulate them on their fine set of marks. "First class, both of you!" my mother cries as we climb up to their cottage porch.

My dad shakes hands with both boys and asks, smiling, "So now I suppose you are going into graduate school, Bob?"

The Spencers all seem to freeze for a minute. Then Mrs Spencer answers, "No, Dan. Not just now. Bob – " She hesitates, and lets her husband complete the sentence.

"Bob has joined the vrc – the Victoria Rifles of Canada."

Colin breaks into a very awkward moment. "But I'll be back in college in the fall," he says. "Harold too," he adds. "Harold's family and my mum and dad ganged up on

15.3
Bob enlists

the two of us. My family convinced me that since Bob is going, I should stay for at least a year. And Harold's parents put pressure on him to stay in college for another year too – to keep me company, they say. Though this year he was so busy with his courses I hardly saw him."

"Me too," I say. I realize that Colin, whether on purpose or not, has swung the talk away from Bob, and away from his parents' feelings about his enlistment. My father, however, reverts to that subject. "When do you start training, Bob?"

"I've started already, Colonel Hillman. I'm waiting for a posting. We have a battalion ready to go overseas, but I'm not sure they'll have a place for me just yet."

"Things seem to be heating up in Greece. Do you think the Canadians will be involved there?"

"Hard to tell. But the rumour is that the Italians will come in openly on the Nazi side soon, officially, and then there will be action in Italy. Manpower is the watchword now. They are pushing recruits through with very little basic training. They're just beefing up the forces, whether or not with trained personnel."

This is a Bob totally different from the quiet friend I have known, the Bob dragging me into college politics. He is addressing my father and his on a new basis. No wonder Mrs Spencer looks so dimmed.

Colin cries, "You're just making me feel worse about staying home, Bob." Bob cuffs him; Colin shoots back a playful punch, and first thing we know the two of them are roughhousing.

"Boys, boys! Fight nicely now!" Mrs Spencer cries as she used to do over the growing-up years.

On May 27, the British sink the *Bismarck*. Somehow "Bismarck," the very name of the German ship, has had mystic significance, and its sinking raises our spirits. Then we think about our own boys at sea, in the small corvettes that form convoys for Allied troop movements and merchant ships. "Sinking" doesn't seem like such a fine word after all.

PART THREE

1941–1942

INTERVAL

In my summer job in 1941, I theoretically do "war work" as one of thousands of girls replacing men gone into the army. It doesn't seem like war work most days, sitting at a desk in one of the accounting offices of the Canadian Pacific Railway. We tally receipts from the transcontinental dining cars, hour after hour. But every so often, the head clerk, Mr. MacCrimmon, appears at the office in his kilt and silver-buttoned jacket, and we know that it is a "troop day." A trainload of soldiers is arriving from the west, to be transferred from the train station to the Montreal docks, where a troop ship waits to transport them overseas.

We office clerks pile into cars to be driven down to the Montreal wharves. From a distance we will hear Mr MacCrimmon's pipe band leading the soldiers as they march from Bonaventure Station down to the harbourfront. With a skirl, the highland band will march onto the docks and form a pipers' circle, while the soldiers stand at ease and we hand out doughnuts and smiles.

And then the bagpipe drones begin again. The soldiers resume their ranks. Young men from the west – from Moose Jaw and Swift Current and Regina – march up the gangplanks. The pipes play the old lyrics and songs of farewell: "Speed bonnie boat …" and "Will Ye No' Come Back Again?"

We working girls go back to our office routine.

Without warning, the war has entered a new and terrible phase. On June 22, Germany invades Russia. The newspapers tell us that "Hitler has ordered 'maximum cruelty' against civilians. Russia prepares unwavering resistance." The non-aggression pact is broken. Russia is on our side now. Will the Canadian communists shift into support of the war they have so urgently opposed?

Another shift occurs in late July. Japanese troops occupy French Indochina. The Far East is drawn now into a new extension of conflict. One more loop and the Americans might be pulled into active participation. We know they are already involved in the Lend-Lease actions that aid the Allied efforts. How long before this new "World War" really becomes worldwide in scope? By the end of summer American sympathy for the Allies seems to us to have grown significantly. They have been helping with convoy duties in an unofficial way, keeping an informal guard on ships sailing between Canadian ports and Britain. We are ashamed of our little spurt of pleasure when we hear that a German U-boat has fired at the uss *Greer*. Maybe this will heighten American antagonism towards the Nazis.

Certainly the German assaults are not lessening. Not only are we still hearing terrible stories about the bombing of England, Scotland, Ireland, and Wales, but we now hear news of the ferocious battles against the Russians (now our allies). Mid-September brings word that the Germans have besieged Leningrad.

Several more of the boys from our high school class have joined up this summer. Jack Liddy is one of them.

Time for the rest of us to go back to college.

HERE ON LEAVE

FLT.-LT. J. W. LIDDY, son of Mr. and Mrs. J. W. Liddy, of 138 Broughton avenue, Montreal West, who has returned to Canada on

I.1

Jack Liddy

CHAPTER 16
CURRICULUM

The McGill campus comes back to life in the fall of 1941, still in many ways unaffected by the war. I am again on the freshman welcoming committee, and my first job is to create a story for the *Daily* that will introduce the campus to the "Frosh."

Elsewhere in the first issue of the *Daily* we read Churchill's view of the current war situation.

AROUND THE GLOBE | WEDNESDAY, OCTOBER 1, 1941

Churchill before parliament. The Prime Minister has considered the possibility of invading the continent but does not feel that the army in the British Isles is capable as yet of such an endeavour. The Home Guard would be invaluable in repelling an invader but the inference to be drawn is that it cannot be used in a general invasion. If Russia were to remain in the field as a first-class war power, Great Britain and the United States would have to aid in every field of production, on the Eastern Front.

We also read eagerly about American moves toward ending the United States Neutrality Act, and hear with patriotic pride about a conference at Moscow between Stalin, Averill Harriman, representing the United States, and Lord Beaverbrook, representing Britain. (How nice to know a Canadian-born magnate is sitting in such auspicious company!)

Less auspiciously, on registration day this year I have trouble putting together a third-year honours English course. Only one half course with Professor Noad is available. He will be on leave from McGill after Christmas, co-opted (as last year's rumours had suggested he would be) by the wartime government because of his

Campus Features for the Frosh

"Moyse Hall, Douglas Hall, Strathcona Hall, — why doesn't someone do something about people who say "he's at the hall," without explaining? enquired a bewildered Frenchman. So the Daily leaps to aid the Green Bow-tied gentleman and his kind with what we hope will describe the appearance and function of some such landmarks as the Redpath library, the Union, Bill Gentleman, and the Three Bares. Here's a short campus tour.

❖ ❖ ❖

At the outset we start where so many a noon-time romance has started . . . at the Roddick Gates, the semi-circular memorial entrance with its four sided clock which stands on Sherbrooke at the head of McGill College avenue. From the gates, the university drive, flanked by a fifty year old row of trees, leads through the campus to the Arts Building. On the right side of the grounds, branch roads lead to the Physics, Chemistry and Engineering Buildings. Directly across the campus from this last building, the Redpath Library and the Redpath museum stand on either side of another branch road. These, with the Biological and Medical Buildings, which lie beyond the Arts Building, are the principal university buildings on the campus.

❖ ❖ ❖

16.1 Back to college

expertise in languages. Dean Macmillan's courses on Old and Middle English, and on Chaucer will not be offered this year. He is too busy with his war-related work in Ottawa and the demands on his time as head of the depleted English Department here. Three of the young academics who had been in the English Department in 1939 have joined up – one in the army, one in the navy, and one in the air force. The most memorable of the three was Dr Newton, the handsome young man who had given us a charming glimpse of Shelley's ethereal poetry in our first-year course. Presumably there is a need for expertise on Romantic poetry somewhere in the war zones.

Two year-long honours English classes are still offered: Victorian Literature and Modern Fiction. I sign up for both. At registration, Professor Files, the teacher of these two courses and my counselor this year, is a bit apologetic about the reduced offerings. He assumes that since I am in the honours program, I want to go on to graduate school, but warns that it is not likely that a graduate school would accept me with such a thin list of undergraduate courses in English. He promises that if I take a second-year course in philosophy, it will be counted in lieu of one of the missing English courses.

Slightly down-hearted, I register for a course in jurisprudence (in case I decide to try for admission to law) and for one called The Chemistry of Everyday Life, a requirement for students contemplating a future as teachers (teaching is a doom I dread.). To fill out my time table, I also register for psychology (goodness knows what future I am contemplating there).

On the first day of classes, Professor Noad, opening his half-course on modern poetry, makes no reference to the war. He sets us back a bit in time. He explains that he won't tackle *contemporary* poetry. We'll be writing that ourselves, he says, and discussing it at Forge Club meetings. By "modern," he amplifies, he means post-Victorian poetry of the First World War; poetry of the 20s and 30s – Vachell Lindsay, Carl Sandburg. We realize with astonishment that he means to include "American poetry." Our syllabus has always adhered to British lists. And at that, mostly English writers, with a mere ritualistic bow to Walter Scott and Robbie Burns. Now Professor Noad adds other dimensions: we will look not only at American poets, but also at Dylan Thomas from Wales, and W.B. Yeats from Ireland. (Still no reference to Canadian writers of course.)

Professor Files is less experimental. His senior course, Modern Fiction, will begin with two rather dim and dated books: Bennett's *The Old Wives' Tale*, and Galsworthy's *The Man of Property*. But he tells us that he will spend more time on James Joyce's *Portrait of the Artist as a Young Man* – a "stream-of-consciousness novel" – and will end the course with a detailed consideration of Virginia Woolf's *Mrs Dalloway*, "very experimental in form." Dr Files's classes will have a special interest this year. Graduate students will take the course for credit since there aren't enough specialized courses now specifically designed for graduate studies. So people in the Master of Arts program will take classes with us lowly undergrads, but prepare advanced seminars as part of their course load. Besides the graduates, Dr Files expects to introduce into the classes some young people already making a name for themselves as writers (John Sutherland and Louis Dudek are among Dr Files's protégés).[74] We will be rubbing elbows with some brilliant young men already intent on changing the course of Canadian literature. *And* learning about that elusive stream of consciousness.

16.2
Red Cross
Corps

16.3
Red Cross
at work

16.4
On the march

I say hello to Neil Compton when the first class ends. He tells me that he is not taking Dr Files's other course, the one on Victorian literature. He is saving it for next year and taking a history course instead. Maybe I should have made that same decision?

At the end of the first day of classes, Sari and I set out together for RVC where we will act as junior hostesses at the freshette tea. I have a new knitted dress, made laboriously this summer, cranberry red, with small cable-stitch inserts at the waist and on the yoke. Today it's still warm enough to go without stockings. Before we go over to the tea, Sari and I apply leg makeup using tan-coloured "stocking sticks," and carefully manipulate eyebrow pencils to draw dark seamlines on the back of our legs. What a nuisance! We had just got used to nylon stockings when they disappeared (we hear that all nylon is going into parachutes). The *Daily* has warned us about such austerity measures.

AROUND THE GLOBE | THURSDAY, OCTOBER 2, 1941

Government announces curtailment of production in non-essential consumer goods such as radios and refrigerators to seventy-five percent of 1940 output in order to preserve steel and release men for labor in war industries.

But we also hear that the boys overseas are able to get nylon stockings to give as presents to their friends in England. Anyway, Sari and I, with our fake stockings, feel elegant enough for the freshie tea.

Wartime uniforms are in the news today. We girls are being kitted out for our new war activity: membership in the Red Cross Corps. No longer just knittin' for Britain, we are training for service in the Home Guard, if, heaven forbid, (but we no longer put that much trust in heaven) an invasion eventuates. Our uniforms are grey.

We wear "civvies" though, when we practice air-raid mop-up procedures.

As for the boys, the new recruits for the COTC march around the campus everyday. They are not yet in uniform, but are clearly more practiced in marching than their predecessors from the last two years.

Things are looking up overseas also as this college year begins.

London: the battle of the Atlantic is beginning to show concrete results for the man in the street ... The British fat ration will be increased 25 per cent and that of sugar fifty percent.

On Friday the opening lecture in psychology introduces Sigmund Freud. We goggle at the revelations of id, ego, and superego. (At home, as this first week ends, my parents tell me that I am showing a little more id than is strictly necessary.) As in sociology, the professor in this course is excited about his relatively new discipline. We will be involved, the professor tells us during his opening lecture, in experiments going on around the campus, experiments in psychology that may have relevance for the war effort. We may be asked to go up to the Allan Memorial Hospital to take part in some secret research. This sounds particularly exciting to Ray Rose, who is also in this class. He is now a pre-med student, and the prospect of hospital research is most welcome to him. But meanwhile: the basics. For this is Psychology I, and we are all novices in this brave new world.

Our fraternity has volunteered for a special kind of "war work" for this term. On Friday afternoons when our classes are over we will traipse along Sherbrooke Street to the mansion that has now been taken over by the Imperial Order of Daughters of the Empire as a base "for the duration." The IODE are doing a variety of things to support the war effort; their Friday contribution is running a tea dance for the men of the merchant marine. These officers who man the merchant ships that convoy military men and ordnance, wheat and butter, bandages and blood supplies to Britain, have a lonesome time in Montreal in the interval when their ships are being refitted and loaded. They need recreation, and they do love to dance. The ladies of the Imperial Order have decided that the men would enjoy dancing with co-eds rather than with matrons like themselves. So on our first Friday, October 3, we prepare to dance.

The merchant marine officers are bigger and stronger than the boys we usually dance with, but they are light on their feet, and delighted to be dancing. Most of them are married; they tell us about their wives in Halifax or Vancouver. The IODE ladies keep the records changing on the record player: "String of Pearls," "Sunrise Serenade," "In the Mood," "Take the A-Train," "Deep Purple." Halfway through the tea dance, the ladies serve us sandwiches and fruit punch. We notice that many of the merchant marines slip out to the conservatory at the back of the mansion. They probably enjoy a smoke and a little liquid lunch in lieu of the sandwiches. By eight o'clock the tea dance is over and then, after we have helped them tidy up, the IODE ladies drive us to our homes, scattered around the west end of the city. War work over for a week. Fran and I agree that this is a much better extracurricular activity than last year's sorting of bottles at the Red Cross lab.

The second week brings the first lectures in my minor courses. On Monday I cross over to the Physics Building for Introductory Science for Arts Students. Professor Hatcher,[75] lecturing to a large class of scientifically innocent students, turns his classes into memorably funny times. I report to my family, "Professor Hatcher says you'd get more iron by chewing nails than by eating spinach." And, "Professor Hatcher says there's less nourishment in a bowl of corn flakes than in the box they're sold in." "Professor Hatcher says …" We're all grateful for a laughing session at the dinner table.

Jurisprudence is a different story. Dry stuff, badly presented, accompanied by a dreadfully long reading list. Law doesn't seem too enticing a prospect anymore. There is a rumour that women are being admitted to the Montreal Bar this year, but even Ruth Hill seems a bit discouraged about the possibility of a really interesting career in law for women here in this province. But she continues to ask good questions in the class – the only bright spot in a dreary afternoon session.

Finally, the first class in philosophy. It is a total joy to be here, though I will miss Neil Compton as a classmate (he took this course last year). But Professor Maclennan's first class fills me with the same sense of peaceful contemplation that I experienced in his first-year course. This term, Philosophy II, will concentrate in-depth on Plato's *Republic*. The second term will turn to later philosophical systems and consider a range of aesthetic theories, concepts of beauty and order. Three hours a week, all year long, with practically no references at all to the war. But oh dear – the war – the war. World news is so confusing these days.

AROUND THE GLOBE | TUESDAY, OCTOBER 7, 1941

Russian high command asserts Germans lost 98 tanks, 160 trucks, one battalion of infantry and 9 aircraft in one day.

AROUND THE GLOBE | WEDNESDAY, OCTOBER 8, 1941

Russians plan counter-attacks; admit that Germans have made dents in their lines.

AROUND THE GLOBE | THURSDAY, OCTOBER 9, 1941

Outnumbered Soviet armies withdrew today from south of Moscow.

16.5 *Old McGill, 1913*, the sixteenth volume

Nevertheless, at the end of the second week, on Friday, October 10, I write in my diary a personal paean of joy: I am to be – oh, glory! – associate editor of the annual, *Old McGill*, whose appearance is awe-inspiring! Whose name is a symbol for long-lastingness and solidity! Whose other editors are Alex Stalker, Ray Rose, Bill Munroe, and Tom Mulligan. Oh! And a whole page of exclamatory "*oh*'s"!

Ray has talked Sandy Stalker,[76] the editor-in-chief of the official annual yearbook, into taking me on as associate editor. We will begin preliminary work now, knowing that the workload will increase exponentially when the publishing date draws near next spring. Everything – and there's an awful lot of "everything" – must be ready to go to press by the middle of March.

Starting now, we will have our own office in the Student Union Building. The annual *Old McGill* has an even longer history than the *Daily*. We three editors begin to pore over old issues, some lighter than others, all packed with images of life on the McGill campus. They inspire us to try to produce a fitting addition to the pile of annuals published since 1897. Ours will be the forty-fifth volume: *Old McGill, 1942*. I haul out a very old copy, Aunt Zoë's *Old McGill, 1914*, and gloat some more.

Work on *Old McGill, 1942* will be increasingly demanding. I will have too much editorial work to do to allow me to take on assignments for the *Daily*. I will miss the excitement of the *Daily*'s tight deadlines, but *Old McGill, 1942* will tie me to a longer and more stringent calendar.

For now, a once-a-month meeting will be enough to get us started on the annual. Ray and I are in psychology together, so the hour after our Wednesday class will suit us and fits into Sandy Stalker's tight schedule at the law school.

AROUND THE GLOBE | WEDNESDAY, OCTOBER 15, 1941

Moscow threatened. Nazis thrust fourth spearhead toward Moscow. Both sides claim heavy casualties.

As we walk over to the Union after Wednesday's lecture on phobias and fetishes, I try to match Ray's scientific response to these perversions and neuroses. Not possible. Psychology is already beginning to give me a queasy feeling, but we are still only in the first month of the course. I have described some of these neuroses to my mother but she remains blithely unmoved. "Never heard of any of these nutty ideas," she says.

At any rate, it is a relief when Ray and I set psychology aside and move into the quiet efficiency of the space assigned to us for the annual. Preliminary work consists of setting up the procedure for getting advertisements, and doing a first draft of letters soliciting official notes of greeting from deans, and the principal and chancellor. Sandy is meticulous in all this. He offers a revelation of concern with detail. The little office has the same atmosphere of calm that I feel in philosophy class.

But the days march on, and the "Around the Globe" news items remind us of a world far from calm.

16.6 Mary on the Arts steps

AROUND THE GLOBE | TUESDAY, OCTOBER 21, 1941

The Empire's sons streamed into a British port today. One of Canada's largest convoys brought men of five continents safely to the shores of Britain: Canadians, Australians, New Zealanders, Rhodesians, South Africans, and Newfoundlanders.

AROUND THE GLOBE | THURSDAY, OCTOBER 23, 1941

Italy prepares for British invasion. Machine gun nests, artillery batteries and barbed wire defences established.

AROUND THE GLOBE | MONDAY, OCTOBER 27, 1941

RCAF blasts three German ships, adding three more Nazi vessels to its score of over 30,000 tons of German shipping.

I must start my first essay for Dr Files. It will be on *The Old Wives' Tale*. None of my friends have enjoyed this novel very much. We sit together in the library and discuss it in whispers. The Arts steps are empty most of the time this autumn. College life is too serious for those dreamy chats we enjoyed there, two years ago in the late fall sunshine.

CHAPTER 17

CONSCRIPTION

Travelling by streetcar from the McGill campus to the Université de Montréal involves transferring three times. I am going to see Dr Paul Geoffrion in his office at the Université. Here, the buildings are beautiful but empty. They spent so much of their big government grant on the building that they had no money left to hire faculty, so goes the gossip. So they rent empty office space to people like Dr Geoffrion. He is the orthodontist who put bands on my teeth when I was in high school; he wants to see me once a year to make sure my smile hasn't slipped.

Dr Geoffrion likes me to speak French to him. I would like to ask him about conscription. It's a very hot topic this November. We believe all French Canadians are opposed to it, but I'd like to get Dr Geoffrion's views. Alas, after two-and-a-half years of university French classes I am still many miles from bilingualism. I leave the office not at all clear about his opinions.

Conscription is the topic hurtling around the *Daily* office when I get back to McGill. On my way to work on *Old McGill, 1942* I hear a group of reporters in their room across the hall. Voices are raised. Tempers

Noted Scholar Becomes Pilot

Malcolm N. Davies, McGill Graduate, Wins Wings in R.C.A.F.

Joining the Royal Canadian Air Force after a brilliant career at McGill University, where he won the highest honors, L/AC. Malcolm Norman Davies has gone on to win fresh honors in this field, heading the order of merit when he graduated to the rank of sergeant-pilot and received his wings at Saskatoon, Sask., yesterday.

L/AC. Davies and four other airmen received distinguished passes during yesterday's ceremony at the No. 4 Service Flying Training School of the R.C.A.F. The others were James D. Sedley, of Moose Jaw, Sask., Ross Herbert Bertram, of Stevensville, Ont. Douglas James Dolphin, of Toronto and John Rennie Barclay, of Winnipeg.

Wings were **Sgt. Pilot Davies** presented to the airmen by Group Capt. A. D. Bell-Irving, commanding officer of the air station.

17.1 Mac Davies

are high. Should the paper take a stand against parliament making military service compulsory? I hear a familiar voice – Ray Ayoub. I haven't seen much of him since my *Flatland* days, but he is now news editor, and rumoured to be in line for editor-in-chief. He is urging the reporters to take it easy.

Their talk swings to a good story in this morning's *Gazette* about Mac Davies, our editor from two years ago. Though the reporters are proud of this story about one of their own, they tend to suspect that the newspaper article is meant to inspire present students with the possibility of heroic action.

AROUND THE GLOBE | MONDAY, NOVEMBER 3, 1941

British and Canadian airmen attacked and damaged some twenty ships over the weekend, parts of convoys travelling off the Netherlands coasts.

Outside the Student Union, a group of young men stride by on a routine march. Their uniforms have arrived early; the McGill contingent of the Canadian Officer Training Corps[77] will take a prominent part in the services at the Westmount cenotaph this year.

Darkening days; and we are preparing for dark observances of Armistice Day as we remember our parents' stories of the last war and how it ended "at the eleventh hour, on the eleventh day of the eleventh month." Maybe the new Armistice will come soon?

AROUND THE GLOBE | TUESDAY, NOVEMBER 11, 1941

Universal conscription for Canada was the keynote of speeches by two MP's in the House yesterday. A.W. Neil, independent Liberal for Vancouver Island advocated compulsory war service for both sexes.

On Wednesday November 12, however, Prime Minister Mackenzie King vetoes conscription, for the present at least.

17.2 **Left … Left …**

A cold wind whistles along Sherbrooke Street on Friday, pushing Fran and Mary and me toward the IODE tea dance. I am finding these afternoons with the merchant marine officers rather difficult. The dancing is fine, but what to talk about between dances? Conscription? Modern poetry? Plato? Psychoses? We have been warned against breaking the wartime secrets regulations by asking questions about the work the merchant ships do. Fran and Mary, who are usually shyer than I am, say they just ask about the food on board the convoys, or the kind of men that serve on the ships. Those sound like safe topics. I'll try them next week.

These tea dances have in fact turned out to be coffee dances. The IODE ladies feed us tiny sandwiches and huge cups of strong coffee. And the men are such vigorous dancers, especially in the polka: they love, "Roll out the Barrel." It's not easy to relax after these caffeinated parties.

And the war at sea does not bear thinking about.

AROUND THE GLOBE | TUESDAY, NOVEMBER 4, 1941

British navy attacked an Axis convoy bound for North Africa, accompanied by two ten-ton cruisers with superior firepower. The British force of two small destroyers sank 10 enemy supply ships.

Axis or Allies, the ships are all filled with endangered men.

On Sunday evening, Tommy Hardwick walks me home from church. Both of us still sing in the choir, both at evensong and at matins. Tommy has developed a fine tenor voice; he is occasionally assigned solos in our anthems. Now as we walk down Brock Avenue, he reprises the part he sang this evening: "*Lead me, Lord; lead me in thy righteousness ...*"

Righteousness has not been a great theme in the books I am reading this term. I am swiveling through *Sons and Lovers* right now.

Tommy sails into another solo:

> Oh, for a closer walk with God –
> Calm and serene my frame;
> A light to shine upon my road ...

"That half rhyme, 'God' and 'road,' is neat," I tell him, not sure how he will take a comment on poetic form. But now Tommy tells me that he is memorizing at least one poem a week. Astonishing!

"But I thought you didn't like poetry? In our first-year class with Dr Macmillan – "

He interrupts. "I didn't like what Dr Macmillan did with the poetry. Poetry is good for me. An antidote to too much math and physics. No – a complement to them. So I memorize whatever I like."

I tell him that there's no point in my trying to memorize poetry. I've completely forgotten all the lines I learned for Dr Macmillan's Shakespeare course last year. "The only poetry I remember are lyrics of popular songs. '*The melody / Haunts my reverie ...*'"

He chimes in, "*The stardust of a song ...*"

I envy Tommy the clarity of his religious faith, and of his math and physics. But as we turn to cross Curzon Street, he recites his "poem of the week" to me: "When I am dead, my dearest ..." Maybe everything is not so clear to Tommy after all.

AROUND THE GLOBE | MONDAY, NOVEMBER 17, 1941

A strong contingent of Canadian troops arrived unexpectedly

at Hong Kong to reinforce the British garrison there.
The crossing took place under
the utmost secrecy.

Canada's volunteer army has suddenly enlarged its sphere. This week, movie theatres show newsreel pictures of the Canadians, marching with pipers into the strange and beautiful oriental city. A friend in the SCM who comes from Jakarta tells me how steamy hot it is in her part of the world. She worries about the Canadian troops who may have to fight in Indochina, since Japanese troops have rushed into the French colony there, taking the western world by surprise.

AROUND THE GLOBE | TUESDAY, NOVEMBER 18, 1941

The Japanese government requested the permission of the
Indochina government to send 50,000 additional Japanese
troops into this French colony, but without waiting for
a reply is already rushing them in.

Setting aside that faraway tension, Ray Rose and I plod together to our Wednesday psychology class. This being McGill, psychology professors, even those giving the introductory course, are strongly affected by the star presence of Dr Wilder Penfield at the nearby Montreal Neurological Institute. Unlike psychology departments at many other universities, McGill places a heavy emphasis on neurology. We have visiting lectures from medical experts introducing new concepts of the brain, as distinct from the mind. Although this is a social science course, we are led to believe that we are entering the fringes of a harder science. We students may soon be asked ("conscripted, more likely" one of our classmates hisses) to take part in one of the secret experiments in brain research developing now in the Neurological Institute at the request of the government.

Ray, who is hoping for admission to medicine next year, is increasingly spellbound by the psychology lectures. He carries this interest back to the *Old McGill* office.

There he argues with our editor-in-chief, Sandy Stalker, a would-be lawyer, about the legal implications of some of the brain research, especially the surgical operations at the MNI.

This is what college life should be, I think: intellectual arguments about real problems, about research, with no military undercurrents. Our *Old McGill* office seems like the famous "ivory tower" while elsewhere battles rage.

In the deserts of Libya, British soldiers push against Rommel's German army through white heat.

AROUND THE GLOBE | THURSDAY, NOVEMBER 20, 1941

A British army of 750,000 men has been advancing into Cirenaica since Tuesday morning.

And in Europe, in sub-zero weather, a German army is directing its full force against Russia. The Russians are responding with ski-borne troops.

Here in our quiet office, we can visualize those skiing soldiers all too well, now that our own weather is dropping into coldness. Sandy cites the relevance of the winter scenes in *War and Peace,* and I tell him that *Ethan Frome,* the book Dr Files is now covering, is joining Tolstoy's story in my own stream of consciousness, as a nightmare of frost. Ray picks up on the idea of a stream of consciousness. "Where does it flow in the brain? What part of the brain is working in dreams?"

In the waking world, weekends bring fierce work, catching up on assignments. Fortunately, in philosophy, Professor Maclennan has decided that instead of asking for two major essays this term, he wants us to hand in a paragraph of comments every week, discussing points from his lectures or from our reading. Poor man – there are sixteen people in the class, many of them honours English students who love to write. But already he is managing to jot a really meaningful comment to each of us, picking up some special point in the assignment. The other professors are not so considerate. Right now I am facing a couple of longish essays, one on *Ethan Frome* for Dr Files's course, and one on the nature of torts, for my jurisprudence class. It is tough slogging.

I miss the kind of writing I used to do every week for the *Daily*. There, assignments were always easy; I could work them up quickly, snatching up facts for my story, whipping off a lead and an ending, writing rapidly, handing in the story without really thinking about it. In comparison, essay writing is grim and onerous.

Well, I can't take on regular *Daily* assignments anymore because of my work on the annual, but at least I can hand in occasional little bits of doggerel, tightly rhymed, and funny (I hope) about campus topics, such as the rejuvenated Mandolin Society, or the smile of the friendly ape in the McCord Museum, or the fashion for argyle-patterned knee-high socks among the girls – a useful fashion, worn over our lisle stockings, now that the thermometer is doing its autumn drop.

On Monday, I hover again in the doorway of the *Daily* office. I am still rather homesick for its messy confusion and the writing assignments that go with it. These people share my excitement about the practical work of putting facts into words. They work hard these days, writing up campus activities in ways that can match the pull of those brief boxed pronouncements in the lower right-hand corner, with their news of the tumultuous world.

AROUND THE GLOBE | MONDAY, NOVEMBER 24, 1941

As the main tank battle rages in its sixth day,
German armored units attempt desperately
to escape trap around Tobruk.
Anzacs and Indians have recaptured Bardia,
Sidi Aziez and Sidi Omar Nuovo.

Back home, I tell my father I really wonder if I shouldn't be seriously thinking about looking for work as a journalist after I graduate.

Luckily, he has an old friend from the days of the last war who is now a big wheel in the newspaper business. Fred Ker[78] is now the top person in the Southam news organization based in Hamilton. My father promises to arrange for me to meet him the next time he is in Montreal.

That "next time" turns out to come more quickly than expected. On Thursday afternoon I go to my dad's office to meet the newspaper magnate. Mr Ker is very kind. Very funny, too. Mostly funny stories about the terrible treatment most women in journalism can expect to face. Jokes about being buried forever in the women's pages. Or horror stories about the very rare woman who aspires to overseas reporting, and gets given "the short end of the stick. Every time she is on the trail of a scoop she is out-scooped by one of the men." And finally, very serious advice: "I wouldn't let my own daughter go into the newspaper business. Better try teaching, Elizabeth. It's much nicer. And much more appropriate for a young lady."

Role of women, status of women, again, as defined by male authority. I remember hearing Dorothy Thompson at the height of her power when she visited McGill in 1940. And what about Judith Robinson of the *Toronto Telegram*? Even my grandmother reads her columns regularly. I don't dare say so, but I think Mr. Ker is wrong about journalism as a profession for women. I say thank you and leave my dad's office somewhat dampened. Maybe I should indeed aim for a teaching job. Or arrange to get married – another job "appropriate for a young lady."

That option comes up as a subject the very next day. Friday, after the "coffee dance," the IODE lady has let Fran and me out at the corner of Strathearn. Then Fran blurts out, "I'm feeling totally confused." It's not the merchant marine parties that are bothering her, she adds. She sounds elated, and a little frightened. "It's about a college student."

"It's not Russ Merrifield, is it?" I ask, remembering the Union dance in our first year, and the sensation Frances created when she danced with the man who was the "big man on campus." No, Fran answers slowly. "No. It's the American med student. You know, Jay, the one who has been coming to fraternity parties with me. I met him in my biochemistry course. He's so serious, Elizabeth. It's kind of scary."

"Doesn't sound scary to me, Fran."

"He wants to marry me."

"That's silly! You're too young. You're still only in third year. You're – "

"I've said all that. But you can't imagine how convinced he is. And if the United States joins the war, he will probably go back and join the American navy, maybe even before he graduates."

"What does your dad think about all this?"

Fran takes off her tam and pushes her fingers through her ash-blonde curls. "My father feels that Jay has no faults. He won't take me seriously when I say I don't want to get married."

"Come on, Fran! Everyone wants to get married!"

"Not me! Not now! Maybe not ever! I've got other things on my mind." She stops talking. I swing away to my own house.

All in all, I am finding it hard to fall asleep on Friday nights after our coffee dances.

AROUND THE GLOBE | FRIDAY, NOVEMBER 28, 1941

President Roosevelt has himself taken over negotiations with Japanese envoys *Numara* and *Kurusu* in an attempt to secure peace or at least a breathing space in the Pacific.

On Monday in the poetry class, Professor Noad tells us officially that he will be leaving at Christmas. "I have been conscripted," he says with a smile. "The government apparently needs me to serve in its decoding section."

We are devastated, we honours English people. We have become something of a clique, tightly bonding in Dr Noad's classes: Mary Margaret Miller, Tom Mulligan, Neil Compton, Honey Dickson. Professor Noad is our ideal of a humane scholar, so learned, yet so interested in our ideas and responses.

Late in the afternoon I suggest to my fraternity sisters that we should invite Professor Noad to one of our professor's teas and ask him to read to us. He will only be here until Christmas; we should give ourselves the treat of listening to him.

Dr Noad reads to us from a really modern poet, William Carlos Williams.

so much depends
upon

a red wheel
barrow

glazed with rain
water

beside the white
chickens.

My fraternity sisters are silent. This is poetry? And I am taking a whole course on this stuff? The thank you to Professor Noad is perfunctory.

I am trying to write poetry myself now, not doggerel, but modern – as stripped down, vortical and imagistic as Williams's. I don't tell the sisters.

CHAPTER 18
HARBOUR

AROUND THE GLOBE | MONDAY, DECEMBER 1, 1941
Cairo: British reach the coast in their African drive against the combined Italian and German forces.

Winter has set in here in Montreal. Soon the port of Montreal will be frozen over; now the marine officers we have been dancing with are working fiercely at refitting and loading so as to leave before freeze-up. Our weekly IODE dances are coming to a close. The men say they'll be back next spring. They look forward cheerfully to the race to be the first ship to enter the harbour after the ice breaks up. "First ship in means a special cane awarded to the captain. A fine Montreal tradition!" they tell us.

I'm rather relieved that the tea dances will soon be over. Too much going on at college. A McGill University Students' War Council has been set up this year to coordinate student efforts. One of the members is Mary Margaret Miller, my friend in the honours English courses.[79] Her position on the Council comes in for questioning, since she is an American. How can a citizen of a neutral country represent Canadian war-minded students? Mary Margaret confides that she is going to become Canadian: she is engaged to a fourth-year medical student from Wakefield, Ontario. The questioning dies down. Fran says, "If I marry Jay, I won't become an American. Not unless they get into the war. That would make a difference I suppose."

All eyes are fixed on the United States right now.

AROUND THE GLOBE | WEDNESDAY, DECEMBER 3, 1941
Roosevelt takes diplomatic offensive against Japan, asking why the Japanese have such a large concentration of troops in French Indochina.

In spite of the build up of tension, it is a total jolt when we hear the sudden news on Sunday: Japan has attacked the United States Navy in Pearl Harbor.

Pearl Harbor? We have never heard of the place. Dad looks it up in the atlas. An American base in Hawaii. What a terrible irony: the lyric names – Pearl Harbor, Hawaii – and the murderous attack!

In the late afternoon of this nerve-racked Sunday, Ray and I decide to take a slow walk down to our own harbour. Here we find a surprising suggestion of pearls, as the early December snow drifts to the cold river. We stand on the esplanade, feeling the force of our island city rising behind us to its hills, like the island hills of Hawaii. It is the start of a ritual for Ray and me, walking down through the city to the Montreal harbour.

I thought we might see some sign of our merchant marine men and their ships, but of course the working part of the docks is now barricaded off. The harbour is getting ready for the winter freeze. I remember standing here in the summer heat, handing out doughnuts to boys getting off the troop train from the west. Soon there will be no more troop trains emptying here. They will go straight through Bonaventure Station and on to Halifax, where the port will stay open all winter. Our harbour will freeze over any day now.

On Monday we learn from the *Montreal Star* that the Japanese have launched attacks on Guam, have invaded Siam and Malaya, and attacked Hong Kong, Singapore, the Philippines, and Shanghai. Japan has formally declared war on both the United States and the United Kingdom. They haven't bothered to declare war on Canada, so our government takes matters into its own hands.

AROUND THE GLOBE | MONDAY, DECEMBER 8, 1941
Canada declares war on Japan.

Holland also declares war on Japan. On Tuesday, China joins in with an official declaration of war.

The *Montreal Star* warns us that Singapore is in terrible danger, and that we must be prepared for the fall of Hong Kong. Canadian troops are there, the Royal Rifles and the Winnipeg Grenadiers. The *Daily* offers comfort, probably picked up from American propaganda releases.

Japs jolted. Japs have made little headway in first 18 hours of attack on Malaya. Jap troops successful in landing have been repulsed and remnants being mopped up.

At our fraternity house a smaller conflict emerges. Jean Douglas warns that our fraternity sisters feel that we Montreal Westerners are too cliquish. Mary Scott, usually so quiet and gentle, flares up in our defence. Not a clique, she cries, just a natural closeness of girls who have been friends since grade one in public school. The critics subside, though we suspect some of them still mutter behind our backs.

The *Daily* reminds us that greater war is getting close to our own town.

Ottawa widens danger zone. New air raid precautions are planned for hitherto unorganized coastal centers. Montreal is placed in the "Medium Risk" raid area.

But nothing dims our excitement about the entry of the States into the war. Good news for embattled Britain; good news for Canadian service people, who have been straining to keep up the bombardment of Germany and the efforts on the Italian front.

It is hard for us English students to keep our minds on what Dr Files is saying about Sinclair Lewis's *Main Street*. With America joining the war, we are all suddenly pro-American and don't like this American novelist's mockery of his own country.

As our fall term nears its end, we hear of one last bit of warmongering: India declares war on Japan. I wonder what Dr Rao, the gentle brown man who impressed me so deeply in first year, would have to say about this new development? In his memory I pick up my little volume of Rabindranath Tagore.

Then I phone Sari. She says that she was in fact about to phone me.

"We have another group of cousins visiting us from the old country," she says, "and it is the wish of my family that you should meet them." Sari's phone calls always seem much more dignified and formal than her laughing self. Perhaps members of her family are listening as she makes the phone call. At any rate, I am pleased to accept the invitation to tea.

Sari's uncle greets me formally – he is usually the one who does the talking when I visit, the mother and aunt knowing very little English, and the grandmother none at all.

"We shall have our tea presently," he says. "But first we have a treat for you." He says the word "treat" as though it is in quotation marks, and as though it is a word he has just recently learned.

The visiting cousin leaves her chair and stands as if at a music recital. Her husband picks up an unusual instrument, something like a guitar, and riffles out a little melody as introduction. Then they sing, words that I cannot understand, but with a charm and grace that carries across the language barrier.

"How does the song seem to you?" Sari's uncle asks when the last notes have died away.

"It seems sad – no, not quite sad, a little mysterious perhaps, and regretful, but beautiful too." I turn to Sari's cousin, Marika. "Your voice is wonderful, Marika."

"Yes but – " the uncle interrupts, "the song itself; you respond to it?"

At this point Sari breaks in. "We must not be mysterious, Uncle. The song is mine, Elizabeth." Then, seeing my puzzlement, "I mean I have written the poem, and Marika and Franzicek have set it to music. It is one of several poems I composed last winter. And now I have almost enough to make a volume to be published."

Sari's grandmother says something quickly in Czech and they all laugh and agree.

Sari's uncle takes over again, recalling us to the tea table. Before I leave, I ask if any of Sari's other Czech poems have been set to music, and a delighted and delightful Marika says, "I shall oblige! This one is of a silver swan caught in the ice of the St Lawrence and wreathed with pearls of snow." The song is quick and sparkling.

Pearls of snow; ice in the silver harbour – fine poetic stuff for a lyric singer. Sari's song offers a dream, a way to escape from the dangers in the real St Lawrence River and the gulf.

I say thank you and accept Sari's uncle's offer of a lift home. It's hard to leave this charmed room filled with song and beauty. Hard to remember the troubles all these sophisticated people have lived through, maybe are still living through.

At home, reading today's *Montreal Star,* I shudder at the winter sufferings of all the belligerents: Germans mired in ice and slush; Russians running out of firewood and food.

How can I keep my mind on poetry in such a blizzard of war? A kind of anesthesia has set in, a lack of ability to process the news, and no offsetting sense of significance in the stuff presented in the final lectures of this term. The faculty seem entranced too, although the assignments continue to be announced and there is no talk of relaxing deadlines for essays and reports.

Days leading up to Christmas bring greetings in thin blue letterforms from the boys I once knew who are now stationed overseas. They can't say much;

18.1 Clyde and Harold Hillman

18.2 Billy Piers and friend

mostly they just reminisce about good times we used to have, or make smart jokes about the English beer – or the ouzo, if they want to hint of imminent deployment to Greece.

One such blue form comes from my cousin, Clyde and his young brother, Harold, both of them now "somewhere in Europe." Cousin Harold spent his embarkation leave with us in August. I paste their picture into my scrapbook, along with a related clipping from the *Gazette* about Billy Piers, another summer cottage friend, now in that same "somewhere."

But the tone of the notes from overseas is changing as news of American involvement spreads. In the past, letters from Britain harped bitterly on America's hesitation to join the war. All that is forgotten now. Franklin D. Roosevelt is a hero to Canadians, here and overseas, even if there are many Americans who still favour the old isolationism. That must be changing, as danger threatens their own boys.

AROUND THE GLOBE | TUESDAY, DECEMBER 16, 1941

US ships lost. Navy Secretary Knox announces loss of *Arizona* and 5 other warships at Pearl Harbour in raid of December 7. Ninety-one officers and 2,638 enlisted men reported dead. Known Japanese losses reported included 3 submarines and 41 aircraft.

Since the attack on Pearl Harbor, news of the tropical isles in the South Pacific has held our attention. We are learning a new archipelago of names.

In the run-up to the end of the term, all of us are also absorbed in polishing off the almost-overdue essays. But in spite of the pressures of assignments, all our English classes are friendly and lively now. We also meet late on Wednesday afternoons at the English Literature Society to discuss new trends, new writers, and sometimes to read our own work to each other. Sari is part of our literary group, though she is honouring in modern languages rather than English literature, and of course she cannot read her poems to us, since she is still writing them in Czech.

place, but our main duty is to pass our courses well, and **to graduate soon.**

Of course, there are difficulties in the road. Many students rely on summer work to provide funds for the winter's expenses. But 89 per cent. of American colleges seem to have got around this difficulty. Why, then, shouldn't we? By adding the extra term, hard-up students will be enabled to graduate all the sooner, thus easing their burden in the long run. The government could assist by setting aside a special loan fund for such students, perhaps stipulating that Canada shall have first call on them after graduation. And by making the summer term **optional,** those students who simply must do summer work will still be able to continue at college.

We must repeat, again, that the difficulties are many and great. Most courses would have to be drastically re-organized. We would all have to work much harder. Fees would have to be altered. But in times like these, we must be prepared to make sacrifices.

And when the war is over, perhaps the ridiculously long five month holiday will be a thing forever past, and students will no longer be students for only half the year.

Neil M. Compton,
Arts III.

18.3 Letter from Neil Compton

We honours English people have become close friends, glad to feel free to share our ambitions and worries. Neil Compton, for instance, is looking forward to an academic career. He makes a habit of writing letters to the *Daily*.

Today he offers proposals rather like Dr James's for changing college patterns once the war ends, such as getting colleges to add an extra term in the summer, so that veterans can get through their college courses more rapidly. He also suggests that veterans' education should be funded by the government as recognition of their service. We applaud his vision. And it's a change to see someone writing in the same key as the principal.

Mary Margaret Miller has become a friend too. She takes me to see the apartment where she lives. She says she has sent sketches of it to her parents, with arrows indicating "→ to the kitchen" and "→ to the bathroom." In fact, as she shows me, the apartment is a single room with kitchen and bathroom in one corner. She can sit on the toilet and stir the soup on the stove, she says. It is my first experience with student housing.

Suddenly our fall term is over. Christmas holidays are imminent.

At the SCM we discuss the possibility of a skiing outing together during the holidays, after Christmas Day. Maybe stay overnight for New Year's somewhere in the Laurentians? But high prices for Laurentian chalets dampen our hopes. I talk the problem over with my parents, and find I can offer an alternative. My SCM friends can stay over New Year's at the cottage on our own snow-bound Île Cadieux. It's not really winter-proof, but with enough sleeping bags and firewood we could keep warm for two or three days.

I mention the idea to Harold and with a little urging he gets his parents' permission to open their cottage too, so that there will be room for the boys to have separate sleeping quarters. General approval; and one of the senior SCM advisers agrees that he and his wife will come along as chaperones.

Best laid plans, but as Burns says, they "gang aft agley."

My family lurches into major trouble. Just before Christmas, Granny Smith's heart trouble intensifies. We organize a quick family train ride to Toronto, but it is too late. Dear Granny dies on December 17. After a dreary time of visitation and funeral we come home a diminished family on the twenty-sixth.

Should I cancel the plans for New Year's with my friends at the cottage? Of course my parents say no to that. So our group of fourteen meets at the SCM and we take the train to Vaudreuil on the thirtieth.

By now, the Lake of Two Mountains has frozen solid, so we all bring our skates. It is a successful venture. Everyone enjoys the sharp cold weather, the fun of skating after dark with flambeaux lighted to augment the moonlight, the singsongs in front of the fireplace, and the gobs of not so nourishing food.

One long-lasting result is that Mary Scott and Homer Brady spend a lot of time together – the start of a life-long romance.

On New Year's Eve after a great day of skating on the beautiful shiny lake we gather around the hearth for a party. The chaperones have been naughty and brought a couple of bottles of wine. None of us are used to drinking. Part of the wartime atmosphere on campus has been a tacit agreement that drinking is not very patriotic. Consequently, a small glass of red wine heats us up. "Auld Lang Syne" brings us into a warm circle of intertwined arms. There is a rather sheepish moment of hugging and kissing all around. Harold says, "Well, I guess it's about time," and puts his hands on my shoulders, bending quickly to kiss me – a first kiss. He misses. Our noses bump into each other, and the kiss lands on my left ear. "That's not good enough!" he cries, and he tries again. This time it is good enough.

We all go out into the snowy darkness and look at the winter stars. Then the boys slip away to the other cottage. Tomorrow we will skate again along the shoreline, under the bridge, and across the thickly iced lake to the harbour at Vaudreuil, change to boots and make our way to the railway station and so home, in the new year brightness of 1942.

CHAPTER 19

EXTRACURRICULAR

Christmas holidays over, it really is 1942, and time for Ray and Sandy and me to knuckle down to work on the annual, *Old McGill, 1942*. Ray hassles the secretaries of all the societies to submit their reports on their this-year activities, and organizes photo sessions for them to get pictures of their this-year executive committees.

Among the first to arrive are the official pictures of the military corps now established on the campus: a naval unit and an air force unit. Principal James welcomes them.

A correlative change impacts more strongly on our lives. Because of military imperatives, the caff in Strathcona Hall is now off limits. The McGill Faculty of Education, ousted from its old home on the Macdonald campus at Sainte-Anne-de-Bellevue by the Canadian Women's Army Corps, has moved into the capacious hall at the corner of McGill College Avenue and Sherbrooke. The CWAC is a new regular army outfit, giving women a more central role to play in the war. But the ultimate consequences of the founding of the CWAC, for us, are dismal. The friendly SCM lounge as a drop-in place will be gone, as well as the suite of SCM offices on the

19.1
Welcome
to war

second floor. Well, the SCM has already found new quarters in the YMCA building on Stanley Street. But the caff in the basement, where coffee and sociable chat have become habit, is gone for good.

Second American ship sunk fifteen miles off US coast causes serious concern on the east coast.

Mid-term exams are now in order. We write our exam on the poetry course rather sadly. How will Dr Noad find time to mark these papers now that he is in Ottawa?

Well, once the mid-terms are over, it's back to the classrooms, back to taking notes, trying to take part in discussions, especially in Dr Files's classes. (He tends to pounce with a question whenever my mind wanders to the annual editing or to events off campus.)

Yes, we honours English students feel at ease with each other; but we all acknowledge a shared loss since Dr Noad departed. We ruefully admit to each other that each of us felt a special bond with him. I myself believed that he was taking special notice of my essays – but Mary Margaret Miller and Tom Mulligan confess they each had the same feeling about their own importance to him! We all agree that we should not waste time now, just because he is gone.

Shades of 1812. Recapture of Mashies by the Red Army marks the failure of the Nazi offensive on Moscow. Hitler faces a direct attack on his headquarters at Smolensk.

Shades of 1812, indeed! I wish we were studying *War and Peace* this term, instead of *Portrait of the Artist as a Young Man.* How about "Portrait of Me as a Young Woman"? Not much of an artist right now. Editing for the annual is not the same as writing. Even writing essays doesn't feel the same as expressing in words the way life seems to change from day to day – in class, at home, in the SCM, at the fraternity.

Our Alpha Omicron Pi fraternity, for instance, has been busy raising money "for the war effort" by sponsoring a Gilbert and Sullivan concert, selling tickets, ushering. Gibson, who chaired this effort, has her picture in the *Montreal Star* as a result.

We AOPi's are missing our first term "war effort," and feeling an extra surge of worry about those nice officers of the merchant marine, especially given today's news.

AROUND THE GLOBE | THURSDAY, JANUARY 29, 1942

Lady Hawkins torpedoed. Two hundred and fifty persons are reported dead or missing after the sinking by an Axis U-boat 11 days ago of the 7,850-ton Canadian National Steamships Lines vessel *Lady Hawkins* in the Atlantic; only 71 of the original 321 passengers reached port after being adrift in an open boat for five days.

Sad, sad news. None of the men we met were on the *Lady Hawkins*, but that doesn't lessen the hollow feeling about the sinking.

Taking up the cudgels for the fraternities on campus, I contribute an editorial to the *Daily* about their attitudes and their contributions to the war effort. The women's Panhellenic Association had presented the Students' War Fund with a check for two hundred dollars – a big hunk of money for us in 1942. I celebrate their effort as an example of wartime cooperation.

I'm on a writing roll now. I produce another *Daily* editorial on equal rights for women, squeezing a little extra juice out of last year's term paper on "The Status of

> "Equal rights for women!" To us in Quebec this has been no ludicrous, long-dead battlecry of a past generation. Within the last few years the League for Rights of Women of Quebec has been fighting to gain not only the right to vote, but to hold office, to make contracts without permission of husband (or other controlling male), to buy and sell property, and so on.

19.2
On the status of women

Women in the Province of Quebec," exploding again with continuing indignation. I submit this editorial as an entry to a competition (and I think it will win). I'm feeling combative.

Gas rationing goes into effect. The amount of gas which may be purchased under Canada's rationing scheme varies from 300 to 580 gallons a year for non-essential to unlimited supply for all times of commercial vehicles.

January 30, 1942: I have won the local editorial contest with my views on the status of women. The prize is five dollars and considerable glory. And the *Daily* editor-in-chief, Harry Lash, tells me that my editorial is to be reprinted in the University of Toronto's *The Varsity*, and other college papers. Professor LaViolette may not have valued my essay last year, but my stand on women's rights has found an audience. Yet in spite of this being a happy day, for some reason I feel listless and dejected. Mid-term blues I guess.

Well, January is over; February will be a shorter month in lots of ways.

In the first week, of course, Sadie Hawkins returns. She is being celebrated twice this year, first in a "Sadie Slide" then, a "Spinsters' Spree." I invite Harold to one, Ray to the other. In both cases it is a payback for a number of nice January dates.

Now I must grind out a series of stories for the *Daily*, hoping to bring more and better material in to the *Old McGill, 1942* office. Sandy, Ray, and I are pushing for people to submit photos for the "Campus Life" section. Sandy says not only is it good publicity, but also the more pictures there are in our book the more copies we will sell.

We run a contest with nice prizes, and I report that. Then we award the prizes, and I report *that*.

While Sandy, Ray, and I begin to collect growing piles of information about the doings of all the college clubs and faculties, the *Daily* collects and publishes reports on far-flung parts of the world and their hostilities.

Informal, Unposed Snaps Required for Contest

Most Entries Lacking In New, Original Angles

The second Campus Life Contest for Old McGill '42, now getting under way has not yet called forth an adequate response of informal unposed pictures the Annual editor stated last night. Most of the pic-—pushing coeds into snow-banks while a colleague snaps the shutter being one of the cute tricks advised by the Editor. . . .

And seriously—skiing shots and pictures of the campus deep in

19.3
Photo
contest

'Nothing Startling' Yet Handed in For Photo Contest, Editor Says

19.4
Nothing
startling

AROUND THE GLOBE | MONDAY, FEBRUARY 9, 1942

RAF cripples foe's communication and supply lines as Rommel's forces are checked at Ain El Gazala, 40 miles west of Tobruk.

By contrast, most of the "Campus Life" pictures coming into the *Old McGill, 1942* office seem to be focused on romantic alliances. Boys and girls holding hands, people dancing at the college hops, even a few shots of couples kissing.

All these nice warm pictures will balance the chillier photos we have been given by the administration, featuring uniformed air force people enrolled at McGill to study physics, with the ultimate hope that they will help advance the development of radar.

Those are exclusively pictures of male students. On the other hand, we are offered lots of pictures of girlish beauty. Mind you, the old Red and White Revue, with its chorus line of co-eds practising high kicks, has gone the way of all flesh. But this year

19.5
Romance

we had a substitute for that kind of titillation: a "Beauty Queen Contest." One of our prize-winning photos depicts student judges deliberating on the choice of a "Campus Queen." In this winning photo three over-reacting boys, two of them in uniform, solemnly consult.

For our final prizewinners, we would like to choose pictures representing the war effort. In the end, however, we award the grand prize to a less-than-heroic shot of a faculty member helping the on-campus effort to put together a "mile of pennies" in order to buy war bonds – "victory bonds," as we must call them. Besides having a good shot of Professor Day plunking down his pennies, we receive another, rather stiff shot of Principal James, almost on his knees as he stoops to place a penny in the mile-long line running from Roddick Gates to the Arts Building. Not a winner, we decide.

AROUND THE GLOBE | WEDNESDAY, FEBRUARY 11, 1942

End in sight. The invading Japanese beat back Imperial British defenders on Singapore Island today.

Study of Beauty Contest Judges Wins Campus Life Competition

19.6 Winners

19.7 Judges of beauty

Work on the photo section of the annual is now complete. All the essays that were due are in. I reckon I can go to the Valentine's dance with a clear conscience. Ray Rose takes me to Victoria Hall, where young people from all over the city gather to dance to Blake Sewell's orchestra. It is a crisp cold evening; I am bundled up in a fur-hooded coat, furry pussy-boots keeping my ankles warm, and a muff to match the hood. So cozy it almost seems a shame to slip out of outdoor clothes when we reach the hall. But I am in good spirits as we climb up the broad stairs to the big dance floor. Ray is in high spirits too, enjoying his one social escape from a regime of study as a pre-med and work on *Old McGill, 1942*.

A great orchestra, a happy crowd, almost as though there was no dark reality of war in the background. Gibby is here with her engineer; Fran with her med student. We cluster and chatter as in the old high school days.

Early in the evening, Blake Sewall comes to the front of the stage and announces, "Special treat for us all. Here's Oscar Peterson – still in high school, but already a GREAT performer. Give him a big hand!"

And there he is, a young boy named Oscar Peterson at the piano, playing eight to the bar, with incredible riffs in the treble and that strong sure bass beat pulling everyone into his special rhythm. High point of the evening, until near the end, when everyone moves into a big circle, and we all join in the chanting, *"Let me call you sweetheart, I'm in love with you."* So much for jazz – even with this wunderkind Oscar Peterson.

Now it is really time to settle down and work on editing the reports from all the college associations that are beginning to drift in to our office. My job is to tidy these reports, which mostly means deleting half of each of them, cutting the first paragraph so as to get a livelier opening sentence; chopping over-long sentences into shorter readable ones; chucking repetitive details.

In their annual reports, most campus associations emphasize their concern with wartime issues. For example, the Political Economy Club claims that "in arranging its program, it considered the need for intelligent and interesting discussion about the war and its problems." It adds a note that during the year, two of the club's executive "departed for active service with the forces … the president joined the navy, while … the secretary joined the RCAF."

In the official photo submitted by this particular group, I note the presence of a rather explosive faculty advisor. Professor Culliton, very popular with the students, is less than popular with the administration. He is a maverick with anti-establishment opinions on many topics. He looks a little impish as he stands at the upper left-hand corner in the club picture, ready to discuss "the war and its problems."

Some of the club reports we have received end with a sad note: "The Women's Union helped in organizing a salvage drive and members did knitting and sewing for the McGill branch of the Canadian Red Cross … The women students heard an address on active service for women. Darker days lie ahead."

19.8
Professor Culliton

The Literature Society's annual write-up wryly notes, "Unfortunately owing to difficulty in obtaining the RVC common room as in past years, because of conflicts with the war training and Red Cross … it was decided that the continuance of the society would be curtailed for the remainder of the session." Small wonder it backed away from conflicts with the Red Cross schedule. No one fights the Red Cross girls, trained for action in case of invasion.

Some of the reports on campus groups seem rather frivolous. Mary Morris appears, centre back row, as treasurer of the Bridge Club (a fitting job for a former debutante). No reference to the war in a half-page summary of bridge activities.

Editing is fun, but it does interfere with course work. If I spend too much time on *Old McGill, 1942* my academic life will founder. Guilt and terror are hard drivers, so I go on editing at full pitch. Ray proofreads and adds his own editorial changes. Sandy Stalker's job as editor-in-chief is to shuffle the whole thing together, keeping some sort of order as the reports and photographs come in. We talk to each other as we work. We discuss what is going on in the Far East, in Singapore, where the British forces have gone down before Japanese attacks.

AROUND THE GLOBE | MONDAY, FEBRUARY 16, 1942

Japanese army announced the unconditional surrender of Singapore, the land fortress which had been held by Britain for 123 years.

19.9

Mary Morris and the Bridge Club

Losing Singapore feels like the beginning of the end of the British Empire. We remember the days when we painted all those spots on the map red. Now they are blood-red.

The news from the United States, on the contrary, sounds a bit like empire-building.

AROUND THE GLOBE | WEDNESDAY, FEBRUARY 18, 1942

President Roosevelt declared today that communications between the United States and Alaska should be improved ... A proposed Alaska highway through British Columbia or Alberta and by way of the Yukon is being considered.

Ray and Sandy and I feel that our work on the annual is a small but important contribution to history. Balancing the news from abroad, we are capturing the way people at home in Canada feel in this moment of drastic change.

A change from the annual, and the war: on Friday, Harold invites me to go skating on the outdoor rink on the campus. This proves less than relaxing, however. He renews our old argument about conscription. For indeed, there was news yesterday about Canada's need to conscript all young men into the armed forces.

Unless barred by the Speaker, the House of Commons will vote directly on the conscription issue today.

"Doesn't affect me, anyway," Harold says. "The navy is going to open a campus corps: 'Royal Canadian Naval Reserve,' they'll call it – RCNVR. I'm going to join. They say that this way I'll go into the navy as an officer next spring when I graduate."

It's pretty cold for skating: Harold takes me home early.

On Monday I go back to editing reports on campus activity. I check off the pictures as they are handed in and turn them over to Sandy, happily pointing out some of my friends to him. Ruth Hill appears in picture after picture, on the executive of almost every group on campus.

In the Fencing Club picture, Gibson appears front and centre; Fran is there too as part of the team.

Of a total of 1,985 men sent to Hong Kong, 1,689 are now in the hands of the Japanese.

On February 27, Harold phones again. "The engineers are having a sleigh ride tomorrow. I was talking to Gibby's friend, Vince, and we wondered if you girls could meet us at the Roddick Gates, about seven. Vince and I both have long labs to finish first that afternoon."

Sounds okay. So on Saturday evening Gibson and I take the streetcar from Montreal West to the Roddick Gates, join the boys, and take a bus to where the sleighs are waiting. Three big wagons, each pulled by a team of workhorses, are lined with a deep layer of straw to make seating comfortable. The snow is deep and powdery, perfect for the sleighs.

We have hardly started when some of the boys begin pushing the girls off the wagon. I am one of the first to land in the soft snow. Harold has heaved me off with

Back row, left to right: Stephanie Zuperko; Frances Tyrer; Margaret McGarry; Pat McCall; Ellen Creaghan; Betty Chisholm.
Front row, left to right: Mr. G. Tully, Coach; Frances Smith; Shirley Jackson; Gibson Beatty; Ruth Harris; Sheila Farquharson; Mary Carmichael; Marguerite Pettes.

19.10 Gibson, Frances, and the Fencing Club

the old twist he used to use on the raft at the cottage. I pick myself up, laughing, stride after the sleigh, and hop aboard again. Another push, and Harold has ousted me again. Back aboard. Back into the snowbank. And again. "Fun, eh, Elizabeth?"

"No!" I gasp, but he laughs and pushes me off one more time.

One time too many. I stay still, puffing, over my boot tops in snow, waiting for the second sleigh to catch up. As it comes abreast, I swing aboard, helped by mittened hands. Before a minute has passed, Harold appears, standing by the side of the road, ready to join me, and ready to begin the roughhousing again. But I am ensconced in the middle of the sleigh, and a kind of mock battle ensues, with some people trying to push me to the edge, while Gibson and Vince and others defend me.

"Fun, eh, Elizabeth?" he calls again from behind the wagon.

19.11
Harold

When the sleighs finally come to a stop he pulls me off and swings me toward the coffee shop where the Engineering Club has arranged a feast – sausages and beans and Coca-Cola. The noise of the party is deafening. I am too upset to eat; glad when it is time to go home on the streetcar with Gibby.

Next day, Sunday, Harold phones. Can I come for a walk after church?

"No thank, you. I'm busy writing an essay." I refuse to add, "Some other time maybe." Then my question erupts: "Just why did you do all that pushing at the sleigh-ride, Harold?"

"Don't know," he says, but adds no apology. Instead, he hangs up without saying goodbye.

On Monday evening, another call. "Finish the essay? Lucky for us engineers, we don't write essays. Just lab reports, and I can breeze through them very quickly. So – would you like to go out for a walk tonight?"

"I'll be working on this essay all week." I add, "Maybe next week too. Probably all month." And if that doesn't send him a message, nothing will.

But his answer is, "Well, I can always phone you."

No, I think – I'm deleting you from my social list. For now, anyway.

It turns out that Harold is deleting me from his list too. I had been looking forward hopefully to the engineers' annual party – the Plumbers' Ball. It is being amalgamated with the Meds Ball this year, so as to lessen the impression of inappropriate festivities on the campus. But no invitation is forthcoming. Maybe Harold, like many others, feels that it is inappropriate in any form. Or maybe he is in a general state of anxiety, feeling the powerful urge to just quit classes right now and join up.

I happen to mention all this to Sari, and she gives me her own bit of news. The boy who took her to the symphony a year ago – the fellow who was so adamantly against talk of war when we first met him – has disappeared. Not in any of his classes, not seen around the campus. "Has he enlisted, do you suppose?"

"Or taken to the woods for fear conscription comes and he is caught?"

"Could be either one or the other!"

CHAPTER 20
WINDING DOWN

In the final phase of our psychology class, Ray and I are invited to volunteer as subjects for an experiment up at the Allan Memorial Hospital. It is a study in thresholds of pain. We will be subjected to increasing heat, applied by a wire attached to the forehead. We will indicate when the pain becomes unbearable. We will be paid a minimal sum for participating in this experiment. Why not? Ray and I sign up. We slither up University Avenue and across to the hospital and are wired up for the experiment. Strapped into a chair, we are attached by wires to a recording machine. A beam of white light is directed at our foreheads. We hold a rubber bulb, which we are to press when the heat becomes hard to bear. It turns out that Ray and I both have a high level of tolerance for pain, though what use will be made of this result we are not told. Something to do with the treatment of prisoners of war, perhaps? That is the rumour at any rate.

20.1
Chemical
weapons
drill

Other, more drastic experiments are taking place on the campus. The Physics Department is participating in wartime research on innovations in warfare: experiments that will help the development of radar and other secret weapons. (Tommy Hardwick has been chosen to join this select group of physics students.) Students in chemistry are playing a part in experiments on poison gas and in ways of resisting gas attacks by the enemy. Chemical weapons drills take place in the Arthur Currie Gymnasium. The administration has sent a picture of the volunteers to us at the annual office.[80] There doesn't seem to be any doubt that we must use it in the "Campus Life" section we are now putting into its final form as March opens.

The *Daily*, however, carries no stories about these experiments in physics and psychology. It does report on Principal James's departure for Britain. The *Montreal Star* fills out the story: Dr James is discussing post-war plans with people like Attlee and Beveridge – plans to solve the unemployment problem that will follow demobilization and readjustment of industry. He is also discussing farther-reaching plans for social adjustments after the war: plans for maternity benefits, workmen's compensation, old age pensions. The *Gazette* and the *Star* both play up these admirable efforts; the *Daily* merely notes his absence from campus – again.

AROUND THE GLOBE | MONDAY, MARCH 2, 1942

Japanese invading forces have driven 40 miles into Java to capture the city of Subbing.

This week's copies of the *Daily* seem thin: the staff is smaller, and the distractions from reporting are greater. The front page notes that the RVC and McGill Men's Glee Club have combined for a concert – historic! But the reporters whisper a rumour that there are too few baritones for the men's club to make up an effective concert program by themselves.

Now that there is less to report by way of sports events, the back pages of the *Daily* are mostly filled with clips from other college papers – the University of Toronto's *The Varsity*, the University of British Columbia's *Ubyssey*, Queen's University's *The Journal*, Acadia's *Athenaeum*, and the University of Saskatchewan's *The Sheaf*. This is a display of effort by Ray Ayoub, now the exchange editor, replacing Sid Schacter, who has joined the army. The exchange editor traditionally also writes a number of the editorials because his perspective has been broadened by keeping up with what is happening at other universities. Ray Ayoub's style shows in a growing number of editorials. He will probably be editor-in-chief next year.

Since I want to make sure of an invitation to the *Daily* banquet, I cross the hall and join the newspaper clan in their office. Some unholy language flies around about the latest crop of rumours.

"The administration plans to tighten control over what the *Daily* can print next year. They say the board of governors is upset about the tone of some of our stories this year, and preparing to punish someone. Anyone," Judy Jaffe tells me. I am glad to leave this office and its explosive atmosphere.

'Daily' Managing Board Names Raymond Ayoub Editor-in-chief At Annual Banquet on Friday

MANAGING BOARD, 1942-43

Editor-in-Chief   *Managing Editor*

RAYMOND AYOUB   EDWARD D. JOSEPH

Major Brown Proposes Toast

Guests Include Many Former "Daily" Editors

The McGill Union Cafeteria was the scene of the annual "Daily" Banquet last Friday evening. Approximately 100 members of the "Daily" heard Major H. S. L. Brown deliver an after-dinner speech in which he commented on the assistance given by the "Daily" to the more efficient performance of military training on the campus.

Besides reporters, editors and managing board, there were present Gerry Clark, former Editor-in-chief; Adam Marshal, also an ex-

20.2
New *Daily* editors

But I am equally glad to accept an invitation to the *Daily* banquet. It is a thrill to learn that next year the editor-in-chief will indeed be my old *Flatland* friend, Ray Ayoub. His picture in the *Daily* announcement looks very serious. He is taking on a big job. In fact, he looks a bit glum. He has always been very serious and there is no doubt that managing to keep the *Daily* afloat as the war goes on and on may be very challenging.

This year's guest speaker, Major Brown, emphasizes "the help given by the *Daily* to efficient … military training on the campus."

AROUND THE GLOBE | TUESDAY, MARCH 10, 1942
Vichy abandons fleet to Nazis.

Ray and Sandy and I have put our heads together to write our own editorial for the annual. The military theme is of course strong here too:

> *This is the third edition of Old McGill, which has appeared since the war broke out, and it has been most affected by wartime conditions. We have entered upon the period of priorities, restrictions, and shortages, and these have left their mark upon our policies and our book. The campus, too, has seen the effects of war, and we have tried to show this. The university's war effort is deserving of being recorded.*

Near the back of our book, we will present a long page titled, "Active Service," listing the names of students who have joined up since October 1941. The list includes three Montreal West boys: Buddy Kimber, Jack Liddy, and John Keys, son of the physics professor who is active in radar and nuclear research. There are also names of boys I met in freshman year at parties and at the scm: Bob Kingsland, Bernard Panet-Raymond, plus the colleagues from the *Daily*, Syd Shachter and Jack Weldon.

Too often we read in the downtown papers the ominous references to friends on active service who are now "missing in action," or worse.

Active Service

This list includes those who have left the University since October, 1941. Some may have been omitted — if so we apologize. We have not included the great number of students who enlisted upon graduation last May, nor those who joined up during the summer and did not come back to complete their courses.

Bailey, John Harvard	B.Com. '42	R.C.N.V.R.
Baker, John Douglas	B.Sc. '45	R.C.A.F.
Barclay, Ian Andrew	B.A. '43	R.C.N.V.R.
Cagney, Alan	B.Sc. '45	Royal Rifles
Capper, John A.	B.Com. '44	R.C.N.V.R.
Cardin, Lucien L. J.	Arts Partial	Active Service
Cluff, Robert Fraser	B.Sc. '45	R.C.A.F.
Ellis, Barton S.	B.Com. '44	R.C.N.V.R.
Flitton, Ralph J.	B.A. '42	R.C.N.V.R.
Freeman, Edwin Leacy	B.Com. '44	R.C.N.V.R.
Frosst, Eliot B.	B.Sc. '45	R.C.N.V.R.
Gibsone, George Derek	B.A. '44	Active Service
Gray, William E. D.	B.Com. '44	Active Service
Hadrill, Peter Geoffrey	B.Sc. '43	R.C.N.V.R.
Harris, Rupert C. T.	B.A. '44	R.C.N.V.R.
Keys, John David	B.Sc. '43	R.C.N.V.R.
Kimber, Gordon Stanley	B.Sc. '45	R.C.A.F.
King, Colin Campbell	B.Sc. '45	R.C.A.F.
Kingsland, Robert R.	B.A. '43	R.C.A.F.
Knox, Stanley H.	M.D. '44	R.C.A.F.
Layne, John Harkon	B.Eng. '44	R.C.A.
Leetham, George E. W.	B.A. '45	R.C.A.F.
Leslie, James St. John	Arts Partial	R.C.A.F.
Lewtas, James L	B.A. '42	R.C.N.V.R.
Liddy, John W.	Dent. '45	R.C.A.F.
MacDonald, John Fyfe	B.Sc. '42	R.C.N.V.R.
McGibbon, James Edmund	B.Com. '43	R.C.A.F.
Main, Robert B.	B.Com. '45	Active Service
Meilleur, Jeanne	B.Sc. '45	R.C.A.F.
Morgan, William Lloyd	B.Eng. '43	Active Service
Noble, William Randolph	B.A. '44	R.C.N.V.R.
O'Neill, Edward Yates	B.Sc. '42	R.C.A.F.
Panet-Raymond, Bernard	B.Eng. '43	R.C.A.
Read, Henry C. C.	B.Sc. '42	R.C.A.F.
Riddle, John A.	B.A. '42	R.C.A.F.
Ritchie, Frank Ivan	B.C.L. '43	Active Service
Savage, James C.	B.Eng. '44	R.C.A.F.
Schachter, Sidney A.	B.Eng. '44	R.C.A.F.
Shannon, Robert C.	B.Sc. '45	R.C.A.F.
Silver, Lee Maurice	B.Sc. '45	American Army
Stevenson, Richard H.	B.Com. '42	R.C.N.V.R.
Stober, Melvin	B.Com. '45	R.C.A.F.
Triganne, Gilles	B.Eng. '45	Active Service
Weldon, John C.	B.Sc. '43	R.C.A.F.
Wilder, William P.	B.Com. '44	R.C.N.V.R.
Wilson, Donald Cliff	B.A. '45	R.C.A.F.

We reserve a page in *Old McGill, 1942*, titled "In Memoriam," for the names of McGill boys who died between 1941 and 1942.

At last *Old McGill, 1942* comes out, handsome in its light grey cover, designed to look like a grey stone castle. We have decided to blend the idea of "oldness" with the new emphasis on war. A bannered medieval knight reappears throughout, recalling, for me at least, Dean Macmillan's glorification of Chaucer's "verray parfit gentle Knight" at the outset of our college experience. Tom Mulligan has drawn clever vignettes.

Anyway, our book is out, and it looks good. Next year, Sandy will be in law and Ray in medicine; both expect to be too involved to have time for extracurricular

[left]

20.3 "Active service"

MISSING OVERSEAS: Flt. Lieut. A. Boyd Ketterson, only son of Major A. R. Ketterson, D.S.O., and Mrs. Ketterson of

20.4

Missing overseas

LOCAL FLIER KILLED

LAC. JOHN RUSSELL D. YOUNG.

20.5

Local flier killed

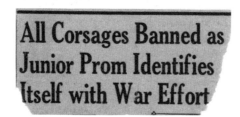

20.6 Editors of *Old McGill*, 1942

20.7
All corsages
banned

activities like this editorial work. So Ray and Sandy take me and Sandy's fiancée to the junior prom to celebrate our publication, and to mark the end of our happy time together.

The war effort haunts us even here. All corsages have been banned from the prom, as its organizers identify with the war effort.

AROUND THE GLOBE | MONDAY, MARCH 16, 1942

In an address to the German people yesterday, Hitler warned that the spring offensive would come in the summer and that the German people would have to suffer more privations.

The pause between the end of classes and the onset of exams seems to be a good time for renewing friendly closeness. Sari calls. "I have something to ask you, something important, Elizabeth. But I think we shall wait until after the examination time, for fear of distracting ourselves."

Indeed it is hard to concentrate, given the daily barrage of unsettling news. A national plebiscite on the issue of conscription will be held while we are writing our exams. French Canadians are the main – though not the only – objectors to the draft. At home my family blaze into indignant commentary, then stifle their anger in order not to upset me during my study time.

My plans for next year are very uncertain. My time at McGill seems to be coming to a premature close. This term I am taking the last two English courses I am eligible to take here, both given by Dr Files. So many other faculty members have been gobbled by the war effort: Dr Macmillan, Dr Noad, Dr Newton, and others – all gone. I must face it: there will be no fourth-year courses left for me to take. I make an appointment to see Professor Files. He says I should still try to get a good honours degree and then go into graduate work.

"Unfortunately we can't give you the courses you need next year. A good graduate school won't take you unless you have studied Old English, Chaucer, Renaissance literature, Victorian prose, and literary criticism. We can't offer any of those next year. Stripped by the war, as you know." He suggests that I transfer. "Maybe to Toronto. They are almost as well-respected as McGill by the big graduate schools."

So during the Easter break I go to Toronto. I have wonderful letters from McGill – from the registrar, Dean Macmillan, and Dr Files. And I have pull. Because she is on the board of the University Women's Club, my Aunt Zoë knows the wives of most of the influential faculty members at University of Toronto. My mother, who went to the University of Toronto before the First World War, is a lifelong friend of the distinguished Dean of Women, Dr Mossie May Kirkwood. So I am kindly interviewed, and forthright accepted into the honours program at Trinity College.

I must give up my CPR scholarship, which is only available at McGill. My parents tell me not to worry; they saved money while I was at McGill because of the scholarship. I know, however, that my brother, Don, will be old enough for college next year, so that will double their expenses.

McGill exams this year have an air of unreality for me, but it is essential that I go to the University of Toronto with a good academic record, so I redouble efforts at reviewing and doing extra reading. When the exam period is over, I feel relatively sure that my marks will be good enough to guarantee me the right to transfer from McGill to Toronto.

Sari phones the day after the end of exams. Another invitation to tea. Gladly accepted. After the first formalities, Sari's uncle says, "We are so very proud of Luissa. She is a very gifted poet. I believe you know her work has already been published in Czechoslovakia?"

I nod, remembering Mrs Grant, the former warden of RVC and her enthusiasm when she first introduced Sari and me, when we were freshettes.

Her uncle continues, "But we want these new poems to be published here in Montreal."

"My family wants them to be published in English, not Czech," Sari says. The aunt, the uncle, even the grandmother, nod eagerly. Sari herself continues in a shy voice, "We want you to translate the poems, Elizabeth. No – not to translate, exactly, because we know that you do not understand the Czech language. We think that if I were to translate them word by word into English, you could twist them into English poetry. Canadian poetry, because these are poems of Montreal."

I have a different idea. "Why don't you write to Tony in Trinidad and ask him to do this for you? He is a real poet and I am not – "

Sari looks a little shamefaced. "I did ask him. He wrote back that his voice was too West Indian. He says, 'You wouldn't want your Montreal winter poems to say, *Oh, Canada, I don' lak yo weathah!* would you?' He is right. You and I, Elizabeth, could work together this summer."

The idea is intriguing, but already I am beginning to worry about whether I can accept Sari's invitation to collaborate. All I can do, in front of her eager family, is say, "I will think about it, Sari. It is very flattering to be asked."

"I do not mean to be flattering," she says. "Only – self-serving!"

They are all laughing as I say, "Thank you and goodbye for now."

It is strange to return from the old-world elegance of Sari's table set under the shimmering chandelier to my own house, where my mother and father sit listening to the radio in our quiet den. Talking to them I realize that I must say no to Sari's idea. Because of the loss of that scholarship when I transfer to Toronto, I must do something this summer that pays well. It is not easy for a girl to make enough money to pay for her college tuition and books. For the coming year, I will face the added expense of living in residence in Toronto instead at home in Montreal.

On Monday I make a date to meet Sari at the Union. There in the empty lounge upstairs I tell her I would love to work with her but I can't. I can't afford not to make money this summer. It is hard to explain this to Sari who, in spite of her refugee status, seems to have no money worries.

Fortunately, I very soon have an interview with the director of a big girls' camp for a job directing drama activities this summer, a job with a reasonably good salary. Gibson worked at this camp last year and has put in the best possible word for me. I wait in hope for a call from the director. It comes. The answer is yes; the job begins in early June, readying the campsite and undergoing training sessions.

So the college year is really over, and so is my time at McGill.

I take as a formal farewell from my alma mater, the letter from Chancellor Beatty, who wrote the solemn note that welcomed us to college in the fall of 1939. He has contributed another letter to *Old McGill, 1942*, containing "hard words" to "the young man" who leaves McGill this year.

[overleaf]
20.8 **Letter from the chancellor**

McGILL UNIVERSITY
MONTREAL

At Victoria, 19th February, 1942.

The Editor-in-Chief,
"OLD MCGILL" 1942,
690 Sherbrooke Street West,
Montreal, Que.

Dear Sir,-

      An annual message to the graduating class of McGill in 1942 is not without its difficulties. At this moment the safety of the homes, the lives, and the liberties of the people of all free nations hangs in the balance. This is no exaggeration.

      In such circumstances, the young man who leaves the halls of McGill to enter the world has no doubt - no hesitation. We spoke for years of the problem of finding employment for our graduates - of offering them a career. The world today offers an unlimited choice of careers to any man who can do anything.

      The one outstanding fact is that these must be careers of service and not of ambition; they must be careers of sacrifice - not of profit.

      These are hard words to speak. What gives hope for the future is that I know our youth do not find them hard words to hear, and do not flinch from the task which is imposed upon them.

      Yours very sincerely,

Eo Beatty

Chancellor.

krp.

CHAPTER 21
AFTERMATH

In June 1942, comes the first of the "happy endings" we girls have been encouraged to dream about – a glamorous white satin wedding for Mary Morris. Her debutante freshman year ended in romance, and now two years later she is being married with all the pomp possible in wartime.

Another summer of 1942 story in the *Gazette* reports that my first editor-in-chief at the *Daily*, Mac Davies, now Flight-Lt. Malcolm Davies, RCAF, has married Pat Neilson, one of our fraternity sisters.

Gibson and I, less romantically, go out to the eastern townships to work at Camp Memphremagog. Gibson's Vince has graduated and gone into the navy; Fran Tyrer's medical student is now in American uniform, remaining at McGill until he can graduate as a doctor, but enrolled as an ensign already in the American navy.

At camp we work hard all week, and then on Fridays we pile into a camp truck and spin away to the nearest barn dance. "*Birdie in the centre and four hands round … Birdie fly out and hawkie fly in … Hawkie fly out and give birdie a spin!*" Strong farm boys, tremendous spinners! As farmers, these young men are not supposed to join the army. (But next fall two of them, Charles and Wellington Brown, will turn up in Toronto at the manning depot in the exhibition grounds, briefly, and take me out to the movies. Briefly, because new recruits will be hustled overseas at a terrible pace now, in the fourth year of the war.)

The worst part of the summer is trying to absorb the brutal August stories about Dieppe and the loss of so many Canadians there.

In the quiet camp morning, I get up before the little campers awake and I sit by the lake and read Milton's *Paradise Lost*. The University of Toronto's Department of English, officially accepting me into its ranks, has reminded me that I am registered for a tough course with Dr Arthur Barker on Milton and Spenser. I also take along *Canterbury Tales* and baffle my way through the Middle English in preparation

rsonal

SECOND LIEUTENANT CHARLES EDGAR MOORE, R.C.O.C., and MRS. MOORE, photographed leaving St. Philip's Church, Montreal West, yesterday afternoon, following their wedding. Mrs. Moore was formerly Miss Mary Dorothy Morris, only daughter of Captain and Mrs. Eric C. Morris, and Lieutenant Moore is the only son of Mr. and Mrs. B. J. Moore, of Outremont.   Peleier Photo.

21.1

Mary Morris's wedding

for another course – a tough one too, I have been warned. Reading *Paradise Lost*, I write a little poem of my own: "Gold-sided birch, still sentinel of dawn ..." A poem about peace. Then I go back to the story of Satan.

Toronto is a long way from Montreal, and the university there proves to be very different from McGill. Small classes, seminar style; many more essays to write. No time for fraternities, or scm, or working on *The Varsity*. New academic idols at the constituent colleges: Marshall McLuhan at St Michael's College, Northrop Frye at Victoria College, A.S.P. Woodhouse at University College, Arthur Barker at Trinity. But that is all part of a different story ...

A long way from McGill. Still, I get letters keeping me up to date about the *Daily* and other Montreal institutions. Letters from my brother, Don,[81] now at McGill and old enough to join the cotc and start the route marches along with his studies. Hardly have his classes begun when he elects to join a bunch of other McGill students. to go west on a "Harvesters' Special" train. These boys will help bring in the prairie harvest in the absence of the many westerners who have enlisted.

Don sends me a *Daily* picture of "McGill Harvesters," in which he is sitting right behind Professor John Culliton, chaperone of the McGill contingent. They all love this popular professor of economics, a legendary friend and fellow humorist of the even more legendary Stephen Leacock. Don has a rollicking good time on the train, and, after some less rollicking times in the wheat fields, a roaring good time on the way back to classes. Professor Culliton is a well-loved teacher, not least because he is said to be rather drunk when he gives afternoon lectures, following liquid lunches at the University Faculty Club. There are unhappy rumours, however, Don writes, suggesting that Culliton may be sent off to Ottawa to lend his economic expertise to the government.

And I get letters from Harold, including one about Professor Culliton. Harold repeats the rumour that Professor Culliton will be drafted. Harold writes that a bold banner has been strung across the façade of the Arts Building – a huge white sheet, with bright red letters spelling out an impertinent message: "Draft James! Leave us Culliton!" Rumour has it that it is a group of commerce students who slung that cocky advice. Whoever the protagonists, the banner disappeared very promptly.

Harold says that the *Daily* is playing the story very carefully. I can imagine Ray Ayoub, as editor-in-chief, pondering carefully whether to mention the incident at all. But clearly it is a campus event, that impertinent flinging of the banner, so the *Daily* has run a picture of it, with a noncommittal cutline.

It is February before I am pelted with more letters from various McGill friends about the aftermath to the banner story. Ray Rose writes to tell me that on February 19, the commerce students took over their traditional job of putting out a special edition of the *Daily*. The *Commerce Daily* has always been outrageous, full of dirty jokes and innuendos about campus personalities, both in the undergraduates and the faculty. This time, though, they have gone beyond the bounds of acceptance, civility, and common sense. Ray sends me a copy of the commerce production. A quick glance and I am repelled and worried by its tone. It is not only full of very dirty jokes, but also full of perilously pointed comments on some of the professors, and, more perilously still, some very nasty cracks about the administration.

A little ditty in one of the columns apotheosizes Professor Culliton, "the late Professor Culliton (that is late of McGill University)":

21.2
The dirty *Daily*

C is for the C's he always gives us
U is for the U's that we deserve;
L is for the lectures that he cancels,
L is for the likker that he serves …

And so on.

Next page, a big photograph of the principal, Dr F. Cyril James, BCom. It appears with the punning title, "Be Calm."

The whole paper looks dangerously close to libel. I turn to the masthead. Who was the night editor in charge of this effort? My goodness! Wallace Beaton, one of the sports editors in my first year at the *Daily*; the son of my mother's old friend Bea Wallace Beaton; the Westmount boy who took me to my first university football game. What will happen to him? Surely there will be some sort of reprimand from the authorities.

Our Principal, Be Calm

DR. F. CYRIL JAMES

21.3
Dr James, Be Calm

Two weeks pass and then Ray Rose writes again to tell me the consequences. Very bad news began to break on Wednesday, February 23, when the *Montreal Gazette* reported, "The chairman of the board of governors of McGill University professes himself discouraged by current student follies." He was, the paper noted, not making an official statement, but the editorial hinted that the board would probably ratify his opinion that the editor-in-chief and the night editor responsible for the scurrilous issue should be suspended from university. The *Gazette* added some fulsome stuff about McGill's principal, Dr Cyril James, internationally known as an economist, respected in the city for his readiness to bring the university into full cooperation with the war effort, and generally regarded favourably by the student body, regardless of what a few radicals might choose to print in the student paper.

In early March, another letter tells me that the *Montreal Star*, in a little story about events on the campus, has noted that "Raymond Ayoub has resigned from the editorial staff of the *McGill Daily*." The board of governors, in fact, has suspended both the editor in charge of the "dirty *Daily*" and also Ayoub, as the *Daily* editor-in-chief, following the old rule that the editor-in-chief is responsible for the paper, even if he had no direct hand in the story. I remember the hubbub in the fall of 1939 over my own very minor mistake, and the high-minded talk then about responsibility. Ray Rose writes further to say that the story of the dirty *Daily* is very complicated, though the officials are paying no attention to the complications. Ray Ayoub was sick that night with flu. The managing editor, who should have checked the copy, was away at Dartmouth with the Debating Union, so the dirty *Daily* went to press with no oversight. For the board of governors and Principal James, Ray Ayoub is indeed responsible for the bad taste of the commerce special, the "dirty *Daily*," along with Wallace Beaton, who actually put it together.

Wallace Beaton I don't care about – but Ayoub? Suspension in his final year means that he will not be able to attend any lectures for the rest of the term. What a blow for him, so hard working and ambitious! Will he even be allowed to write his final exams?

It seems likely that the suspension is really a punishment because the *Daily* ran that picture of the banner hung last month over the Arts Building door, and because Dr James has harboured hostility ever since that first "stolen" *Daily* interview with him two years ago. He has boiled over at the open rudeness, and the board of governors backed up their principal. The *Daily*, through its editor, must be punished for fomenting the foolish student unrest.

Ray Rose ends his letter sadly: "Ayoub is home, studying on his own. I think he is getting some tutoring from some of the professors that feel sympathetic toward him. He is still hopeful of getting good final marks. He wants to go on to graduate school at Columbia." The letter concludes: "Someone should make the board of governors see Ayoub's side of the story. Do you know anyone who has pull with any of the governors?"

I know it's none of my business, but I do know someone. Gibson's father is secretary of the Montreal board of trade; he undoubtedly deals with people on the board of governors. When I am home for Easter and visiting at Gibson's house, I pour out Ray's version of the story to Mr Beatty, remembering that long ago he had himself been the editor of the *Daily.*

"It does seem over the top," Mr Beatty admits. "Still, it's wartime, and the governors are anxious not to let the students appear in a bad light. Not everyone agrees that students should remain at college rather than enlisting, like other young men. They would have no use for students putting out a disrespectful, ugly paper."

"But regardless," I tell him, "the editor taking the brunt of the governors' wrath was actually out of commission on the night of the dreadful *Daily,* and in no way capable of stopping it from going to press."

"Doesn't seem right, I agree. I'll try talking to someone I know." That sounds hopeful. But before the Easter holidays ends, Mr Beatty tells me that he has indeed "had a word" with, I presume, one of the governors and to little avail, as it turns out. The powers have decided to reinstate Wallace Beaton. The chairman of the board knows the Beatons, "an old Westmount family." The board, however, feels unable to exonerate Ayoub, who is ultimately responsible for the paper as its editor-in-chief.

"Is Justice the Interest of the Stronger?" our first-year philosophy course had asked. It seems now that a WASPY Westmount boy is stronger than an Ayoub, a young man of Syrian extraction, who comes from goodness knows where – St Urbain Street, perhaps. My sociology course on Montreal's strata should have prepared me for this outcome.

There is a postscript to this story of the "dirty *Daily.*"

At the end of the 1942–1943 final exams at the University of Toronto, I go home for a brief holiday, then board the train going back to Toronto. I lurch through the corridor on the way to the dining car. One coach is filled with soldiers on their way to a training camp out west, all too eager to delay my progress down the aisle. A little scary, a little exciting; but I continue through the cars, and flop into the nearest seat in the dining car.

"Good afternoon, Elizabeth." It is Miss Hibbard, the librarian, my Aunt Zoë's friend.

Embarrassed by my graceless arrival, I can only reply, "Good afternoon. How nice to see you."

"Indeed," says Miss Hibbard. "I hoped to see you sometime. I did want to tell you that I missed your columns in the *Daily* this year." She stirs her tea, taps the spoon against the side of the cup and continues, "I read the *McGill Daily* very carefully. It is always illuminating."

Not the word the authorities have been using lately, but I venture politely, "I'm very glad you enjoyed my columns, Miss Hibbard."

"Indeed," says Miss Hibbard. "They were good. Light but good."

Neither light nor good, there comes a sudden interruption. Who should slouch into the diner but Ray Ayoub, dishevelled as usual, horn-rimmed glasses so speckled it is hard to imagine anyone seeing through them. ("Breaks the glare," was his usual response to any comment on those famously dirty glasses.) Ayoub, sliding into the seat across from me, seems pleased to see an acquaintance and is obviously prepared to join me for dinner.

I sit up very straight and do a proper introduction. "Raymond Ayoub, Miss Hibbard. Miss Hibbard the librarian, Ay – "

"Ray," he says sourly.

"*Assistant* librarian," Miss Hibbard replies equally starchily. And then, "I know your name of course. In bad odour at the university, I'm afraid." Before Ayoub can bristle or make an obnoxious retort, Miss Hibbard continues, "I must confide in you that the university authorities are in even worse odour, as far as I am concerned."

To my astonishment, Miss Hibbard continues with a litany of grievances. The board of governors, always stingy, is now using the outbreak of war to refuse any and every request for money. The library is falling behind; and the librarians, especially the junior ones, "are, frankly, being exploited in a disgraceful way. Longer hours, reduced pay. Reduced!" Miss Hibbard brandishes her teaspoon across the table. "When the pay for juniors is already so bad that they can't go to church because they haven't enough change to put in the collection plate!"

"The board of governors is a bunch of fat cats!" Ayoub snarls (and barely breaks his tirade to order an omelette from the hovering waiter). "You don't see them reducing the executive salaries in their own corporations just because of the war!"

"Furthermore – " Miss Hibbard is in full steam, barely pausing for breath whenever Ayoub tries to break in, " – the administration is putting pressure on certain members of the faculty, whose political beliefs don't jibe with authority – "

Ayoub thunders, "Authority, indeed!" and I begin to feel like a spectator at a tennis match, my head swivelling from one side of the table to the other as the two surprising allies send volley after volley of heretical opinions – surely treasonable ones? – across to each other.

Finally, Miss Hibbard sets her teaspoon neatly onto her saucer, dabs at her mouth with the table napkin, and stands erect in spite of the lurching of the train. "A pleasure to meet you, Mr Ayoub."

Ayoub doesn't rise in response, but he is smiling amiably as she asks, "What will you do now?"

I have been wondering the same thing, not just today but for weeks.

The answer is surprising. "The university let me write my final exams even though I had been suspended from classes since March." He turns directly toward me. "I got help from the head of my department. Math, you know."

"Professor Sullivan?" I ask.

"Himself. Professor Sullivan put in a word with his friend the registrar. It was quietly arranged." At last he is grinning, a boyish grin. "Final marks aren't out yet of course, but – well, I'm hopeful."

"And you know what your marks are?" I goggle at his answer, his smug answer. "Tops in every class except economics."

"Attaboy!" Miss Hibbard's slang is no more surprising than the beaming smile that transfigures her thin prim face.

I can't help asking, "What next?"

"Another problem. The University of Illinois had accepted me into their graduate school to do mathematics, dependent on my marks – and my letters of reference. Well, even if my marks are good, the letters are not forthcoming, you can bet. What professor is going to put on paper something good about the editor of that scurrilous *Daily*?"

"So what will you do?"

Ayoub's eyes are inscrutable behind the foggy glasses. "Go to work, I guess, in my

Wins Scholarship

Miss Judith Jaffe

Daughter of Mr. and Mrs. Simon Jaffe, of Montreal, Miss Jaffe has been awarded a Carola Woerishoffer resident graduate scholarship in the department of social economy and social research at Bryn Mawr College, Bryn Mawr, Pa. A graduate of Westmount High School, she expects to receive her degree of B.A. this month from McGill University, where she was president of her class and women's editor of the McGill Daily in her final year.

Wins Law Honors

Miss Ruth Hill

Woman Beats Men Students

Has Highest Standing In 2 Years at McGill

Male supremacy in the domain of law is tottering, it is disclosed by the award of prizes today in the first two years of law at McGill University.

The special prize for the highest standing in first year law has been awarded Miss Ruth Hill, who was last year elected president of the McGill Women's Union, the top executive post for co-eds on the campus. Miss Hill, who also took her arts course at McGill, is a daughter of Mr. and Mrs. A. H. Hill, of 304 Union boulevard, St. Lambert.

Another campus leader, Alex McT. Stalker, who in March last was elected president of the Students' Society, won the Alexander Morris exhibition for the highest standing in second year law. He is a Westmount student.

Walter A. Johnson, of Montreal, won the Adolphe Mailhiot prize in second year law. The final year law standing will be announced following a Senate meeting tomorrow.

[above]
21.4 **Judy Jaffe**

[right]
21.5 **Ruth Hill**

uncle's shop in Toronto. I'm on my way to talk to him now." At last he too stands up, looming beside Miss Hibbard and looking down at me as I spoon up the last of my ice cream. "But I'll get to graduate school by hook or by crook!"

Miss Hibbard looks as though she might repeat "Attaboy," but her face is already settling back into its disapproving, disappointed lines. She turns, ready to leave the dining car. "Goodbye, Elizabeth."

I can only answer sadly, "Goodbye, Miss Hibbard. And good luck, Ray," knowing that his chances of getting lucky are not very strong.

The summer of 1943 brings happier endings to some threads in this story of wartime and university. Many of my friends from McGill days graduate. Judy Jaffe, my first-year mentor on the *Daily*, wins a graduate fellowship at Bryn Mawr College near Philadelphia.

Ruth Hill has entered law school and has done very well indeed. The *Gazette* turns the story of her triumph into a tale of the battle of the sexes.

Sandy Stalker is also on his way to legal glory. The paper makes nothing of his "beating" women students.

Jean Douglas, my sponsor for joining the fraternity, is now a second lieutenant in the Canadian Women's Army Corps, looking very smart in her khaki uniform.

For others, the happy ending is marriage. First Gibson and Vince. Then Fran and Jay, her med, now an ensign in the American Navy. Mary Scott, after studying at Banff School of the Arts and finishing a teachers' course, will marry Homer Brady.

Colin has left McGill to join the infantry. He spends the summer of 1943 in khaki, in classes at Kingston.

Harold has followed a different path. On graduation he has joined the navy. In mid-summer I have the dubious pleasure of going downtown to watch a parade of the Royal Canadian Naval Reserve. There is Harold, looking handsome in the naval uniform. He expects to be assigned to convoy duty, probably in a corvette. His picture is in the *Gazette*.

I write a little poem for him:

> When Samarcand and Timbuktu
> Were magic names, enthralling you,

Their Forthcoming Weddings of Interest

—Photos by Jacobs.

Miss Gibson A. Beatty, daughter of Mr. and Mrs. Harry C. Beatty, of Montreal, and Mr. Vincent O. Griffin, son of Mr. and Mrs. Morley V. Griffin, of Brighton, Ont., whose engagement is announced. Their marriage will take place on June 19th in St. Philip's Church, Montreal West. Both are graduates of McGill University. Mr. Griffin, B.Eng., class of '42 and Miss Beatty, B.Arts, class of '43.

21.6

Gibson and Vince

—Photo by Posen

CUTTING THEIR WEDDING CAKE: Ensign Jason Kline Moyer, jr., U.S.N.R., and Mrs. Moyer, photographed as they cut their wedding cake at the reception at the home of the bride's father, following their wedding which took place on Saturday afternoon in St. Philip's Church, Montreal West. The bride was formerly Miss Frances Hope Tyrer, daughter of Mr. David J. S. Tyrer, of Montreal West. The bridegroom is the son of Mr. and Mrs. Jason K. Moyer, sr., of Binghamton, N.Y.

21.7

Frances and Jay

DAILY STAR, THURSDAY, MAY 20, 1943

McGILL TRAINED: Navy Engineers on Active Service

McGill University's engineering faculty, unsparing in its contribution to all three fighting services in this war, trained the above group of young Canadians to take their place in the naval service. With one exception, Warrant Officer John Inglis, of Shawbridge, (first from left in front row), they are all probationary sub-lieutenants (engineer). From left to right, are: front row—W/O Inglis, E. W. Montgomery, Winnipeg; J. H. Richer, Westmount; J. E. Freeman, Iroquois Falls, Ont.; and R .E. Mainguy, Montreal West; back row, A. A. Berry, St. Lambert; H. A. Norton, Montreal; A. H. Coote, Pointe Claire; R. G. Wilson, Winnipeg; J. R. Irwin, Montreal, and J. D. Anderson, Lunenberg, N.S. Not included in the picture is ~~Sub-Lieut S. C. Lowe, of Coch-rane, Ont., v~~ ~~ct Montreal with this draft for activ~~

21.8 Harold in the Navy

My sluggish spirit stayed at home.
But now that you sail off to roam
Somalia Straits, Mombasa Sea
These names are pulling, pulling me.
You write to say the only call
Entrancing *you* – is Montreal.

The war will go on and on and on: 1943, 1944, 1945.

In July 1943, Canadian troops will participate in the invasion of Sicily; Mussolini will be overthrown, although the Germans will continue to fight in Italy.

On June 6, 1944, D-Day, Canadians will play a costly part in the Allied landings on the coast of France.

On November 22, 1944, conscription will be enacted in Canada for overseas service. That winter, Canadian soldiers (including my brother, Don, now a gunner in the Royal Canadian Artillery) will take part in the Allied advance into Germany along the Rhine, and in spring 1945 Canadians will help in the liberation of Holland.

On May 8, 1945, VE Day, Victory in Europe will be celebrated by the Allies, and July 1945 Canadian troops will enter Germany as part of the occupying forces.

The war effort will swing to the Far East and the hope of defeating Japan, with the US forces spearheading this hope, culminating in VJ Day, August 15, 1945.

Canada will sign the United Nations Charter in San Francisco.

The world will settle, momentarily, into peace.

When the *McGill Daily* resumes in fall of 1945, it will be filled with stories of a strange new student corps of "young veterans" and a new post-war hustle on the old campus.

EPILOGUE

This book is a catchment – a netting of the past. In memory, in reveries, and in dreams, we all catch parts of a bygone reality, distorted, probably, by emotional realities of the remembered time: fear, or love, or self-delusion. Ultimately, we sift those memories through more recent intervening emotions: prejudice, embarrassment, vainglory. In this book I have caught memories of events of the opening years of World War II, as experienced on a Canadian university campus, and as filtered, now, through emotional sieves, new and old.

Because I am a writer as well as a rememberer, I have dramatized this story. I have created possible as well as probable dialogue to enliven provable scenes. A real historian would eschew these made-up embroideries, the "might-have-saids." I cannot give them up. Dreaming of the past, I hear the remembered voices. When I have asked all my old friends if this is the way they would have spoken, they all say, "Well – something like that anyway. We all talked so much none of us remember exactly what we said." If I have to make up for gaps in what I remember someone saying, so be it!

All writers work for audiences, even if the memoirist writes for an audience of only three or four. Try recounting one of your own memories three times to three different audiences. You may well find yourself editorializing, and you will do it differently each time you recount the incident.

I am particularly conscious of the way diarists and memoir writers embellish facts because, since 1982, I have been involved in editing the wonderful journals of L.M. Montgomery, author of *Anne of Green Gables*. The longer I work on these diaries, the more I find historical evidence that refutes many of her statements. Montgomery's life was more complex than mine, but her way of wrestling her experiences into readability offered an irresistible model. Perhaps only half-consciously, she refurbished events with a novelist's sense of drama, structure, and style. I plead guilty of the same writerly tendency. *Blitzkrieg and Jitterbugs* is to some extent a "fictionalized memoir."

By good fortune, however, I have been restrained from straying too far from fact. To turn dimming memories into this book, I have been able to rely on other kinds of nets, each catching verifiable aspects of the early years of World War II, as I experienced them at McGill University in Montreal. These are my reality-nets:

- A scrapbook of press clippings. Local reality was filtered for McGill students through a college paper. The *McGill Daily* reported briefly, six days a week, on campus events. As a *Daily* reporter for three years, I wrote about frivolities, meetings, and campus controversies. I clipped and pasted precious copies of my compositions.

- Simultaneously, the *Daily* reported in a small box titled "Around the Globe" on battles, bombings, advances through the southern desert, and retreats through the northern snows between 1939 and 1942. Some of these I clipped also; the rest I have consulted and pondered over in the McGill archives.

- Yearly handbooks. Each year the university gave every student a very small bright red day timer. Line by line I recorded dental appointments and dances, due dates for essays and choir practices. I added brief anecdotes about encounters with friends and – inevitably in Montreal – about the weather. I kept a second, sporadic diary, with emotional eruptions and effusions recording my reactions to unfolding events.

- Yearbooks: *Old McGill, 1940, 1941,* and *1942.* I was one of the editors of the last of these; the annual roundup of campus life added a broader than personal scope.

- Photograph albums, mine and my mother's. She was the one who preserved the scrapbooks and diaries after I left home, and she was the one to pull out the Brownie camera and record life at home with my parents, brother, grandparents, cousins – all another part of college years. My album caught new friends and old: Gibson on the ski slopes, Mary on the Arts Building steps, Frances at a fraternity dance.

NOTES

1 Sir Edward Wentworth Beatty (1877–1943), president of the Canadian Pacific Railway since 1918, became chancellor of McGill from 1920 to 1942. Lewis Williams Douglas (1894–1974), former adviser to Roosevelt, was principal of McGill from 1937 to 1939, returned to the US at the outbreak of war, and later served as ambassador to Great Britain. Russell Merifield (1916–2005), BCL, QC, captain of McGill's championship football team 1938, and president of the Student Council for the 1939/1940 academic year, returned to a career in law and business after serving in the navy.

2 The Roddick Gates, named for a former dean of medicine, have stood since 1924 at the formal entrance to the McGill campus. Photo: McGill University Archives, PR002675.

3 The Arts Building, central edifice on the McGill campus since 1843, fronted by James McGill's tomb. Photo: McGill University Archives, PR017145.

4 Charles S. Hendel was educated at Princeton. He came to McGill in 1929, and was dean of Arts from 1937 to 1940 before accepting a professorship at Yale.

5 Royal Victoria College, the women's residence, stood at the corner of Sherbrooke Street and University Avenue. Since 1884, all women at McGill were considered members of RVC.

6 Seven girls and four boys from Montreal West High School entered McGill in 1939.

7 Born in France, Lucie Touren Furness came to McGill in 1918 as a lecturer in the French Department, served as the assistant director of the French Summer School from 1939 to 1954, and was named professor emeritus of romance languages in 1956.

8 This and all further entries from the "Around the Globe" headlines are copied from the volumes of the *McGill Daily*, 1939–1943, held in the McGill University Archives in McLennan Library. These daily digests of world news usually contained three or four sentences.

I have selected and sometimes edited single sentences from each of the news headlines.

9 "Resurrected: Editors of the McGill Daily," *McGill News*, 1995.

10 Professor Paul F. McCullagh (1903–1999) taught classics at McGill from 1926 to 1988, and was named professor emeritus in 1981.

11 Cyrus Macmillan (1882–1953), BA, MA, McGill; PhD, Harvard; chairman of the McGill English Department from 1923 to 1940; became dean of Arts and Science, 1940, and MP and cabinet member from 1940 to 1945. He published two anthologies of Canadian folk tales (1918, 1922), and *McGill and Its Story, 1821–1921* (1922). Photo: McGill University Archives, PR009102.

12 The Student Union Building opened in 1906 as a club for male students. In 1971, a new student building opened and the Union was taken over by McCord Museum. Photo: McGill University Archives, PR009034.

13 Maude Parkin Grant, among the earliest female graduates of McGill, became warden of RVC after the death of her husband, William Grant. Daughter of George Parkin and daughter-in-law of George Munro Grant, she was the mother of philosopher George Grant. Mrs Grant did not hold an academic position at McGill, but as warden she was expected to wield a good influence on young women.

14 Peter Wyman, BA, 1940; pilot officer, RCAF; was killed in 1942 in an aircraft crash near Khartoum.

15 *McGill Daily*, XXIX, 1, October 2, 1939. All quotations from the *Daily* come from my "Press Clippings" scrapbook, 1939–1943.

16 Buildings and institutions endowed and named for Sir William Macdonald, head of Imperial Tobacco Company, appear on campuses all across Canada, including McGill's Macdonald College of Agriculture at Sainte-Anne-de-Bellevue, Photos: McGill University Archives, PR000681; McGill University Archives, PL028671.

17 A.H.S. Gillson, MA, Cambridge; served in the Royal Navy in World War I. He later became a professor in the McGill Mathematics Department in 1935, vice-principal of Dawson College in 1945, and principal of the University of Manitoba in 1948.

18 Ruth Hill became a gold medalist in law and went on to a career

as a justice in juvenile courts. In 1946 she married George Stanley, military historian at UBC, RMC, and Mount Allison University; he later became lieutenant-governor of New Brunswick and designer of the Canadian flag. They had three daughters.

19 Thomas J. Hardwick, enlisted by Professor David Keys to participate in wartime secret experiments on radar and nuclear fission, became a leading chemical physicist at Atomic Energy of Canada, Chalk River, and author of articles on radioactivity.

20 Roderick Diarmid Maclennan (1900–1977), MA, Edinburgh University; veteran of World War I; professor and chair of the Department of Philosophy at McGill from 1933 to 1956; later ordained as Presbyterian minister in Scotland.

21 Neil Compton (1922–1973), BA, McGill, 1943; MPhil, Cambridge; professor and chair of the Department of English at Sir George Williams College of Concordia University in 1948. After contracting polio, he worked valiantly from a wheelchair, revered by his students until his untimely accidental death.

22 "Conversat" is short for "Conversazi-one," meaning a party that did not include dancing.

23 Colin Spencer (1922–) BEng, McGill, 1948; interrupted his engineering studies in 1943 to serve in artillery, and later, infantry. He took part in the occupation of Germany in 1946, and later became a successful businessman in hardwood lumber.

24 Gerald Clark, BSC, 1939; *Daily* editor for the 1938/1939 academic year; wrote in a later *McGill News*, "I was the first Jewish editor and that was a big thing. McGill had quotas for Jewish students but, incredibly, nobody questioned or challenged that at the time. We were so grateful to get into McGill, the attitude was 'don't rock the boat.'" The quota policy finally ended when Samuel Bronfman (as rumour has it) exerted pressure on the principal.

25 Wallace Beaton (1922–2007), BCom, McGill, 1943; was a fellow of the Chartered Accountants Association Canada, and leader in appraisal theory at the time of property revaluation.

26 Margaret Hibbard, BA, McGill, 1915; librarian in charge of Wood Zoologi-cal Division of the Redpath Library where she organized an important exhibition on falconry in 1939.

27 Montreal West High School, a small school proud of its academic leadership, renamed Royal West Academy in 1983, now serves Montreal as an alternative school for highly motivated anglophone students.

28 Madeleine Parent (1918–), BA, McGill, 1941; early fighter for women's rights, worked as an undergraduate for organized unions in war industries, leading to imprisonment by the Duplessis provincial government.

29 Mac Davies later wrote in the *McGill News*, "Mrs MacMurray gave me early warning that F. Cyril James would replace Lewis W. Douglas. As a result, I was able to scoop the *Gazette* … I had to bend the truth a wee bit to the doorman of his apartment building. He asked if I were a reporter; I replied innocently that I was a student coming to see Professor James."

30 Malcolm Davies (1920–2011) BA, McGill, 1940 (honours classics); after serving in the RCAF, pursued a career in business and eventually became vice-president of Bell Canada.

31 Edward Archibald, MD, CM, McGill, 1896; joined the Royal Victoria Hospital in 1904, developed new techniques in treatment of war wounds during World War I; senior professor of surgery McGill in 1923; became surgeon-in-chief at Royal Victoria Hospital in 1939.

32 Statue of Queen Victoria, executed by Princess Louise, was erected in front of the college at the time of the opening of RVC, 1899. Photo: McGill University Archives, PR036670.

33 In 1914, my father had helped raise a regiment, the CORCC (Canadian Overseas Railway Construction Corps); engineered the construction of roads and bridges in advance of the British marches through France and Belgium; then supervised their destruction behind the retreating Allies, returning to Canada as a Lt-Colonel with the DSO.

34 The Arts Building in winter. Photo: McGill University Archives PN028704.

35 *Three Bares*. American sculptor, Gertrude Vanderbilt Whitney, created the marble statue of three male figures shouldering an ornamental bowl, and presented it to McGill as a celebration of international friendship. Its installation in a fountained pool was finalized in 1933. From 1937 on, it has been protected against winter damage, boxed in a wooden case. (*McGill News*, Fall 2005).

36 In the character of Sari I have blended memories of two McGill friends: Louise Skutezky and Charlotte Ferencz, whose families had been displaced from Europe before the war. Louise lived in the Gleneagles and wrote poetry; I have not been able to discover what happened to her after graduation. Charlotte (1921–) came to Montreal West from Hungary just before we all began college; she graduated from McGill, BSC, 1944, and MD, 1945; served at Johns Hopkins University School of Medicine in pediatric cardiology from 1954, and in 1973, joined the departments of epidemiology, preventive medicine, and pediatrics at the University of Maryland.

37 Robert A. Spencer, BA, McGill; MA, Toronto; PhD, Oxford; published his first work as a military historian while overseas in the Canadian army. Following the war, he became professor of history at Trinity College, University of Toronto, and later director of the Centre for International Studies there. His publications include, *Canada in World Affairs* (1959). His memoir, *A European Affair* (2007) includes reminiscences about his years at McGill from 1937 to 1941.

38 Thérèse Casgrain (née Forget), a leading twentieth century Canadian reformer, had argued for women's suffrage before World War I, led the cause in the 1930s, and during World War II she raised women's concerns with the Wartime Prices and Trade Board.

39 Katherine Haverfield (Wilson), BA, McGill, 1941; first woman to become managing editor of the *McGill Daily,* an activist in many causes, died at Kamloops in 1999.

40 The Canadian Student Assembly, organized in 1937 as a national association primarily to find funding for bursaries for students from poor families. It agitated in wartime to keep students in class and out of the armed forces, and 1939, came under police surveillance.

41 Lord Tweedsmuir in the regalia of St George and St Michael. Photo: Library and Archives Canada, C8507 / McGill University Archives, PR011211

42 Al Tunis, a later editor, recollected this process in an article in the *McGill News*: "It was set in hot type and printed at the *Gazette*, in its old building on St. Antoine Street, near Peel … How many late nights we

spent at the *Gazette*, looking over the shoulders of the tolerant compositors who set the columns of the hot metal type, as suggested on our mock-ups!"

43 After several years as a junior lecturer at McGill, Jock Dando eventually taught at Trinity College in Hartford, Connecticut.

44 Elected in March, 1940, Dr Macmillan became chairman of three committees preparing for the end of the war: one on land settlement of veterans of the present war, one on honours and decorations, and one on pension and war veterans' allowance. Later he played an active part in the Ministry of National Defence for Air.

45 Theodore Newton (1903–), BA, 1925, and MA, 1927, McGill; MA, Harvard; taught at Harvard from 1929 to 1937, returned to McGill as associate professor of English, and assistant warden of Douglas Hall from 1937 to 1943. He joined the Wartime Information Board in 1943, and served as Canadian representative to the United Nations Information Board until 1945.

46 Canadian Officers' Training Corps ceremony in Redpath Library, colours presented by Principal F. Cyril James, McGill University. Photo: McGill University Archives, PR010014.

47 Raymond G. Rose, MA, McGill; FRCP; began publishing on experimental cancer treatments in the 1950s at the Montreal General Hospital. He ended his career in Arizona.

48 Harold Norton (1922–1996), BEng, McGill, 1943. He settled in the Maritimes after the war and died in Kentville, NS.

49 Professor McCullagh was awarded a PhD from the University of Chicago in 1939, perhaps in response to Principal James's pressure on tenured professors to up-grade. This pressure led to a battle with Eugene Forsey, who, like Professor McCullagh, had not completed a doctoral degree.

50 Gerald Clark's later publications included *Memoirs of a Reporter* (1995) and *Montreal: The New Cité* (1982). In 1994, Monty Berger published, *Invasions Without Loss*, the story of the Royal Canadian Air Force's 126 Wing.

51 Algy Noad (1898–1952), BA, 1919; MA, 1921; tutored the son of President Mario Garcia Menocal of Cuba from 1919 to 1920, taught English at McGill from 1921 to 1951, and became an author, editor, and authority on comparative literature. At the time of his death he

was working on a study of imaginary voyages in literature.

52 Dorothy Thompson (1893–1961), American journalist, was noted by *Time* magazine in 1939 as one of the two most influential women in America, the other being Eleanor Roosevelt.

53 Dr F. Cyril James (1903–1973) came to the McGill Economics Department from the University of Pennsylvania in 1939. Installed as principal and vice-chancellor in 1940, he remained in charge until 1962. Photo: McGill University Archives, PR000440.

54 Harold Files (1885–1982), BA, 1915; MA, 1916; and PhD, 1923, Harvard; joined the English Department at McGill in 1923, became chairman in 1947, and taught with distinction until his retirement in 1964.

55 Charles Sullivan, BA, MSC, PhD, FRSC, taught all the honours courses in mathematics at McGill at this time.

56 David Keys, BSC, 1915, University of Toronto; PhD, Harvard; PhD, Cambridge; joined McGill Physics Department in 1922. During World War II, he trained two thousand radar technicians for the RCAF.

57 Forrest LaViolette, BA, Reed College, Oregon; PhD, University of Chicago;

assistant professor of sociology at McGill in 1940. In mid-1943, on leave from McGill, he spent six months at the Heart Mountain concentration camp as an administrator-community analyst for the War Relocation Authority (WRA), dealing with relocated Japanese-Americans.

58 Accepted sociological theory about Montreal had been developed by the chair of LaViolette's department, Carl Dawson, a recognized pioneer in the teaching of sociology in Canada, born in Prince Edward Island; PhD, University of Chicago.

59 Muriel V. Roscoe (1898–1990), BA, Acadia; PhD, Radcliffe at Harvard; professor of biology at Acadia; warden of Royal Victoria College from 1940 to 1947. She was head of botany from 1952 to 1962, publishing extensively in her field. In 1964, a new wing of RVC was named in her honour, and lectureships and other awards were established in her name. Photo: McGill University Archives PR009579.

60 Donated by Peter Redpath in 1893, the library was expanded in 1901, 1921, and 1952. When the new McLennan Library was built in 1969, it was connected to the old library so that the Redpath stacks continued to

be used. Photo: McGill University Archives, PRO32175.

61 Raymond Ayoub, BA, honours mathematics and physics, 1943; PhD, University of Illinois, 1950; published "Transfinite Numbers" (1946) while a graduate student. He became a noted numbers theorist, with works including, *Introduction to Analytic Theory of Numbers*, (1983) and concluded an academic career as professor emeritus at Pennsylvania State University.

62 The Royal Grammar School, established in 1816, had developed into the High School of Montreal, situated on University Street, across from the McGill campus.

63 Montreal West was incorporated in 1897 with a population of three hundred fifty. After World War I, it reached 5,474. From 2002 to 2005 it was merged, unwillingly, into the greater City of Montreal. Re-established in 2006, it stabilized in 2010 at a population around five thousand.

64 By 1945, 549 people, one-sixth of the Montreal West population, had enlisted. This was regarded locally as a record within the British Empire.

65 The McGill Debating Union helped launch the public careers of many later graduates, including Leonard Cohen, Moses Znaimer, and Justin Trudeau (*McGill News*, winter 2010).

66 Stanley Frost, *The Man in the Ivory Tower: F. Cyril James of McGill* (Montreal: McGill-Queen's University Press, 1991), 103, 107, 134.

67 Sydney Segal, MD, FRCP (1920–1997) became a noted neonatologist; he retired as professor emeritus at University of British Columbia.

68 Although Wodehouse's books continued to hold their devoted audience, there were uneasy rumours about the author's present life. Remaining in Europe in spite of the war, he was said to be contributing broadcasts perilously close to fascist propaganda.

69 Palmer Savage later worked for Dominion Bridge in publishing and public relations.

70 Another editor mentioned the survival of this habit: "Another tradition of the *Daily*, not deliberate but nevertheless valued, was being 'hauled on the carpet' by the principal for some journalistic misdemeanor. Mrs MacMurray, the principal's secretary, would call early and say, 'Do you have a free period today?

Dr James would like to see you.'"
(*McGill News*, 1953).

71 Madeleine Thornton Sherwood moved from Montreal to New York in 1953 where she originated the role of Abigail in Arthur Miller's *The Crucible*, and the role of Mae in Tennessee Williams' *Cat on a Hot Tin Roof*. She enjoyed a long later career in film and television.

72 Harry Lash, BA, 1947; MA, 1949; after briefly lecturing at McGill, moved to Vancouver, where he worked in urban planning. The Harry Lash Memorial Library is named for him. He died in 1995.

73 *The Man in the Ivory Tower*, p.71.

74 John Sutherland (1919–1956) and Louis Dudek (1918–2002), associates in writing and publishing poetry and criticism. Their group included Stephanie Zuperko, one of my classmates, who married Dudek in 1941. Irving Layton, BSc(Agr), 1939, married to Sutherland's sister, joined them in launching *First Statement* in 1942, a seminal journal that changed the direction of Canadian poetry (1942–1945). After earning a PhD from Columbia in 1951, Dudek was appointed to the McGill English Department.

75 William Hatcher (1893–1969), born in Newfoundland and educated at McGill, BA, 1916; MSC, 1917; and PhD, 1921. He joined the Department of Chemistry in 1920, became assistant professor in 1921, associate professor in 1929, and professor in 1936. In 1949, he became vice-principal of Dawson College, the campus created for World War II veterans.

76 Alexander McTavish Stalker (1920–2004), BA, 1941; DCL, 1944; became a Queen's Counsel and a judge in Montreal.

77 Canadian Officers Training Corps outside of Christ Church Cathedral, 1940. Photo: The *Montreal Star* / McGill University Archives, PR001371

78 Frederick Innes Ker of Hamilton, a major promoter of the St Lawrence Seaway project, developed programs for financing the Canadian war effort during World War II. He lost his son, Fred Southam Ker of the Royal Canadian Navy, in September 1940.

79 Mary Margaret Miller married David Geddes while he was a medical student. On graduation they moved to Wakefield, north-east of Ottawa, where she sadly missed her connections with the vibrant literary circles in Montreal.

80 Students wear gas masks in a chemical weapons drill. Photo: McGill University Archives PR009903.

81 Donald Hillman (1925–2004), MD, PhD, FRCP; taught at McGill, Memorial, McMaster, and many other universities and hospitals around the world. He and his wife, Dr Liz Sloman Hillman, were invested with the Order of Canada for their work in medical education.

ACKNOWLEDGMENTS

To all the people who helped me catch and fix these memories of youth and war, studies and romances, my thanks and love. Gibson Griffin, Mary Brady, and Frances Moyer, still all going strong, helped me recreate the mood of those days. Mary Rubio, dear friend and colleague, through many years of working together on L.M. Montgomery's life and works, deepened my sense of the intersect between fact and fiction. Sarah Waterston, my granddaughter, and Zoë Greenwald, my great-niece, when they were undergraduates at McGill, spent long hours in the McLennan Library Archives, helping check the "Around the Globe" details. My writer friends in Florida critiqued early versions of the book. Carole Gerson and Muriel Gold Poole offered brilliant suggestions for improving the manuscript. Robert Spencer, a genuine historian, kept me semi-honest in historical details. At the McGill University Archives, Mary Houde and Laura Markiewicz assiduously located illustrations, and archivist Theresa Rowat graciously helped locate illustrations and gave permission for their use. Patricia Desjardins at the *Montreal Gazette* okayed use of material from the newspaper files. Rob Turner, Jim Peters, and Fred Sgrosso produced scans of some of the pictures. Michael Bliss framed the story with a fine-tuned preface. Most importantly, my indefatigable daughter, Rosemary, proofread insightfully and cheerfully readied the many illustrations for the printing process. As always, my husband, Doug, and the rest of the family – Dan, Jane, Christy, and Charlotte, Francois, Jennifer, Phil, and Tom – cheered us all on as we got the book ready for publication. At McGill-Queen's University Press, Jacqueline Mason hailed the manuscript with enthusiasm and carried it forward firmly. Jennifer Charlton, a gifted copy editor, gave it a modern polish. Finally, I am very grateful to all the students who were in my classes over the years at Sir George Williams, the University of Western Ontario, and the University of Guelph. They always kept me poignantly aware of the travails and triumphs of undergraduate life.